A Book Of

MARKETING MANAGEMENT

For
M.B.A. (Semester - II)
And Other Allied Courses
As Per Pune University's Revised Syllabus
Effective from June 2013

Aparna Tembulkar
D.E.R.E, BA (Social Sciences), DMM, MMS (Marketing)
Assistant Dean –Director's Office & Corporate Relations
IndSearch
Pune 411004

MARKETING MANAGEMENT　　　　　　　　　　　　　　　　　　　ISBN 978-93-83750-58-0

First Edition : December 2013

© : Author

The text of this publication, or any part thereof, should not be reproduced or transmitted in any form or stored in any computer storage system or device for distribution including photocopy, recording, taping or information retrieval system or reproduced on any disc, tape, perforated media or other information storage device etc., without the written permission of Authors with whom the rights are reserved. Breach of this condition is liable for legal action.

Every effort has been made to avoid errors or omissions in this publication. In spite of this, errors may have crept in. Any mistake, error or discrepancy so noted and shall be brought to our notice shall be taken care of in the next edition. It is notified that neither the publisher nor the author or seller shall be responsible for any damage or loss of action to any one, of any kind, in any manner, therefrom.

Published By :　　　　　　　　　　　　　　　　　　　　　　　　　　　　　　　**Printed By :**
NIRALI PRAKASHAN　　　　　　　　　　　　　　　　　　　　　　　Repro Knowledgecast Limited,
Abhyudaya Pragati, 1312, Shivaji Nagar,　　　　　　　　　　　　　　　　　　　　　　Thane
Off J.M. Road, PUNE – 411005
Tel - (020) 25512336/37/39, Fax - (020) 25511379
Email : niralipune@pragationline.com

DISTRIBUTION CENTRES
PUNE

Nirali Prakashan　　　　　　　　　　　　　　　　　*Nirali Prakashan*
119, Budhwar Peth, Jogeshwari Mandir Lane　　　　　　S. No. 28/27, Dhyari,
Pune 411002, Maharashtra　　　　　　　　　　　　　　Near Pari Company, Pune 411041
Tel : (020) 2445 2044, 66022708, Fax : (020) 2445 1538　　Tel : (020) 24690204 Fax : (020) 24690316
Email : bookorder@pragationline.com　　　　　　　　　Email : dhyari@pragationline.com
　　　　　　　　　　　　　　　　　　　　　　　　　　　　　　bookorder@pragationline.com

MUMBAI
Nirali Prakashan
385, S.V.P. Road, Rasdhara Co-op. Hsg. Society Ltd.,
Girgaum, Mumbai 400004, Maharashtra
Tel : (022) 2385 6339 / 2386 9976, Fax : (022) 2386 9976
Email : niralimumbai@pragationline.com

DISTRIBUTION BRANCHES

NAGPUR　　　　　　　　　　　　　　　　　　**JALGAON**
Pratibha Book Distributors　　　　　　　　　　　*Nirali Prakashan*
Above Maratha Mandir, Shop No. 3, First Floor,　　34, V. V. Golani Market, Navi Peth, Jalgaon 425001,
Rani Jhanshi Square, Sitabuldi, Nagpur 440012,　　Maharashtra, Tel : (0257) 222 0395
Maharashtra, Tel : (0712) 254 7129　　　　　　　Mob : 94234 91860

BENGALURU　　　　　　　　　　　　　　　　**KOLHAPUR**
Pragati Book House　　　　　　　　　　　　　　*Nirali Prakashan*
House No. 1, Sanjeevappa Lane, Avenue Road Cross,　New Mahadvar Road,
Opp. Rice Church, Bengaluru – 560002.　　　　　　Kedar Plaza, 1st Floor Opp. IDBI Bank
Tel : (080) 64513344, 64513355,　　　　　　　　　Kolhapur 416 012, Maharashtra. Mob : 9855046155
Mob : 9880582331, 9845021552
Email:bharatsavla@yahoo.com

CHENNAI
Pragati Books
9/1, Montieth Road, Behind Taas Mahal, Egmore,
Chennai 600008 Tamil Nadu, Tel : (044) 6518 3535,
Mob : 94440 01782 / 98450 21552 / 98805 82331, Email : bharatsavla@yahoo.com

RETAIL OUTLETS
PUNE

Pragati Book Centre　　　　　　　　　　　　　　*Pragati Book Centre*
157, Budhwar Peth, Opp. Ratan Talkies,　　　　　　676/B, Budhwar Peth, Opp. Jogeshwari Mandir,
Pune 411002, Maharashtra　　　　　　　　　　　　Pune 411002, Maharashtra
Tel : (020) 2445 8887 / 6602 2707, Fax : (020) 2445 8887　Tel : (020) 6601 7784 / 6602 0855

Pragati Book Centre　　　　　　　　　　　　　　*PBC Book Sellers & Stationers*
Amber Chamber, 28/A, Budhwar Peth,　　　　　　　152, Budhwar Peth, Pune 411002, Maharashtra
Appa Balwant Chowk, Pune : 411002, Maharashtra,　Tel : (020) 2445 2254 / 6609 2463
Tel : (020) 20240335 / 66281669
Email : pbcpune@pragationline.com

MUMBAI
Pragati Book Corner
Indira Niwas, 111 - A, Bhavani Shankar Road, Dadar (W), Mumbai 400028, Maharashtra
Tel : (022) 2422 3526 / 6662 5254, Email : pbcmumbai@pragationline.com

www.pragationline.com　　　　　　　　　　　　　　　　　　　　　　　　　　info@pragationline.com

Preface

It is indeed a pleasure to present the book titled Marketing Management for the students of MBA Semester II. The book has been written according to the new revised syllabus prescribed by the University of Pune for the students of the MBA programme.

The book brings out the various theories and practices in the area of Marketing Management in a very simple and lucid manner making it easy to understand. The concepts are explained in detail and have been substantiated with examples. Also it incorporates caselets and to give students an insight into the real life business scenarios. Care has been taken to ensure that all topics mentioned in the syllabus have been covered in totality.

Different types of questions have been given at the end of each chapter. In addition to multiple choice questions, there are application or project based questions that will help students to apply the theoretical concepts.

I would like to express my heartfelt gratitude to Dr. Ashok Joshi- Director IndSearch and President Association of Management Development Institutions in South Asia (AMDISA), Dr. Sunita Joshi – Associate Dean – IndSearch, Dr. N. M. Vechalekar – Associate Dean – IndSearch and all my colleagues for the encouragement they have given me.

I would also like to express my sincere thanks to Shri. Dinesh Bhai Furia and Shri. Jignesh Furia and their staff for the opportunity and support provided during the writing of this book.

I am also obliged to all my family members for their continous support and encouragement to complete this book.

Any constructive suggestions or comments for improving the content of this book are most welcome.

Aparna Tembulkar

Syllabus ...

1. **New Product Development and Product Life Cycle** (7 + 2)
   1.1 **New Product Development:** Need for New Product Development, Booz Allen and Hamilton Classification Scheme for New Products.
   1.2 **New Product Development Process:** Idea Generation to commercialization.
   1.3 **Branding:** Introduction to Branding, Product Vs. Brand, Meaning of a brand, Brand Equity and Brand Elements.
   1.4 **Packaging and Labeling:** Meaning and Role of Packaging and Labeling, Primary, Secondary and Shipment Packages.
   1.5 **Product Life Cycle:** Concept and Characteristics of Product Life Cycle, Relevance of PLC, Types of PLC and Strategies across stages of the PLC.

2. **Price** (6 + 2)
   2.1 **Pricing Basics:** Meaning, Importance and Factors influencing Pricing Decisions.
   2.2 **Setting the Price:** Setting pricing objectives, Determining demand, Estimating costs, Analyzing Competitors' pricing, Selecting Pricing method, Selecting Final Price.
   2.3 **Adapting the Price:** Geographical Pricing, Price Discounts and Allowances, Promotional Pricing, Differentiated Pricing.
   2.4 **Price Change:** Initiating and responding to Price Changes.

3. **Place** (6 + 2)
   3.1 **The Role of Marketing Channels:** Channel Functions and Flows, Channel Levels.
   3.2 **Channel Design Decisions:** Analyzing customers' desired Service Output Levels, Establishing Objectives and Constraints, Identifying and Evaluating Major Channel Alternatives.
   3.3 **Channel Options:** Introduction to Wholesaling, Retailing, Franchising, Direct marketing, E-Commerce Marketing Practices.
   3.4 **Market Logistics Decisions:** Order Processing, Warehousing, Inventory and Transportation.

4. **Promotion** (10 + 2)
   4.1 **Introduction:** The role of marketing communications in marketing effort.
   4.2 **Communication Mix Elements:** Introduction to Advertising, Sales Promotion, Personal Selling, Public Relations, Direct Marketing, Concept of Integrated Marketing Communications (IMC).
   4.3 **Developing Effective Communication:** Identifying Target Audience, Determining Communication Objectives, Designing the Communications, Selecting Communication Channels.
   4.4 **Deciding Marketing Communications Mix:** Factors in Setting Marketing Communication Mix, Measuring Communication Results.

5. **Marketing Planning and Control** (6 + 2)
   5.1 **Product Level Planning:** Preparation and Evaluation of a Product Level Marketing Plan, Nature and contents of Marketing Plans - Executive Summary, Situation Analysis, Marketing Strategy, Financials, Control.
   5.2 **Marketing Evaluation and Control:** Concept, Process and types of Control - Annual Plan Control, Profitability Control, Efficiency Control, Strategic Control, Marketing Audit.

Contents ...

1. **New Product Development and Product Life Cycle**   1.1 – 1.62

2. **Price**   2.1 – 2.30

3. **Place**   3.1 – 3.40

4. **Promotion**   4.1 – 4.46

5. **Marketing Planning and Control**   5.1 – 5.46

Chapter 1...

New Product Development and Product Life Cycle

Contents ...

Introduction
1.1 New Product Development
    1.1.1 What is a Product?
    1.1.2 Difference between Goods and Services
    1.1.3 Levels of a Product
    1.1.4 Product Hierarchy
    1.1.5 Product Classification
    1.1.6 Product Mix
    1.1.7 Components of the Product Mix
    1.1.8 Product Line Decisions
    1.1.9 Need for New Product Development
    1.1.10 Booz Allen and Hamilton Classification Scheme for New Products
1.2 New Product Development Process
    1.2.1 Types of New Products
    1.2.2 The New Product Development and Decision Process
1.3 Branding
    1.3.1 Levels of a Brand
    1.3.2 Product/Commodity Vs Brand
    1.3.3 Concept of Branding
    1.3.4 Purpose and Significance of Branding
    1.3.5 Branding Decisions
    1.3.6 Brand Equity
    1.3.7 Brand Elements
1.4 Packaging and Labelling Decisions
    1.4.1 Purpose of Packaging
    1.4.2 Requirements of a good Package
    1.4.3 Types of Packaging
    1.4.4 New Trends in Packaging
    1.4.5 Labelling
    1.4.6 Role of Labelling
    1.4.7 Functions of Labels
    1.4.8 Classification of Labels

1.5 Product Life Cycle
   1.5.1 Concept and Characteristics of Product Life Cycle
   1.5.2 Relevance of Product Life Cycle
   1.5.3 Alternate Patterns of Product Life Cycle
   1.5.4 Special Categories of Product Life Cycle
   1.5.5 Strategies Across Stages of the Product Life Cycle
   - Points to Remember
   - Questions for Discussion
   - Project Questions
   - Case Study
   - Questions from Previous Pune University Examinations

Learning Objectives ...

- To Appreciate the need for New Products.
- To study the Classification scheme for New Products.
- To understand the entire process of New Product Development and the various stages involved in it.
- To acquire an understanding of Branding.
- To study the concepts of a Brand, Brand Equity and Brand Elements.
- To understand the relevance and Role of Packaging and Labeling and to study the various types of Packages.
- To develop an understanding of the Product Life Cycle, its Relevance, and the various types.
- To gain an understanding of the requirement and development of different strategies across the Product Life Cycle.

Introduction

The marketplace is never static: it is dynamic and fast changing, and demand for products is constantly shifting as needs, wants, and technology all change. As a result, companies must always evaluate their existing product line and look for ways to ensure that it is up to date and in line with consumer desires. Continuous decisions must be made about whether new products should be added (and whether old products should be removed).

This chapter deals with the need for the development of a new product, the process discussed step by step and the entire gamut of functions involved in the process.

Every function in the New Product Development process has a bearing on the success of that product in the marketplace. Often one sees instances of quality products failing in the market when at the same time one hears success stories of some other not so great products.

Developing a new product that is good and saleable is not enough. A marketer needs to understand the pulse of the market and translate this understanding into products that are need satisfying, affordable, suitably branded, packaged, promoted and distributed. Test marketing is a crucial stage in the new product development process and is discussed in detail in this chapter.

The chapter introduces the concept of Product Life Cycle (PLC) and also focuses on the various stages and phases in the Product Life Cycle. It deals with the types of Product Life Cycles and delves deeper into the varying strategies that are required for the various stages of the cycle.

1.1 New Product Development

Before we commence with the new products and the development of the same, let us begin by understanding the concept of a Product.

1.1.1 What is a Product?

In day to day language, we refer to a product as anything that can be used to satisfy a particular need. The word product is generally associated with tangible offerings. But it is more than just tangible offerings. In broad terms we can say that a product is anything that can be offered to a customer to satisfy a want or a need.

More specifically, we can define a product as Physical goods, services, experiences, events, persons, places, properties, organisations, information and ideas that can be offered to a market for satisfying a particular want or need.

A Product is defined as goods, services or ideas that are offered to satisfy the needs and wants of customers.

According to **Philip Kotler** *"A Product is a bundle of physical services and symbolic particulars expected to yield satisfactions or benefits to the buyer".*

So the concept of a product is not restricted to physical goods alone. Let us look at some common examples of products that we encounter in our day to day lives.

When we are purchasing a toothpaste, it is an example of physical goods; purchase of a train ticket is an example of purchase of a service, similarly purchase of a ticket to a movie is the purchase of an experience (the entertainment experience), purchase of a ticket for a concert is purchasing for an event, purchasing a house is purchase of a place and so on with various other products.

These are all day to day examples that we experience and it is a fact that products are an integral part of our lives. As mentioned earlier, products can be tangible or intangible. For example, toothpaste is a tangible product (goods) where as a doctor's service is an intangible product (service).

Before we proceed further it is necessary to understand the differences between goods and services.

1.1.2 Difference between Goods and Services

Goods are tangible objects that can be offered to a customer to satisfy his need or want.

A Service as an act or performance that one party can offer to another, that is essentially intangible and does not result in the ownership of anything. Its production may or may not be tied to a physical product.
... Philip Kotler

Hence the differences between goods and services are:

(a) Goods are tangible while services are intangible. The important point here is that goods have a physical form and shape; they can be seen and touched whereas a service is an intangible offering, that is, it does not have a physical form or shape and it cannot be touched or seen, it can only be experienced.

(b) Goods result in the ownership of the physical product whereas services do not result in the ownership of anything. To clarify let us take an example. When we purchase a pen, we own the pen, or in legal terms, we have the title to the pen. On the other hand, when we go to the doctor to get treatment for an ailment, neither do we own the doctor, nor the treatment that he gives us nor his diagnosis of the ailment for that matter. So the purchase of a service does not result in the ownership of anything.

(c) Goods are generally first manufactured at the place of manufacture, then distributed through the various distribution channels, then sold to the customer and finally consumed. In case of services, the manufacturing, selling and consumption happen simultaneously almost always. This also brings out another important difference. Physical goods can be separated from the manufacturer of the goods and also from the customer. Services cannot be separated from the service provider and the service receiver (customer). That is services are inseparable.

(d) Manufacturers of goods differentiate their goods on the basis of services whereas manufacturers of services differentiate their services on the basis of goods. Let's see an example. Manufacturers of Consumer durables like washing machines will differentiate their product from that of the competitor on the basis of the service like extended warranty etc. whereas manufacturers of services like Gymnasiums or health clubs will differentiate their services on the basis of physical goods like the latest equipments.

(e) Goods are generally consistent in nature whereas by nature services are inconsistent. That is if we buy a particular soap today and the same brand and variety of soap a month later, there will be no difference in the two goods purchased. However, if we avail the service of a beautician, it may vary from one occasion to another. This is mainly because services are provided by people. The services may vary because of change in the beautician offering the service, change in the time when the service is availed, change in the place where the service is availed, change in the mindset of the customer at both the occasions. All these could lead to a change or variation in the experience of the customer on both occasions.

(f) Moving further, another point of difference is that goods can be stored or inventoried. By this we mean that goods can be stocked depending upon the demand and supply situation. If a retailer of shoes knows that there is a good demand for a particular brand of shoes he will stock them in larger quantities so as to meet the demand of the customers. If he has stocked 500 pairs of shoes and has been able to sell only 100 pairs on a particular day, the rest of the shoes can be carried forward for sale in the coming days. However, the same does not hold true for services. Let us take the example of a restaurant that has a seating capacity of 100 people. If on a particular day there are 400 people wanting to eat at the restaurant, the restaurant owner cannot create and store additional capacity. The capacity here is finite and cannot be inventoried. Similarly, if on a particular day he finds that only 50 people have availed the service, the balance capacity of 50 expires on the same day. He cannot carry it forward to another day.

Table 1.1: Difference between Goods and Services

No.	Goods	Services
1.	Goods are tangible.	Services are intangible.
2.	Goods result in the ownership of the product.	Services do not result in the ownership of anything.
3.	Goods are manufactured then stored then distributed then sold and finally consumed.	Incase of services the manufacturing and selling happen simultaneously.
4.	Goods can be separated from the manufacturer and the customer.	Services cannot be separated from the service provider and the service receiver.
5.	Goods can be inventoried.	Services cannot be inventoried.
6.	Often, we find that Manufacturers of goods differentiate their goods on the basis of services.	Manufacturers of services differentiate their services on the basis of goods.
7.	Goods are consistent in nature.	Services are variable or inconsistent in nature.

1.1.3 Levels of a Product

While planning the offering that a marketer wants to make to satisfy a particular need or want of the market, the marketer has to think through the five levels of the product. These levels are:

(a) Core Benefit Level
(b) Basic Product Level
(c) Expected Product Level
(d) Augmented Product Level
(e) Potential Product Level

Each of these levels add more customer value and the five levels together constitute the Customer Value Hierarchy. Diagrammatically, these levels can be represented as shown below in Fig. 1.1.

Let us look at each of these levels in greater detail and try to understand what they mean to the marketer.

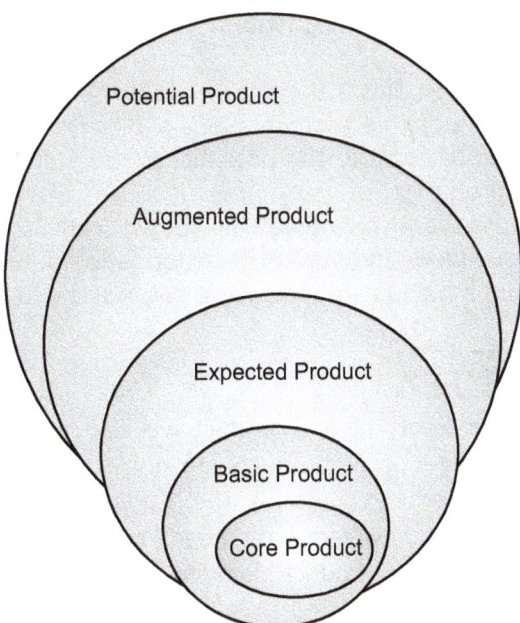

Fig. 1.1: Five Levels of a Product

(a) **Core Benefit Level:** At the most fundamental level is the core benefit level that the customer seeks or the need that the marketer tries to satisfy.

Example: If a customer is going to a restaurant to eat food, the core benefit level is that the product food satisfies the hunger of the customer. Here the benefit that the customer seeks is to satisfy his hunger by means of food.

Marketers need to look upon themselves as benefit providers rather than product sellers.

(b) **Basic Product Level:** This is the second level, where the marketer must now turn the core benefit into a basic product.
Example: The food that is the hunger satisfying core product is turned in to a basic product that is an edible tasty dish.

(c) **The Expected Product Level:** At the third level the marketer now prepares an expected product, which is a set of attributes and conditions that customers will normally expect.
Example: It is a normal expectation to have the food set in neat clean dishes with good cutlery, served on a properly laid table, having a proper seating arrangement, with sufficient lighting arrangements.

(d) **Augmented Product Level:** At the fourth level the marketer will further enhance the product by augmenting it and trying to meet the customer's desires beyond his expectations.
Example: Fresh flowers laid on the table, a live band playing music, etc. From the marketers' point of view this level is very important because in today's world, competition happens at this level only. Upto the expected level all marketers will stand at a more or less same platform. The differentiation will happen at the augmented level.

(e) **Potential Product level:** This is the fifth level. At this level the marketer has to take into consideration all possible augmentations and transformations that the product is likely to undergo in the future. The potential product describes the future possible innovation of the product.
Example: The restaurant providing the Guest with a facility to oversee the preparation of the food and having it tailormade to the requirements of each customer or having a menu card that would suggest menu combinations at the click of a button.

1.1.4 Product Hierarchy

Having studied the five levels of the product we also need to look at the Product Hierarchy. As seen in the product mix, products are not isolated. Each product belongs to certain product classes and product categories. The Product Hierarchy is a way of grouping the products in a way that stretches from basic needs to particular items that satisfy those needs. There are seven levels in the product hierarchy. The seven levels are explained below with the help of an example.

(a) **Need Family:** The core need that is beneath the existence of the product family.
Example: Clothing is the need family

(b) **Product Family:** All the product classes that can satisfy the core need in a reasonable manner.
Example: Garments

(c) **Product Class:** A product class is a group of products within a product family that are known to have certain functional consistency or coherence.
Example: Men's Clothing

(d) **Product Line:** A group of products within a product class that are closely related and perform the same function, are sold to the same group of customers and marketed through the same channels and have a similar price range.
Example: T-Shirts

(e) **Product Type:** A group of items within the product line that share one or several possible features of the product.
Example: T-Shirts with a collar

(f) **Brand:** The name, term, symbol or sign associated with one or more items in the product line that identifies the manufacturer or producer of the product and differentiates it from that of the competitor.
Example: Nike'

(g) **Stock Keeping Unit (SKU) or Item:** A distinct unit within a brand or a product line that can be distinguished on the basis of size, price, appearance or some other attribute.
Example: Size - 40.

So in this example we have seen a size 40, brand Nike', T-shirt having a collar and belonging to the product line T-shirts, Product Class Men's clothing, Product family Garments and Need family clothing. The chart below depicts the Product Hierarchy.

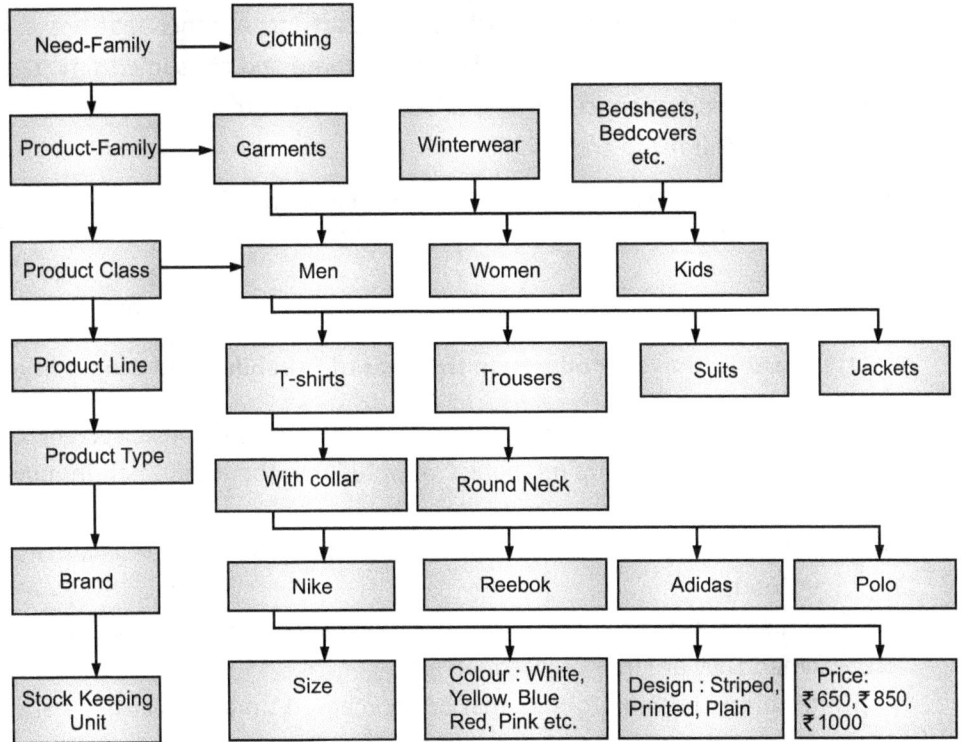

Fig. 1.2: Product Hierarchy chart

1.1.5 Product Classification

After studying the levels of a product and product hierarchy, we will now look at Product Classification. In order to understand the marketing strategy that applies to each classification of the product, it is necessary to study this in addition to the levels and the hierarchy. The basis used by Marketers to classify the products are:

(a) On the basis of durability and tangibility of the product
(b) On the basis of Consumer Shopping Habits
(c) On the basis of use in industry

(a) **On the basis of Durability and Tangibility:** Products are classified as Non-durable Goods, Durable goods and services on the basis of durability and tangibility.

- **Non-Durable Goods:** These represent the tangible goods that are consumed in one or few uses.
  Example: Soap, Salt, coke etc.
- **Durable Goods:** Tangible goods that go on or survive many uses.
  Example: Refrigerator, Clothing, television etc.
- **Services:** They are acts provided by one party to another that are essentially intangible in nature and are usually manufactured and consumed simultaneously.
  Example: Medical services, Transportation Services etc.

On the basis of Durability and Tangibility

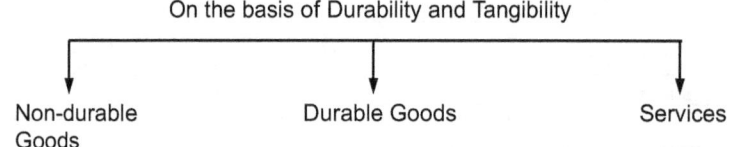

Fig. 1.3: Classification of Products on the basis of Durability and Tangibility

(b) **On the basis of Consumer Shopping Habits:** Here the products are classified depending upon the shopping habits adopted by the consumer in buying the product.

They are classified as Convenience Goods, Shopping Goods, Speciality Goods and Unsought Goods.

- **Convenience Goods:** Goods that are purchased for the convenience of the consumer. They are further classified as:
  - **(i) Staples:** These are goods that are purchased on a regular basis and form a part of the daily food and lifestyle requirement of the consumer - Rice, Wheat, Sugar, Toothpaste etc.

(ii) **Impulse:** Goods that the consumer buys when he has not gone with the intention of buying these goods; mainly they are not a part of his pre-decided shopping list. They are purchased on an impulse.
   Example: Chocolates, Ice creams, Shirts etc

(iii) **Emergency:** Goods that are a must and need to be purchased depending upon the situation.
   Example: Umbrella, Footwear, Medicines.

- **Shopping Goods:** Goods that a consumer will go specifically shopping for are shopping goods. They are further classified as:
  (i) **Homogenous Goods:** In homogenous goods, product features are more or less the same, only price difference is noticeable, e.g. Salt, Soap etc.
  (ii) **Heterogeneous:** In these types of goods, product features vary and they are compared while buying.
      Example: Television, Music System.
- **Specialty Goods:** These are goods which have unique characteristics and Brand identity. These generally hold a "snob appeal" for the buyer.
  Example: Mercedes Car, Nakshatra Diamonds
  Unsought Goods: Not known to consumers or known but not sought.
  Example: Burglar Alarms, Smoke detectors

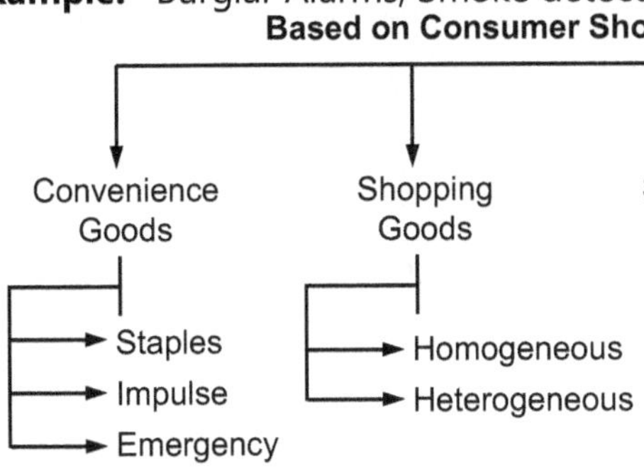

Based on Consumer Shopping Habits

```
                     Based on Consumer Shopping Habits
        ┌──────────────┬──────────────┬──────────────┐
        ▼              ▼              ▼              ▼
   Convenience      Shopping      Speciality      Unsought
     Goods           Goods          Goods          Goods
        │              │
        ├─► Staples    ├─► Homogeneous
        ├─► Impulse    └─► Heterogeneous
        └─► Emergency
```

Fig. 1.4: Product Classification based on Consumer Shopping habits

(c) **Product Classification Based on use in the industry:** Under this classification the Products are classified depending upon their application in the Industry as Materials and parts, Capital Items, Supplies and Services.

Materials and parts are further classified into raw materials and manufactured materials. Raw materials are further classified into Farm Products and Natural Products and manufactured materials are further classified into Component Materials and Component parts.

Similarly Capital items are classified into Installations and into Equipments and Supplies and Services are classified into Operating Supplies and maintenance and Repairs.

Raw materials are materials that are processed to make the finished products. They are further classified as materials that are natural and extracted from the nature and farm products that are grown in the farm.

Example: Natural raw material – iron ore, Lumber

Farm produced raw material – Wheat, Cotton

Manufactured Materials are materials that are manufactured in the manufacturing unit using some raw material. They are classified into Component Material and Component Parts. The difference between component material and component parts is that while component material goes into a finished product it forms an undistinguishable part of the product, whereas a component part is usually a distinguishable part of the finished product.

Example: Component material – Cement, Yarn

Component part: Tyres, Small Motors

Capital Items: Capital items are those items whose purchase amount to a capital expenditure for the organisation. These are further classified into Installations and Equipments.

Example: Installations – Buildings, Factories, Elevators

Equipments – Trucks, Forklifts, Cranes

Supplies and Services: Supplies and services are allied products that though not a part of the end product or finished product, they aid in the manufacturing of the product. These are classified into Operating Supplies and Maintenance and repairs.

Example: Operating Supplies – Lubricants, Oils, Paints etc.

Maintenance and Repairs –Consultancy, Annual maintenance Contracts

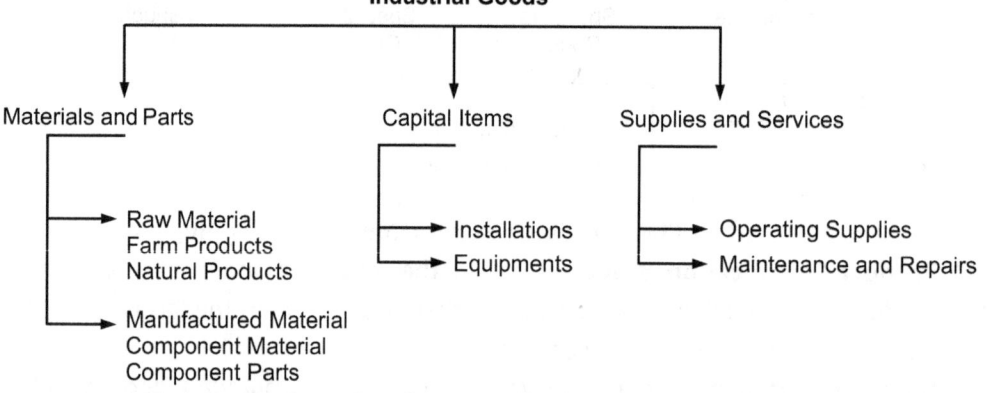

Fig. 1.5: Product Classification based on the use in Industry

1.1.6 Product Mix

The product mix is part of the marketing mix. The marketing mix is defined as a set of tactical tools in the hands of the marketer that he blends; depending upon the situation faced by the organisation, to elicit the desired response from the target market. It comprises of the 4 P's that is Product, Price, Physical Distribution (Place) and Promotion. Each of these has a set of variables known as the product mix, the price mix, the place mix, and the promotion mix, which can be modified or blended to suit the situation. In this chapter we will study the product mix in detail.

When we discuss the marketing mix, we talk about the various elements of the 4 P's. These are the elements that a marketer can vary or modify to suit the situation that the organisation faces.

To cite an example, when Tata Docomo became the first private sector service provider to launch 3G services on 5th November 2010 enhancing its services protfolio, a threatened Reliance Telecommunication followed suit in December 2010 and Vodafone did the same in mid March 2011 *(http://en.wikipedia.org/wiki/3G)*. What these firms essentially did was added a new service to their existing portfolio to overcome the threat posed by Tata Docomo. That is they modified the element product variety. Similarly other elements or variables of a product are quality, design, features, packaging, sizes, and brand name. Depending on the situation that the organisation is facing, it will modify one or more of these elements to get a desired response from the target market. The entire bouquet of products that arise out of all such modifications and that are offered to the customers constitute the product mix.

A product mix is defined as a set of all the products that a particular seller offers to the buyer for sale. It is also called as the product assortment.

1.1.7 Components of the Product Mix

A product mix comprises various product lines. Each product line has a length and product line depth. The Product mix also has a product mix width or breadth. Let us see these terms with the help of examples.

- **Product Line:** A product Line is a group of products that are closely related because they perform similar functions, and are sold to the same consumer groups and through the same marketing channels and fall within a given price range.
  Example: In LG Consumer Appliances, the various product lines are Refrigerators, Washing Machines, LCD's etc.
- **Product Line Length:** The length of the product line is the sum or total of the number of products that are available in that line.
  Example: If three types of washing machines are available under the LG range of washing machines namely front loading, top loading and semi automatic, then the length of the Product line of the Washing machines is three.
- **Product Line Depth:** It is the total of the number of variants in each type of the product in the product line.
  Example: If in each of the three types of washing machines, the following variants are available:
  Front Loading – 8 (Eight) variants (variation in capacity and features)
  Top Loading – 19 (Nineteen) variants (variation in capacity and features)
  Semi Automatic – 15 (fifteen) variants (variation in capacity and features)

Then the product line depth is forty two:
- **Width or breadth of the product mix:** It is the sum total of the number of product lines a company carries.
  Example: If LG carries a total of seven product lines namely TV/Audio/Video, Mobile phones, Computer products, Washing Machines, refrigerators, Microwave Ovens, Air Conditioners then its Width or breadth is seven.
- **Length of the Product Mix:** The length of the product mix is the sum total of the lengths of all individual product lines in that mix.
- **Depth of the Product Mix:** It is the sum total of the depths of individual product lines in that mix.
  (source of examples http://www.lg.com/in/home-appliances)

1.1.8 Product Line Decisions

Generally in most organisations that operate various product lines, Product Line Managers are entrusted the responsibility of separate product lines. Each product line is seen as a separate profit centre or business unit with a Manager responsible for running it successfully and ensuring profits. It is in this context that the Manager has to evaluate the market demand, the competitive situation, match those with the available resources and take decisions to ensure the optimal results from the product line. These decisions are product line decisions.

The various product line decisions are:
(a) Line stretching – Upwards and Downwards
(b) Line filling – Only in between
(c) Line Modernisation
(d) Line Featuring
(e) Line Pruning

(a) **Line Stretching:** The product line of any organisation covers a certain part of the total possible range of products in that line. A Manager is said to have done Line stretching when he adds products to the product line beyond the current range. This addition can happen at the down market, up market or both ends. An organisation that has positioned itself in the middle market or up market, may want to introduce low-priced products for the lower end market. This is a downward stretch. Similarly, an organisation that has products positioned in the middle market or low end market may aspire to introduce products in the up market range. This is an upward stretch.

When products are introduced both at the lower and upper end, it is called as a two way stretch.

An example of a downward stretch would be the launch of the C-Class by Mercedes Benz.

An example of upward stretch is launch of the Lexus by Toyota.

To cite an example of a two way stretch we can look at Zen LXI and Zen VXI by Maruti Suzuki.

(b) Line filling: An organisation can also lengthen its product line by adding products within or in between the present range of products. This is known as line filling. There are several motivations for an organisation to go for line filling. These are:

Using excess capacity, earning extra profits, satisfying dealers who complain of the loss of the customers because of insufficient items in the product line, and most importantly plugging holes to keep out the competition.

Example: In the last four years, the automobile manufacturer BMW AG has transformed from a single brand, five model carmaker to a three brand, 10 power house. In addition to the upward and downward stretch, BMW has done line filling by introducing its X3 and X5 sports activity vehicles and the Z3 and Z4 roadsters and a 6 series coupe.

(c) Line Modernisation: The Product Managers need to consistently review the Product Lines. In a highly competitive and rapidly changing market scenario, modernising the product line is of prime importance. This is done by continuously upgrading the products and incorporating in them the latest developments.

Example: Bajaj Pulsar upgraded to Bajaj Pulsar DTSI

(d) Line featuring: Here the Product Manager will typically select one or a set of items or products to feature. That is, the focus is on one item or a set of items not on the entire line. This is typically seen when an organisation finds that one end of its line is doing well, while the other end is not. In order to attract buyers from the other end, line featuring is done.

(e) Line Pruning: Many a times it is seen that products over a period of time start performing poorly, eating into the profits of the organisation. At such times, the Product Line Managers need to identify these products and remove them from the product line. Removal of products from the product line to shorten the length of the line is known as pruning.

Uptil now we have tried to understand "Product" in a little detail. We have looked at the definition of a Product, the difference between goods and services, levels of a product, product hierarchy, the product mix, components of the product mix and the product line decisions.

As discussed the decisions regarding the product line that are taken by organisation are often related to adding products to the Product Line or deleting products from the product line. Adding products to the product line is a way to introduce new products into the market. However, there are various types of new products and it would be appropriate at this point to understand the various types of new products and the classification of the new products.

1.1.9 Need for New Product Development

In dynamic markets companies must constantly introduce new products and services to keep up with changing consumer wants and needs.

Every business needs to innovate to stay ahead of the competition. No business can continue to offer the same unchanged product; otherwise sales would decrease and profits reduced.

New product development (NPD) is the process of bringing a new product to the marketplace. An organisation may need to engage in this process due to changes in consumer preferences, increasing competition and advances in technology.

Innovative business organisations thrive by understanding what their market wants, making smart product improvements, and developing new products that meet and exceed their customers' expectations.

'New products' can be:
- products that a business has never made or sold before but have been taken to market by others.
- product innovations created and brought to the market for the first time. They may be completely original products, or existing products that have been modified and improved.

Before we start discussing the new product development process, it is necessary to understand the rationale behind the launch of new products i.e. the need for new product development. "Why do organisations launch new products?" – This is the question that needs to be addressed.

There are in fact several reasons as to why an organisation would want to launch new products.

- Many a times the existing technology that has been used to manufacture a product becomes obsolete. In such cases an organisation would want to come out with a product that incorporates the latest technology and gives a better performance.
- Similarly, if a competitor launches a new product in the market, an organisation may be forced to launch another similar new product that is competitive and equally (if not better) good in terms of performance, features, quality price and other aspects.
- Another instance is when the organisations unearth a need in the market that is not being met currently and invests in research and development to come out with a new product that meets the said need.
- Yet another reason for launch of a new product could be the upgradation of the existing product with newer features and facilities.
- Apart from the above said reasons organisations look forward to minimising risks by increasing their product portfolio and not by investing all resources on a single product.

- Consumer "needs and wants" continuously change. Organisations should respond to these changes through their products and services. Otherwise consumers will switch to competitor products that satisfy their "needs and wants".
- The product maybe at the end of its Product Life Cycle, so the company may introduce new and improved updated versions.
- If an organisation's products are experiencing poor sales or suffering from a negative reputation it is time to change the product offering.

1.1.10 Booz Allen and Hamilton Classification Scheme for New Products

Quite similar to the above mentioned classification of new products, the **Booz Allen** and **Hamilton** classification scheme goes one step further giving six types of new products. These are:

(a) Technological Breakthroughs/New to the world products
(b) Significant improvements
(c) Modified Products
(d) Products new to the company
(e) Repositioning
(f) Cost reductions

Let us look at these six types of new products in greater detail.

(a) **Technological Breakthroughs/New to the world products:** These products are absolutely new to the world and will create their own market. (Similar to the truly innovative products studied above)

(b) **Significant improvements:** These products are not born out of a major invention but carry significant improvements over their existing counterparts. They offer superior performance and hence replace existing products. (Similar to Replacements in the market that are significantly different from existing products)

(c) **Modified Products:** These products are modifications of the existing products. These may include new flavours, new perfume, new package, a revised size etc.

For example: Recently Procter and Gamble has launched the Ariel Laundry Products - Ariel Complete, Ariel Anti Bacteria and Ariel 24 Hours fresh

Ariel Complete™

Ariel has a multiple cleaning system and built in additives for a Complete™ wash. Ariel has pink noodles, green speckles, and blue speckles which have the power of bar, brush and blue, which helps remove the toughest of stains with 100% stain removing power. Keep your clothes Shine like New* with Ariel Complete™. Can be used in Hand wash or in Top loading washing machines.

Ariel AntiBac

Ariel AntiBac combines Ariel Complete™'s superior cleaning properties to remove stains effectively^ with the determining power which, unlike ordinary detergents, removes up to 99.9% germs on clothes#. They can be used in Hand wash or in Top loading washing machines.

Ariel 24-hour Fresh

Ariel 24-hour Fresh combines Ariel Complete™'s superior cleaning properties to remove stains effectively with advanced perfume technology which gives long-lasting fragrance for 24 hours. They can be used in Hand wash or in Top loading washing machines.

Source:(http://www.ariel.in/en-IN/Products/variant.aspx?product=Ariel&utm_source=google&utm_medium=cpc&utm_term=mdm&utm_content=textads&utm_campaign=Phrase_Consideration_Ariel&gclid=CNXK3q6_zLkCFUJU4godR3MASg

(d) Products new to the company: These products are new to the company but not to the market. (Similar to imitative or "me too" category of New Products)

(e) Repositioning: These products are existing products, but targeted at new segments or new markets for the reason like increasing market share, fighting local brands etc.

Example: Tata Nano which was earlier positioned as the World's cheapest car at ₹ 1 lakh will now be repositioned as the Smart City Car. Faced with steep fall in sales of the Nano, Tata Motors today said it will reposition the budget car as 'a smart city car' with added features such as power steering, apart from introducing a CNG version.

"We are now focusing on increasing the features and the perceived value of the Nano with every subsequent model launch," Tata Group Chairman Cyrus P Mistry told shareholders at the 68th annual general meeting

Source: (http://articles.economictimes.indiatimes.com/2013-08-21/news/41433281_1_ tata-nano-cyrus-mistry-tata-motors-limited)

(f) Cost reductions: These products are functionally similar to the existing product but launched at a reduced price.

Example: Apple's newest iPhone costs $650 without a subsidy whereas Samsung has introduces a variety of Smartphones in markets like India, China and Indonesia priced below $100.

Source:(http://www.forbes.com/sites/timworstall/2013/09/09/why-samsung-beats-apple-or-perhaps-vice-versa/)

The Booz Allen and Hamilton scheme for classification is also depicted through the graph which gives an approximate percentage of the six types.

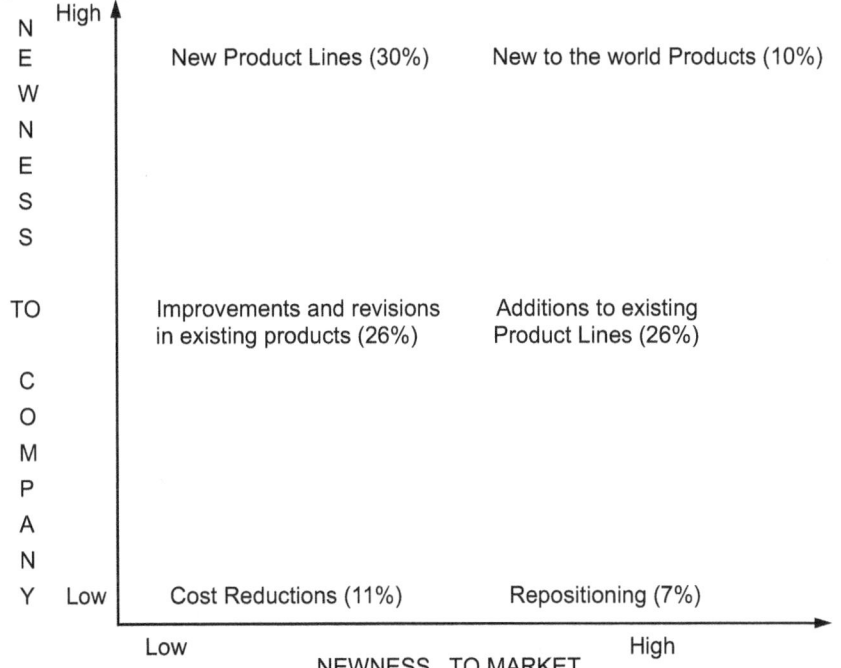

Fig. 1.6: Booz Allen and Hamilton Scheme for Classification of New Products

1.2 NEW PRODUCT DEVELOPMENT PROCESS

1.2.1 Types of New Products

When we talk of new products, we can easily classify them into categories or types. For example, there are products that we have never heard of and similarly there are new products from a particular organisation but not necessarily unknown to the market.

Generally the new products are classified into three main categories, namely,

(a) **Truly Innovative New Product:** It satisfies a real need that is not being met presently. These are truly new products that the market has not seen earlier. They are the first of their kind products and they satisfy those needs that were not being met.
Example: Telephone when it was invented.

(b) **Replacements in the market that are significantly different from existing products:** These are products that serve a need that is currently being met, but in a better and more efficient manner.
Example: Disposable Contact Lenses, Ball Point pens.

(c) **Imitative products new to the organisation but not to the market "ME TOO":** These are products that already exist in the market. When an organisation that does not have the said product in its portfolio, launches the said new product, it is called as an imitative or "me too" product.
Example: Two months before Cadbury–Kraft India launched its global best-selling Oreo Biscuits (Chocolate Flavoured sandwich Cookies) in March, arch-rival Britannia Industries stole its thunder by launching an exact me-too product called Treat-O.

The various types of new products are displayed in the following figure:

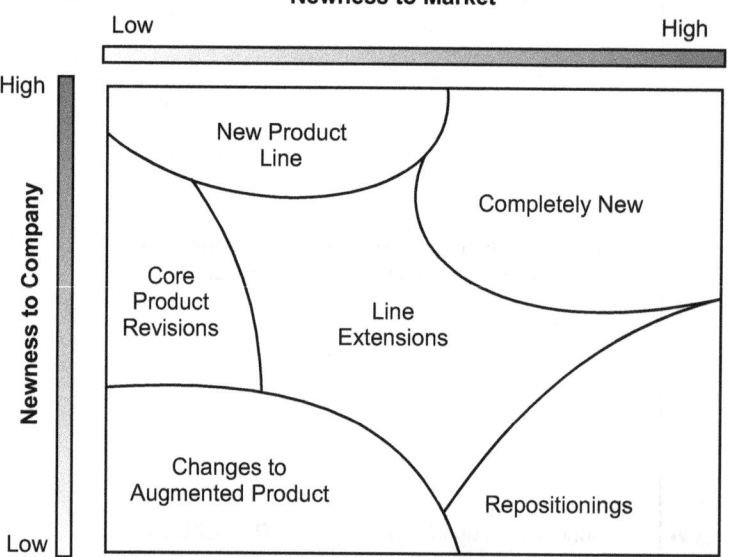

Fig. 1.7: Types of New Products

Nevertheless, the decision of whether to launch a new product or not is a difficult one and organisations need to be very careful while taking this decision.

1.2.2 The New Product Development and Decision Process

Let us now take a look at the new product development process and the various stages involved in it. Fig 1.8 below is a pictorial representation of the New Product Development Process.

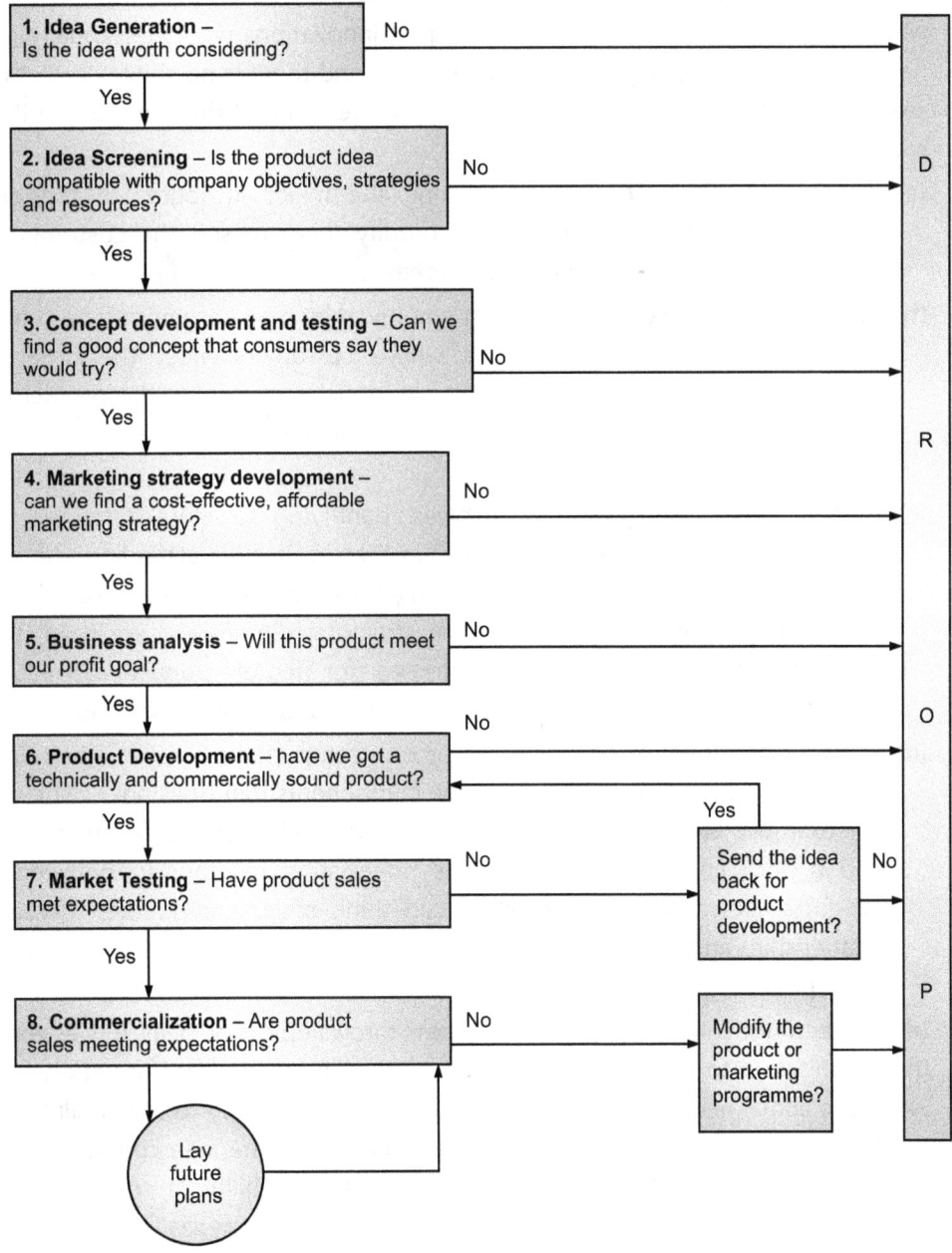

Fig. 1.8: New Product Development Process

Let us now look at this process step by step and how the process is managed.

1. **Idea generation:** Having seen the need for launching of new products, the first and foremost question facing most organisations is what kind of new product is to be launched. Here begins the search for ideas. While some experts do believe that the best way to get ideas for new products is to uncover unmet needs of the customers, while some others believe that technological innovations would essentially lead to new product ideas. Idea generation is a process and there is no single correct way of searching for or generating ideas. Given below are some of the common methods in which ideas are generated:

   (a) **Attribute Listing**: This involves listing the major attributes of the existing products and then finding ideas to modify them to suit the customer needs better. This gives rise to new product ideas.

   (b) **Brainstorming**: A common method employed by many organisations, it involves the running of informal sessions where customers meet the organisation personnel like engineers and design personnel and discuss the problems with current products and how they can be improvised, giving rise to new product ideas.

   (c) **Morphological Analysis**: This involves identifying structural dimensions of a problem and examining the relationship therein. It aims at finding some novel combinations and thereby new solutions, for example, if the problem is that of transportation on the city roads. The structural dimensions are road, type of traffic density, fuel etc. A small electric car for densely populated roads which also saves on fuel costs can be an ideal solution and a new product idea.

   (d) **Forced relationship**: Studying various components of a situation and establishing a relationship between the components that does not exist currently. For example, an office would normally house a telephone, a facsimile machine, and a photocopier. Per say there is no existing relationship between these products. However an organisation can think of combining these (creating a relationship) and coming out with a new product that is a combination of all the three products in one product.

2. **Idea Screening:** The idea generation process throws up many ideas. It is essential for the organisation to check the feasibility and viability of the transformation of these ideas into actual new products. For this purpose it is necessary to screen all the ideas. Most organisations form an idea screening committee. The idea committee reviews all the ideas and checks these ideas for overall probability of success. Here the probability of technical completion, probability of commercialisation as well as probability of economic success is taken into consideration.

At this stage there are typically two errors that the idea committee must avoid making. These are the "GO" error and the "DROP" error.

The "GO" error occurs when the idea screening committee gives a go ahead to a bad idea or an idea that is likely to fail while the "DROP" error occurs when the idea screening committee does not approve a good idea and the idea is dropped.

3. **Concept Development and Testing:** Every product idea must be made into a concept that appeals to the buyer, and it must also be tested to understand how well it is accepted by the customers.

   Concept Development: Let us take an example. Let us assume that an organisation evolves a new product idea to prepare a new kind of nutritive milk additive (nutritive powder to be added to milk) to increase its nutritional value and taste.

   This is a product idea. It must now be converted into a product concept. The concept should be such that it appeals to a buyer or groups of buyers. The concept can be:

   (a) An instant breakfast drink for adults - providing nutrition and energy to carry out their duties all day long.

   (b) A tasty drink for children - which gives them the required nutrition and owing to the taste, children drink it happily.

   (c) A health supplement for older people or senior Citizens- to help them regain nutrients.

   Concept Testing: According to the organisation that wants to launch the new product, the idea that is picked up, will indeed be a good idea. However, no matter how good the idea according to the organisation that wants to launch the product, it is necessary to find out what the customers feel about it. This calls for concept testing. It involves testing the concept with an appropriate group of target consumers and getting their reactions. The more the tested concept represents the final product; more dependable are the results of the testing process.

   (a) **Conducting a consumer survey:** A consumer survey can be conducted to understand the acceptance level of the concept. Given below are some questions that can be asked to ascertain the acceptability of the concept.

      (i) Are the benefits of the product clear to you and do you think that the product will really be beneficial to you?

         This question would help the organisation understand the communicability and believability of the concept.

      (ii) Are you using any other products that currently meet this need and satisfy you?

         This question will help understand the gap level of what is available and what is required.

(iii) Do you find the price reasonable with respect to the value you will get from the product?

This question gives an idea of the perceived value according to the customer.

(iv) Would you buy the product?

This question is to gauge the purchase intention of the customer.

(v) Who would use the product, how often would it be used and when would it be used?

This question will give an indication regarding the target audience, frequency of usage and purchase occasions.

(b) Conjoint Analysis: When more than one product concept need to be tested so as to narrow down to one concept, a research technique called conjoint analysis can be used. Conjoint Analysis is mainly used to test consumer preferences for alternative product concepts.

In this method respondents are shown different hypothetical offers, formed by combining varying levels of product attributes, and the consumers are asked to rank the offers. Based on the ranks given by the consumers the most suitable product concept is selected.

4. **Marketing Strategy Development:** A marketing strategy is a game plan that the marketing manager must prepare for introduction of the new product into the market. A marketing strategy comprises of three parts:

(i) The first part of the strategy should essentially look at the target market size, its structure and behaviour, the planned product positioning in the market, the projected sales and market share and profit goals sought in the initial years of launching the product.

(ii) The second part of the strategy focuses on the products to be launched, the pricing of the products, the distribution strategy and the promotional and marketing budget.

(iii) The third part of the marketing strategy looks at the future of the product and its benefits to the organisation. This part would mainly focus on long term sales and profit goals and the marketing mix over a period of time.

5. **Business Plan:** After concept development and testing and designing of the marketing strategy, it is now time for the organisation to look at the overall attractiveness of the business proposal as a whole. Here the Management would look at estimating the sales, costs and profit projections and assess whether they can be aligned with the organisation's overall objectives. If the plan is found to be suitable, then the product concept moves to the product development stage.

6. **Product Development Stage:** It is at this stage that the product concept is transformed into a physical product or we can say that the product actually comes into existence. Upto this point the product has existed in the form of a drawing or as a description. Now the product concept passes on to the Research & Design team and the Engineering team to be actually made into a physical product (A prototype). At this stage there is a large jump in the investments. It is at this stage that the organisation determines whether the product idea can be transformed into a technically and commercially feasible product.

   Developing and manufacturing a successful product can take a lot of time. Once the organisation is ready with the prototype, it is necessary to put the prototypes through rigorous functional and consumer tests. Functional tests are conducted under laboratory and field conditions to ensure the safe functioning of the product.

   There are various techniques for conducting Consumer tests and finding Consumer preferences. Some of the common techniques are:

   (a) **Simple rank order method**: Here the consumer is asked to rank the items in order of preference. This is a fairly simple method, though it does not measure the intensity of the preference for the particular product.

   (b) **Paired Comparison:** This calls for presenting pairs of items to the consumers and asking which is the most preferred item in the pair. For example, You present the consumer with item A and Item B and ask them which of the two they prefer. Then present them with B and C and ask for the preference between the two and then again present them with Item A and c and ask for a preference. This way the marketer can find out the most preferred item/product.

   The major advantage of this method is that people often find it easier to make a choice between two products/items and consumers are able to concentrate on two items noting their similarities and differences and make a fairly good and correct choice.

   (c) **Monadic Rating method:** Here the consumer is asked to rate his or her liking for each product on a scale of 1 to 10 where 1 represents Intense Dislike and 10 represents Intense Like.

7. **Market Testing:** Once the product performs satisfactorily in the functional and consumer tests, the product is now ready to be adorned with a brand name and packaging and go into the market. Before a full scale launch of the product a preliminary marketing programme is run to test the new product in a more authentic consumer setting so as to learn how consumers and dealers behave with regards to using, handling and repurchasing the actual product. This is the market testing stage.

The three common market testing techniques used in the consumer goods industry are:

(a) **Sales Wave Research:** In this method consumers who initially try the product at no cost are reoffered the product or the competitor's product at a slightly reduced cost. This process is repeated upto as many as 5 times (sales wave), with the organisation making a note of the number of customers who have repeatedly selected the organisation's products and their level of satisfaction.

Although this is a quick method and does not require the product to be packed and advertised, one of the major disadvantages is that it does not give an indication of the trial rates, as also it does not indicate the Brand's power to gain favourable shelf position and distribution.

(b) **Simulated Test Marketing:** In this method of test marketing, 30 to 40 qualified shoppers are questioned about their brand familiarity and preferences in a specific product category. The consumers are paid a token amount and invited to a store where they are asked to make purchases. The organisation makes a note of how many shoppers buy the new brands and how many of them buy the competing brands. Consumers are also questioned about the reasons for purchase as well as for non-purchase. Those consumers who have not purchased the product are then given a free sample of the product and then re-interviewed to understand their opinions about the product attributes, usage, satisfaction and repurchase intention.

(c) **Controlled Test Marketing:** In this method, the organisation identifies a panel of stores (retail outlets) that carry the newly introduced product for a fee. The organisation selects the location of these stores and also decides the number or stores in the panel. The organisation also has a say in the shelf positioning of the product, number of face-ups, displays, point-of-purchase promotional material etc. Sales results are then measured either through the sales record or through electronic scanners at the checkout point of the store. One major advantage is that, controlled test marketing allows the organisation to check out the impact of in-store factors on the consumer buying behaviour.

8. **Commercialisation:** Having completed the Market Testing stage the organisation is now in a position to decide regarding the launch of the product. While going in for commercialisation, the organisation must take a decision on a few aspects. It must decide when to launch the product (timing), where to launch it (Geographical strategy), who the target audience should be (target market) and how to launch (Introduction strategy). Let us take a look at these aspects.

(a) **When (Timing):** In commercialising a product the market entry timing is very crucial. There are generally three choices that an organisation has in this regards:

  (i) **First Entry:** The first firm entering the market with a new product generally enjoys the "First mover advantages" of locking up distributors and customers and gaining a reputation in the market.

  To cite an example, as reported in the Economic Times dated Friday 10th June 2011, Oralcare Giant Colgate announced the launch of Colgate Sensitive Pro-Relief toothpaste for tooth sensitivity. However, this did not create the desired impact because just two months prior to this launch, an associate company of Glaxo Smithkline Consumer Healthcare had launched Sensodyne in the same space of pain relief. As such the first mover advantage was taken by Glaxosmithkline Consumer Healthcare's Sensodyne.

  (ii) **Parallel Entry:** A firm that times its entry to coincide with that of the competitor is making a parallel entry. The company tries to play it safe, by doing things exactly as the competitor.

  (iii) **Late Entry:** Here a firm enters the market only after the competitor has launched its product. Here the advantage is that the competitor has already borne the cost of educating the market, besides if there is a flaw in the competitor's product, the organisation can learn from the competitors' mistake and introduce an improvised product and this also helps the organisation to gauge the size of the market.

(b) **Where (Geographical Location):** Here the decision that the organisation has to take is whether to launch the product in a single locality, in one region, several regions or nationally or even enter the international market. Depending upon their financial strength and capacity, most companies would progress from launching in a few regions to then launching nationally and finally entering the international market.

(c) **Who (Target Market):** When the product is being launched the organisation must ensure that the product reaches the best prospect groups through its promotion and distribution. The best prospects are those who would adopt the products early, and be heavy users. So also they would be opinion leaders and reaching them would be essentially cost effective. Although all prospect groups may not have all the above characteristics, the organisation needs to target those which are most attractive to them.

(d) **How to launch:** Again this is very crucial to the success of the new product, as to how the Product is launched and what introductory marketing strategy the organisation employs. It is necessary that the organisation develops an action plan to roll out the new product into the market. It is necessary to allocate sufficient resources and also give sufficient time for the process of new product introduction in the market.

9. **Consumer adoption process:** In the marketing context, the term adoption is used to imply an individual's decision to become a regular user of a product/service. Let us take a look at the stages in the adoption process:

   (a) **Awareness**: The consumer becomes aware of the new product or the innovation but does not have detailed information about the product.

   (b) **Interest**: The interest of the consumer in the product is awakened and the consumer is motivated to seek more information about the product.

   (c) **Evaluation**: In this stage the consumer takes a decision whether to try the new product or not.

   (d) **Trial**: The consumer tries out the product and forms his opinion also comparing the experience against his/her initial estimate/judgement of the value of the product.

   (e) **Adoption**: The consumer decides to make regular use of the product.

10. **Test marketing a new product:** Although we have studied test marketing in the preceding section, we will see the same in greater detail in this section. The main reason to carry out test marketing is to be able to gauge correctly the consumer's response to the product. It is an attempt to test in an authentic setting how consumers and dealers receive the product, how it is handled and used and how willing the consumer's are for repurchase.

    Let us take a look at Test Marketing for consumer goods and business goods.

    (a) **Consumer Goods test marketing:** The consumer goods test marketing attempts to estimate four variables viz. trial, first repeat purchase, adoption and the purchase frequency. There are four common methods that are used. Out of these three methods viz. Sales Wave Research, Simulated Test Marketing and Controlled test marketing have been discussed in earlier sections. We shall now take a look at the fourth method, which is said to be the most costly or expensive method of conducting market tests.

    Test markets: The best way to test a new product is to put it into a full blown test market. Here the organisation has to choose a few representative cities, where the organisation's sales force will try to sell the product through dealers and retailers giving the product a good shelf exposure. The organisation also runs a full scale advertising and promotion campaign, in the representative cities, similar to the one it would probably use in the national market. Also, the marketing plan is varied in different cities to understand the impact of alternate marketing plans. In this type of market testing, there are several crucial decisions that the organisation must make. These are:

(i) **Number of test cities:** Needless to say the more the number of test cities higher will be the cost of test marketing. Also the threat of competition ambushing the product is there by testing the product in more number of cities. As a standard most organisations use, two to six cities.

(ii) **Choice of cities:** While choosing the cities for launching the new product, the organisation must have some pre-determined criteria such as media coverage, presence of cooperative chain stores, and level of competitive activities.

(iii) **Time given to run the market test:** Market tests can be conducted for anywhere between a few months to a year. It depends largely on the average repurchase period for the product.

(iv) **Information Gathering:** While conducting market tests it is necessary that the organisation decides well in advance what information it needs to gather. Information relating to various areas must be gathered. For example, information regarding weekly sales, buyer behaviour etc.

(v) **The action plan:** The last stage is the decision about launching the product. If the market tests show a high trial and repurchase rate, the organisation should consider launching the product nationally; on the other hand if the trial and repurchase rates are low, the organisation can either drop the product or increase communication to enthuse more consumers to try the product.

(b) **Business goods test marketing:** Given the expensive and technical nature of most business goods, the methods used for test marketing business goods differ from those used for consumer goods. Expensive business goods and new technologies are first test marketed using Alpha testing and later using Beta testing.

(i) **Alpha Testing:** The goods are tested within the organisation or under laboratory conditions.

(ii) **Beta Testing:** Here the potential adopters are invited to conduct confidential tests at their sites or premises. During Beta testing the organisation's technical personnel observes how the test consumers (potential adopters) use the product. Often this is helpful in revealing unanticipated problems with regards to safety issues and servicing.

(iii) **Trade Shows:** The organisation can test market the product by launching it at trade shows and getting the opinions and feedbacks from potential users.

(iv) **Display in Distributor and Dealer showrooms:** Here the organisation displays the product at the Distributor's showroom or the Dealer's showroom, where the product is kept alongwith competing products or similar line of products. This method helps the organisation to gather information regarding product preference and pricing.

Some Examples of New Product launches are given below:

1. **TATA I-Shakti chana flour introduced in Mumbai; Available in 500g SKUs**

   Tata Chemicals launched its I-Shakti brand of besan (chana flour) in Mumbai recently. The flour is processed from 100 per cent chana dal and bears an Agmark Grade-I certification. It is now available in 500g stock-keeping units at retail outlets across the metropolis.

   With the launch of the product, Tata Chemicals entered the second phase of its consumer product category expansion. Speaking at the launch, Ashvini Hiran, chief operating officer, consumer products business at Tata Chemicals Ltd. said, "After successful launch of Tata I-Shakti Besan in the northern markets, we hope to leverage our established distribution channels across the country, and aim to offer Tata I-Shakti Besan along with our range of quality pulses to Indian households."

2. **Café Coffee Day launches Friends of Frappé, comprising three offerings**

   Café Coffee Day (CCD) recently introduced the Friends of Frappé range at its Cuffe Parade outlet in Mumbai. The range comprises three frappés – Blushberry Frappé (a shake with chunks of strawberry topped with whipped cream); Crunchy Vanilla Frappe (also called Snowy Vanilla Frappe, a vanilla shake with butterscotch bits topped with whipped cream), and Crunchy Frappe (a mixture of crunchy Oreos dunked in a chocolaty meltdown).

   An array of bite-sized eats was also launched alongside the range. These include the Egg Wrap (a spiced scrambled egg with traditional flavours in a scrumptious wrap); the French Croissant (which has a crunchy buttery taste) and the Creamy Choco Donut (which is dark and sinful).

   The frappes and the bites together make for three Combos – namely the Egg Wrap Combo (Egg Wrap plus Cappuccino or iced tea), the Crunchy Combo (Crunchy Frappe plus Chilli Cheese Toastizza) and the Choco Donut Combo (Creamy Choco Donut plus Cappuccino or iced tea).

   Friends of Frappe are available at all 1,497 CCD outlets across India. The prices range between ₹ 25 and ₹ 94. Those of the Bites combos range between ₹ 79 to ₹ 99.

Speaking on the occasion, K Ramakrishnan, president, marketing, CCD, said, "As pioneers and trendsetters in the café retail space in India, we can proudly say that we at CCD have succeeded in keeping our customers content through various offerings at great values."

"The launch of Friends of Frappe is another novelty from CCD to keep our customers delighted with our café experiences and keep them coming back for more. We are positive that the new range of frappes and appetising bites will appeal to our customers," he added.

Source: (http://www.fnbnews.com/article/detnews.asp?articleid=34237&sectionid=31)

We have now looked in detail at the New Product Development Process. However, one major aspect that a marketer must look into is Branding of the New Product. In the next section of this chapter we will look at various aspects of Branding a Product.

1.3 Branding

A Brand is a name, term, sign, symbol or design or a combination of them intended to identify the goods or services of one seller or group of sellers and to differentiate them from those of the competitors.
— **Philip Kotler**

The American Marketing Association (AMA) defines a brand as a "*name, term, sign, symbol or design, or a combination of them intended to identify the goods and services of one seller or group of sellers and to differentiate them from those of other sellers*".

A brand is essentially a seller's promise to consistently deliver a specific set of features, benefits and services to the buyers. Best brands convey a warranty of quality.

1.3.1 Levels of a Brand

A brand conveys upto 6 levels of meaning. These can be briefly described as follows:
- Attributes
- Benefits
- Values
- Culture
- Personality
- User

Attributes: A brand first brings to mind certain attributes, e.g. a Mercedes suggests expensive, well built, well engineered, durable, high prestige fast and so on.

One or more of the attributes are generally used to advertise the car. Tagline "Engineered like no other car in the world".

Benefits: A brand however is more than a set of attributes. A customer does not buy attributes; he buys benefits that these attributes offer. Hence the attributes need to be transferred into functional/emotional benefits.

Example: Durable – I do not need to buy a new car for next 10 years – Functional Benefit.

Example: Expensive – The Car helps me feel important and admired – Emotional Benefit.

Values: A brand also says something about the producers' values.

E.g. Mercedes stands for High performance, safety and prestige, TATA's stand for quality, fair price and so on.

Culture: The brand may represent certain culture.

Example: The Mercedes represents German Culture: Organised, Efficient and High Quality, Coke is an icon of American Culture, Shilpa Bindis represent typically Indian culture.

Personality: The Brand can also project certain personality. To understand this one needs to ask, if the brand were a certain person, animal or object, what would come to your mind?

Example: Animal –Mercedes might suggest a reigning, royal Lion, or Object - An austere palace, Personality – A No-nonsense Boss

MRF suggests a muscle man; Cherry Blossom refers to Charlie Chaplin.

User: The Brand suggests the kind of a consumer who buys or uses the product.

Example: An advertisement showing a 20 year old secretary driving a Mercedes would seem out of place, whereas a 55 year old CEO or top executive driving a car would fit the image.

1.3.2 Product/Commodity Vs Brand

While studying brands, it is important to contrast/compare a commodity (Product) with a brand.

A product or commodity is anything that can be offered to a market for attention, acquisition, use or consumption that might satisfy a need or a want. Thus a product may be,

(a) Physical goods

(b) Service

(c) Idea

A brand on the other hand is therefore a product, but one that adds another dimension that differentiates it in some way from the other products designed to satisfy the same needs.

The differences may be rational and tangible (Related to product performance of the brand) or more symbolic, emotional and intangible (related to what the brand represents).

What distinguishes a brand from its unbranded commodity counterpart is the sum total of the consumers' perception and feelings about the product's attributes and how they perform, about the brand name and what it stands for, about the company associated with the brand.

1.3.3 Concept of Branding

Let us now look at the concept of Branding.

Branding is not about getting your target market to choose you over the competition, but it is about getting your prospects to see you as the only one that provides a solution to their problem.

To succeed in branding you must understand the needs and wants of its customers and prospects. You do this by integrating your brand strategies through your company at every point of public contact.

1.3.4 Purpose and Significance of Branding

Branding is not a new concept. It has been around for centuries as a means to distinguish the goods of one producer from those of another. Although primarily used for the purpose of distinguishing, branding today has evolved as a tool that helps the marketer in more ways than one. Brands today play a number of vital roles that improve the consumer's lives and help organisations fulfill their objectives.

(a) Brands help the consumer to identify the source or the maker of the product and allow consumers to assign responsibility for its performance to a particular manufacturer or producer.

(b) Brands help consumers in decision making and help them to reduce the risk associated with the purchase of products and services.

(c) Brands help organisations to organise inventory and maintain accounting records.

(d) Brands offer organisations legal protection for unique features of the product/service. The brand name can be protected through registered trademark; and similarly manufacturing processes can be protected through patents.

(e) Brands help organisations by influencing consumer behaviour. They can also be bought and sold and are a source of future revenue for organisations.

(f) Organisations are known to have paid large earnings for brands in mergers and acquisitions, justifying the premium paid on the basis of extra profits to be extracted and sustained from the brands.

Thus we can see that strong brands lead to better earnings, and profit performance for the organisation, and create greater value for shareholders as well as other stakeholders.

1.3.5 Branding Decisions

The organisations have to make several decisions with regards to branding of their products.

The stages of branding decisions can be explained with the help of the following figure.

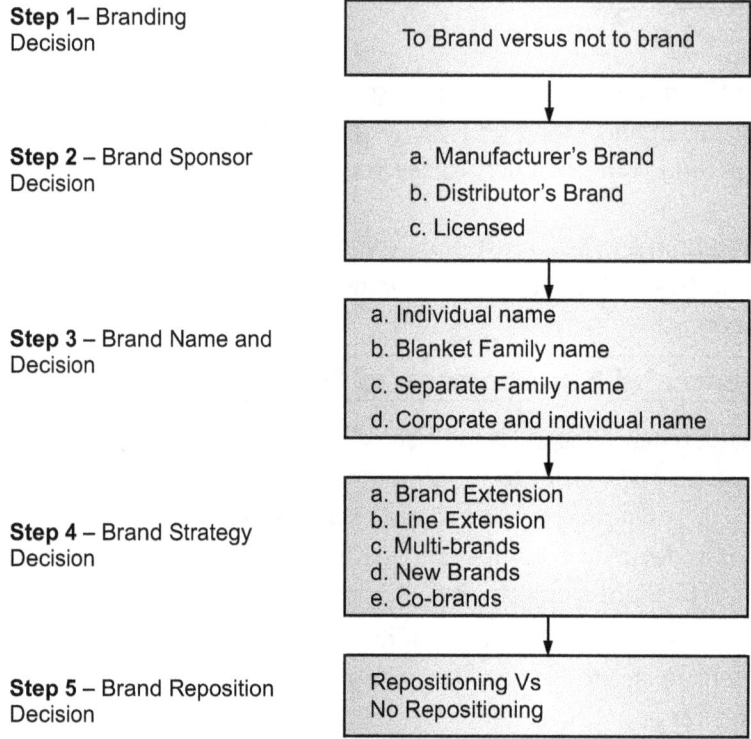

Fig. 1.9: Branding Decision Hierarchy

Let us take a detailed look at this process.

Step 1: Branding Decision: The first branding strategy decision is whether to develop a brand name for a product. In today's competitive situation, this actually is a foregone decision. It is quite difficult to find an unbranded product today.

Step 2: Brand Sponsor Decision: This decision is about the control of the brand and with whom it stays. If the organisation produces or manufactures a product and wants to brand the product on its own, it is called as a manufacturer's brand. As against this the manufacturing organisation may decide to let the stores that sell the product to brand their product and sell it; in this case it would be a Distributor's brand. Similarly an organisation can license a brand and use it on their product. Here it is a licensed brand.

Step 3: Brand Name Decision: The organisation now has the responsibility of choosing a brand name for its product.

Four general strategies are often used to choose a brand name:

(a) Individual names: Here the organisation gives different names to different products, even within the same product line. To cite an example – Hindustan Unilever gives different names to its various products like Lux, Lifebuoy, Dove, Liril for the Soaps (Personal Care), Surf, Wheel and Sunlight for the detergents (Fabric care) and Lipton,

Red Label and Taj Mahal (Tea Brands). A major advantage of using individual names is that the organisation does not tie up its reputation to the brand. That is if, the product fails for some reason, it does not hurt the image of the organisation.

(b) **Blanket Family Names:** Organisations using this strategy, use the same blanket family name for the diverse product categories. This strategy is seen with the TATA group. TATA brand name is used for diverse categories such as salt, tea, automobiles as well as for steel. The advantage of this strategy is that the organisation does not have to spend heavily on advertising and promotion as the brand name is already known and consumers are able to identify with it.

(c) **Separate Family Names for all products:** Here the organisation uses separate names for separate category of products. The Aditya Birla Group follows this strategy. Hindalco for aluminium, UltraTech fro Cement, Grasim and Graviera for fabrics.

(d) **Corporate Name combined with individual product names:** Here the organisation combines its corporate brand name with the individual product names, for example, Nestlé. Nestle Munch and Nestlé Kit-kat in chocolates, and similarly Nestlé Everyday Dairy Whitner, Nestlé Milkmaid and Nestlé Slim Milk in Milk and dairy category. Another example is Cadbury, which has Cadbury Five Star and Cadbury Dairy Milk in chocolates.

Step 4: This step is about the brand strategy decision. The organisation needs to take a call on the type of strategy that it will follow. The organisation can select from the five common strategies:

(a) **Brand Extensions:** An organisation may decide to use an existing brand name to launch a product in a new category. The advantage of this strategy is that a well established brand name gives the new product instant recognition and quicker acceptance. This also helps in saving advertising costs that would be required otherwise to familiarise consumers with the brand.

However there are also certain risks associated with this strategy. The new product may not be upto the consumers' expectations and may end up damaging the organisation's reputation. Although it is a good strategy, the brand name should suit the new product category as an inappropriate brand name may end in a marketing disaster for the organisation.

(b) **Line Extension:** In this strategy, the organisation introduces additional items in the same product category, under the same brand name, usually with new features like Flavours, Colours, and Sizes etc. The advantage is similar to that of Brand Extension strategy. Infact recognition and acceptance is more, since the newly introduced product belongs to the same product line.

The risk however is that if the product fails, it may damage the reputation of the entire product line. Besides, the brand name may lose its specific meaning.

(c) Multi-Brands: An organisation that introduces additional brands in the same product category is said to be using the multi-brand strategy. This strategy is generally used when the organisation is trying to establish different features or target different customer segments/markets having different buying motives.

The main advantage of this strategy is that it helps organisations to lock up more of the distributor shelf space and to protect its flagship brands or major brands by introducing other brands which are also called as flanker brands.

The risk associated with this strategy is that, each brand might obtain only a small market share with none of the brands being particularly profitable, with one brand cannibalising the others.

(d) New Brands: In certain cases the existing brand names do not suit the new product category or are found inappropriate for the new product category. In such cases the organisation finds it suitable to create new brand names.

While this strategy gives the new brands a distinct image and detaches it from existing brands, the advertising costs to familiarise the consumers and create a trust amongst them is considerable.

(e) Co-Brands: Also known as dual branding, it is a strategy in which two or better known brands are combined in an offer. Each brand stands to benefit from the others in terms of influencing the preference or purchase intention of the consumer. In case of co-packaged products, organisations entering into co-branding hope to reach newer audiences by associating with the other brand.

There are various forms of co-branding. When Lenovo advertises its laptops indicating the usage of Intel processors, it is component co-branding. Another form is same-company-branding, as in when an organisation brands two of its products. Another form is joint venture co-branding when two or more organisations brand their products together.

Step5: Brand Repositioning Decision: No matter how well a brand is positioned, a company may often have to reposition its brand. This happens when a competitor may place a brand next to the organisation's brand, or there may be a decrease in demand for some reason.

1.3.6 Brand Equity

Brand Equity is the differential effect of brand knowledge on consumer response to the marketing of the brand. It can be positive or negative. Brand equity incorporates the ability to provide added value to the company's products and services. This added value can be used to the company's advantage to charge price premiums, lower marketing costs and offer greater opportunities for customer purchase.

What is Brand Equity?

Brand equity is an intangible asset that depends on associations made by the consumer. There are atleast three perspectives from which to view brand equity:

- **Financial:** One way to measure brand equity is to determine the price premium that a brand commands over a generic product. For instance, if consumers are willing to pay ₹ 5000/- more for a branded television over the same unbranded television, this premium provides important information about the value of the brand. However, expenses such as promotional costs must be taken into account when using this method to measure brand equity.

- **Brand extensions:** A successful brand can be used as a platform to launch related products. The benefits of brand extensions are the leveraging of existing brand awareness thus reducing advertising expenditures and a lower risk from the perspective of the consumer. Furthermore, appropriate brand extensions can enhance the core brand. However, the value of brand extensions is tougher to quantify than a direct financial measures of brand equity.

- **Consumer-based:** A strong brand increases the consumer's attitude strength toward the product associated with the brand. This importance of actual experience by the customer implies that trial samples are more effective than advertising in the early stages of building a strong brand. The consumer's awareness and associations lead to perceived quality, inferred attributes and eventually brand loyalty.

Benefits of Brand Equity

- Facilitates a **more predictable income** stream.
- **Increases cash flow** by increasing market share, reducing promotional costs and allowing premium pricing.
- **Brand equity in an asset** that can be sold or leased.

However, brand equity is not always positive in value. Some brands acquire a bad reputation that results in negative brand equity. Negative brand equity can be measured by surveys in which consumers indicate that a discount is needed to purchase the brand over a generic product.

Building and Managing Brand Equity

In his 1989, **Managing Brand Equity**, Peter H. Farquhar outlined the following three stages that are required in order to build a strong brand:

1. **Introduction:** Introduce a quality product, with the strategy of using the brand as a platform from which to launch future products. A positive evaluation by the consumer is important.

2. **Elaboration:** Make the brand easy to remember and develop repeat usage. There should be accessible brand attitude, that is, the consumer should easily remember his or her positive evaluation of the brand.

3. **Fortification:** The brand should carry a consistent image overtime to reinforce its place in the consumer's mind and develop a special relationship with the consumer. Brand extensions can further fortify the brand, but only with related products having a perceived fit in the mind of the consumer.

Advantages / Importance of Brand Equity:

(a) It allows the company to charge a price premium compared to competitors with less brand equity.

(b) It maintains higher awareness of company's products.

(c) It is used as 'leverage' while introducing new products.

(d) It is often interpreted as an indicator of quality.

(e) High brand equity makes sure that the company's products are included in most consumer consideration set.

(f) It offers a strong defence against new products and new competitors.

(g) It can lead to higher rates of production trial and repeat purchasing due to buyer's awareness of brand, approval of its image/ reputation and trust in its quality.

1.3.7 Brand Elements

(a) **Brand Image:** A great brand has the power to create and reinforce a visual image. Often it takes a lots of advertising to imprint a brand image into the hearts and minds of the company customers.

A great brand is nothing if the product doesn't deliver or if the business plan is flawed. Creative advertising may be writing, but if people don't remember the brand name or message, it has failed in building the brand image. All companies are vulnerable. A brand image can live on, or it can lose its luster.

A brand is a visual image, a cure that people associate with a company. Building quality and purpose into a brand helps to sell the product and create a loyal customer base. Many products have become commoditised, that is, one brand is (perceived) as good a substitute as the other.

(b) **Brand Identity:** 'Brand Identity' is the total proposition that a company makes to consumers - the promise it makes. It may consist of features and attributes, benefits, performance, quality service support and the values that the brand possesses. The brand can be viewed as a product, a personality, a set of values and a position, it occupies in people's mind.

Brand identity is everything the company wants the brand to be seen as. It represents what is true and authentic about a brand. It is the cognitive and emotional understanding of the products, or organisation in the minds of existing customers and future customers. It is a state of mind that the marketer attempts to create in customers he wants to reach. To create this state of mind, all kinds of marketing techniques such as advertising, logos, celebrity endorsements, musical themes, event sponsorship etc. may be employed.

Through brand identity, the marketer's goal is to create a compelling connection in customer's mind between the product or company and some other attributes of value to the customer.

(c) Brand Franchise: The essence is to build up steadily the brand franchise or privilege. Branding enables a company to influence customers and develop customer preferences towards brands. Advertising and sales promotion can create initially **brand awareness** and **recognition**. Then, it can develop **brand preference** and, if possible, **brand loyalty**. The most desired objective is **brand insistence**. It is the stage when consumers so prefer a given brand that they will insist upon buying it and will not settle for substitute.

A seller has a brand franchise if customers exhibit brand insistence, brand loyalty or brand preference towards his product or service, rather than gaining mere brand awareness or recognition. A seller would always try to move buyers from brand awareness to brand preference, loyalty and insistence. Brand preference indicates that customer regards the brand favourably but he will accept a substitute if the said brand is not available in the market.

Brand recognition indicates the customers, favourable attitude towards the brand. This is the minimum expectation of the advertiser while developing brand franchise.

(d) Brand Preference and Brand Patronage: Branding not only gives separate identity and easy recognition to the product but it also creates special brand preference and brand loyalty. Branding is a powerful instrument of demand creation and demand retention. Popular brands such as Lux, Liril, Vimal, Colgate etc. have very great pulling power in the market.

Development of loyal customers, acting as a talking advertisement and repeat buyers is the greatest reason in favour of branding. Such customers will always insist on buying their favourable brand. In a competitive market, a clear message of service and appreciation, responsiveness to the customers, and value in the brand and brand name produces consumer loyalty to the brand.

1.4 Packaging and Labelling Decisions

Packaging is often referred to as the fifth P, in addition to the 4 P's of the marketing mix. This is because of the vital role that packaging plays as a part of the product strategy.

Packaging includes all activities of designing and producing the container or wrapper for a product.

1.4.1 Purpose of Packaging

Packaging has various purposes. Some of these are mentioned below:

(a) **Product Protection:** Packaging provides protection to the product, specially in case of products that are made of glass or are fragile in nature. It protects the products from damage due to handling, Pilferage, Contamination by dust or dirt, insect attack etc.

(b) **Product attractiveness:** The size, shape, colour and design of the package help in attracting the attention of the consumer.

(c) **Product Identification:** Packages help in differentiating similar products.

(d) **Product Convenience:** The package is also for convenience of use for the consumer.

(e) **Effective Sales Tool.**

(f) **Segmentation.**

1.4.2 Requirements of a good Package

1. **Package Design:** The package design must be such that it is in line with the image of the firm.
2. **Packaging Materials:** Though there is a wide choice with regards to packing material, the organisation should choose materials that are attractive and at the same time easy to use and do not increase the overall weight of the product.
3. **Convenience of Usage:** Packaging should be such that it provides maximum convenience and ease of handling to the consumer.
4. **Package should be eco-friendly:** Organisations must be socially responsible and packaging used must essentially be eco-friendly and not have an impact on the environment.

1.4.3 Types of Packaging

The container or wrapper in which the product is placed is called as a package. There may be upto three levels of material in package. This would largely depend on the type of the product and the requirements of the packaging.

For Example – a perfume is at first packed in a bottle. This is the **primary package.** The bottle is then placed in a cardboard box having the brand name and other informative details to be provided to the customer like the expiry date, ingredients etc. This is the **secondary package**. Lastly, all such boxes are placed in various corrugated boxes together for shipping purposes. This is the shipping package or the **tertiary package.**

Packaging is increasingly being used as a marketing tool, because it conveys meaning to the customer and is often a silent sales person in prompting the customer to buy the product. *The factors that have contributed to the increasing use of packaging as a marketing tool are described below:*

(a) **Self-service:** With the increase in the number or organised retail outlets, most products are sold at self service counters at the outlets. Statistics state that on an average a shopper passes by some 300 items in a minute. It is here that an effective package will help to catch the attention of the consumer and stand out in a crowd of products.

(b) **Consumer affluence:** A rise in consumer affluence has lead to consumers aspiring for better packaged products.

(c) **Organisation and Brand Image**: Organisations today recognise the power of packaging in contributing towards brand loyalty and instant brand recall and hence are paying more and more attention towards packaging.

(d) **Innovation opportunity**: Innovative packaging offers marketers an opportunity to differentiate their product in highly competitive markets.

1.4.4 New Trends in Packaging

1. **Squeeze bottles and tubes**: Bottles and tubes made of a variant of plastic are now a days used in packaging of products like toothpastes, personal care products etc.

2. **Sheet formed containers**: The examples of this type of packaging include skin packaging where a thin film of plastic is drawn across the product by vacuum, Blister packaging where a rigid bubble of plastic containing a product is attached on top of a product, and Semi rigid packaging in which semi-rigid plastic sheet is used as a complete product container.

3. **Sachets:** Sachetisation is when products are sold in small packets. This is commonly used for shampoo, hair oil, toothpaste, chocolates etc.

Today, the "going green" phenomenon has introduced a new aspect to packaging and labeling trends - conserving the earth's resources by simplifying packaging.

Packaging trends are heading toward smarter, more eco-friendly packaging. Not only will this help to reduce waste and conserve resources, but this may also help to lower overall packaging and labeling costs. Packaging trends and labeling trends will challenge manufacturers to balance attractive and functional designs with sustainable packaging options.

Downsizing Packaging: Less excessiveness and possibly less extravagance are some of the supplement packaging trends. Consumers are getting smarter.

Eco-friendly Solutions: Research is showing that consumers want to do their part to help and preserve the world for future generations. Packaging trends for eco-friendly packaging are no longer becoming an option! Eco-friendly packaging makes more sense and attracts more consumer appeal.

Convenience: Consumers are always looking for easier delivery forms and convenient packaging options. Packaging trends are definitely moving towards individual pouches that are portable and travel-friendly. As global travel increases, many consumers are looking for single dose pouches that they can take on a business trip or on a family vacation.

1.4.5 Labelling

Labelling is actually a part of packaging or can be termed as a subset of packaging. *The label can be something as simple as a tag attached to the product or something that is elaborately designed and presented along with the product.* The main function of a label is to identify the product.

1.4.6 Role of Labelling

- Labelling gives essential information to the customers about products.
- Customers can gain knowledge about the quality and features of product without tasting the product.
- Customers can recognise standard and grade of the product.
- A label provides information about the price, quantity, quality etc. of the product, due to which the customers buy the product without doubt and hesitation. They compare the product with the same nature products of other firms on the basis of the information provided on the label.
- A label becomes helpful to sellers to sell out the product. It protects the customers from malpractices of the middlemen.
- Labelling is a very key element affecting sales and distribution process of a product, which provides clear information about the grade, quantity, price, brand name, features etc. to the customers.

1.4.7 Functions of Labels

In marketing, the importance and necessity and functions of labeling of a product can be mentioned as follows:

1. **Labelling identifies the product:** Label helps to identify the product and brand and gives it a name that differentiates it from other products in the same category. It also helps to popularise the product and its brand name.

2. **Labelling grades the product:** A label helps to depict the grade of a product. For example, wheat can be expressed with the grades such as 1, 2, 3, 4. A label thus becomes useful in grading any product according to its quality.
3. **Labelling describes the product:** The label describes the product. Information and instructions about, who manufactured the product, when and where it was manufactured, how many and what ingredients have been used in it, how to use the product, how to keep the product safe, etc. are given on the label. This becomes helpful to the customers.
4. **Labelling promotes the product:** Label helps to promote the product. Customers' attention is drawn by attractive and fascinating graphs, figures or marks. This motivates the customers to buy the product. Label plays an important role in sales and distribution as it makes the customers take buying decision.
5. **Labelling protects the customers:** A label protects the customers. As maximum selling price, quantity, quality etc. are mentioned on the label, the customers are protected from the possible malpractice of middlemen.
6. **Labelling encourages the manufacturer or producer to make only standard products.**
7. **Manufacturer buyer relation is established.**

1.4.8 Classification of Labels

Labels can be classified depending upon its specific function:

(a) **Brand Label**: This is a label which gives the name of the Brand of the product only. These are exclusive labels which are meant for popularising the brand name.
Example: Lux, Taj Mahal etc

(b) **Grade Label**: When the manufacturer has many variants in one product category, he uses grade labels to describe the variant to the consumer.
Example: Dust Tea, leaf tea etc.

(c) **Descriptive and Illustrative labels:** These labels are descriptive in nature. They provide full information such as date of manufacturing, date of expiry, quantity, quality, ingredients etc.

1.5 Product Life Cycle

Products form an integral part of our lives. We are continuously using products from time to time throughout our lives. Our experience with products helps us make certain observations about the product. These are:

(a) All Products have a limited life.
(b) Throughout the life, the sales of any product does not remain consistent i.e. it passes through distinct stages, each posing some challenges and problems to the seller.

(c) Just as the sales are not consistent, it follows that profits also rise and fall at different stages in the life of the product.

(d) To cope with this, varying strategies are adopted by marketers.

The above observations now bring us to the concept of a Product Life Cycle (PLC).

Product life cycle *is the cycle through which every product goes through from introduction to withdrawal or eventual demise.*

Product life cycle is the period of time over which an item is developed, brought to market and eventually removed from the market. First, the idea for a product undergoes research and development. If the idea is determined to be feasible and potentially profitable, the product will be produced, marketed and rolled out. Assuming the product becomes successful, its production will grow until the product becomes widely available. Eventually, demand for the product will decline and it will become obsolete.

The product life cycle is the graphical representation of the various stages that a product goes through in its life. It comprises four stages. They are:

(a) Introductory stage

(b) Growth Stage

(c) Maturity stage, and

(d) Decline stage

However, while studying the concept of Product Life Cycle we must keep in mind that it applies to a generic category of a product and not a specific brand.

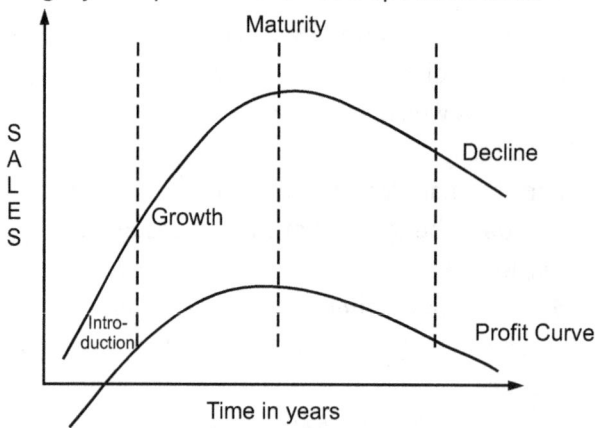

Fig. 1.10: Product Life Cycle

1.5.1 Concept and Characteristics of Product Life Cycle

The product life cycle concept derives from the fact that a product's sales volume and sales revenue follow a typical pattern of four phase cycle. The life cycle is a fact of existence for every product. It is similar to the human life cycle. The length of the life cycle, the duration of each phase and shape of the curve vary widely for different products.

A product passes through certain distinct stages during its life span; this is termed as Product Life Cycle. The 'Product Life Cycle' (PLC) indicates that a product is born or introduced, grows, attains maturity in a particular market and sooner or later it is found to enter in its declining stage. The 'Product Life Cycle' (PLC) should be termed as product market life cycle as it is related to a particular market.

(a) Introduction Stage: Also known as the pioneering stage. It is characterised by very little competition. Heavy promotional activities are required to create an awareness and demand for the product. This stage is expensive and risky. It is a no-profit stage because of the heavy promotional expenses.

  (i) Product is introduced in the market with the intention to build a clear identity and heavy promotion is done for maximum awareness.

  (ii) Before actual offering of the product to customers, the product passes through product development, involves prototype and market tests.

  (iii) Companies incur more costs in this phase and also bear additional cost for distribution. On the other hand, there are a few customers at this stage, means low sales volume.

  (iv) During the **introductory stage** company's profits shows a negative figure because of huge cost but low sales volume.

  (v) At this point in the life cycle, the organisation will typically control very little market share and the sales volume will be very low. This is usually due to the simple fact that not a lot of people are aware of the product.

  (vi) As a result, the fixed costs cannot be spread out very well, which leads to a high cost per customer. The combination of low sales volume and a high cost per customer typically result in negative profits.

  (vii) At this point in the life cycle, the organisation will want to create a marketing mix strategy that has the sole purpose of educating the target market.

  (viii) Likewise, the organisation should ensure that market segmentation is considered and it is important to determine whether or not the organisation is actually targeting the right customers. Often times, post-launch market research can be much more beneficial that pre-launch market research.

(b) Growth or the Market Acceptance Stage: Sales and profits are on the rise. Competitors enter the market in large numbers. It is in this stage that the product establishes itself in the market.

  (i) As the product enters the growth phase of the product life cycle, sales volume should start to rise rather rapidly.

  (ii) As people become aware and start to buy the product, the overall cost per customer will ultimately decrease.

(iii) With more customers and a lower cost per customer, the product's profitability should start to increase. During the growth phase, competition will start to take notice and will likely enter the market with a similar product.

(iv) At this point in the product life cycle, the organisation will want to adjust their marketing mix strategy to address the concern about competition. When laying out the revised marketing mix strategy, the following questions should be looked at:
- What has been learned about market segmentation and how accurate were the initial assumptions?
- In regards to competition, which competitors present a real threat to the business?
- How much would it cost to implement the necessary marketing mix strategy?
- Is there a substantial profit motive to move forward with the product?
- How much market share could be ultimately captured as the product moves through the product life cycle stages?

(c) Maturity Stage: It is also known as the stagnation or plateau stage. In the beginning part of this stage sales do increase but at a decreasing pace, because of intense competition.

(i) This is the stage where sales increases at a decreasing rate. New users cannot be added indefinitely and sooner or later the market approaches saturation.

(ii) Normally, this is the longest stage of the product life cycle. Many major household appliances are in the maturity stage of their life cycles.

(iii) For shopping products and many specialty products, annual models begin to appear during the maturity stage. Product lines are lengthened to appeal to additional market segments. Service and repair assume more important roles as manufacturers strive to distinguish their products from others. Product design changes tend to become stylistic (how can the product be made different?) rather than functional (how can the product be made better?)

(iv) As prices and profits continue to fall, marginal competitors start dropping out of the market. Dealer margins also shrink, resulting in less shelf space for mature items, lower dealer inventories, and a general reluctance to promote the product. Thus, promotion to dealers often intensifies during this stage in order to retain loyalty. Heavy consumer promotion by the manufacturer is also required to maintain market share.

(v) Another characteristic of the maturity stage is the emergence of "niche marketers" that target narrow, well-defined, under-served segments of a market.

(vi) Because the product is selling in such large volumes, the overall cost per customer should be very low. As a result, the product's profitability should be at its highest point yet.

(vii) During the maturity phase, it's likely that the number of competitors in the market has become stable, possibly even declining some.

(viii) At this point, how the product has performed as it's moved through the different product life cycle stages is to be considered. This insight will help in creating a marketing mix strategy for this particular stage of the life cycle.

(ix) Some questions that need to be looked at in this stage:
- Is there a profit motive to continue to put in money into marketing this product?
- Is there still market share to be captured? And how much would it cost to capture that market share?
- What has been learned from the previous product life cycle stages and how can that knowledge be applied at this stage in the life cycle?

(d) Decline Stage: For most products decline is inevitable. Here profits and sales volumes both decline.

(i) A long-run decline in sales signals the beginning of the decline stage. The rate of decline is governed by how rapidly consumer tastes change or substitute products are adopted. Many convenience products and fad items lose their market overnight, leaving large inventories of unsold items.

(ii) Due to the declining sales volume, the product's profitability will eventually start to decline. During the decline phase, competitors will likely leave the market.

(iii) Some firms have developed successful strategies for making products in the decline stage of the PLC. They eliminate all non essential marketing expenses and let sales decline as more customers discontinue purchasing the products. Eventually, the product is withdrawn from the market.

(iv) Consumers can be grouped according to how quickly they adopt a new product. On the one extreme, some consumers adopt the product as soon as it becomes available. On the other extreme, some consumers are among the last to purchase a new product.

The table given below summarises the Characteristics, Marketing Objectives and strategies in the various stages of the Product Life Cycle.

Table 1.2: Table depicting the characteristics of various stages of the Product Life Cycle

	Introduction	Growth	Maturity	Decline
Characteristics				
Sales	Low	Rapidly rising sales	Peak sales	Declining Sales
Costs	High cost per customer	Average cost per customer	Low cost per customer	Low cost per customer
Profits	Negative	Rising	High Profits	Declining
Customers	Innovators	Early adopters	Middle Majority	Laggards
Competitors	Few	Growing number	Stable number beginning to decline	Declining number
Marketing Objectives	Create Product Awareness and trial	Maximize Market share	Maximize profit while defending Market share	Reduce expenditure and milk the brand
Strategies				
Product	Offer basic product	Offer product extensions, service, warranty	Diversify brands and items models	Phase out weak products
Price	Charge Cost-plus	Price to penetrate market	Price to match competitors	Cut price
Distribution	Build Selective distribution	Build intensive distribution	Build more intensive distribution	Go selective; phase out unprofitable outlets
Advertising	Build product awareness among early adopters and dealers	Build awareness and interest in mass markets	Stress brand differences and benefits	Reduce to levels needed to retain hard core loyals
Sales Promotion	Use heavy sales promotion	Reduce to take advantage of heavy consumer demand	Increase to encourage brand switching	Reduce to minimal level

Source: Marketing Management Kotler, Keller, Kosh and Jha 13th Edition, Pearson Education

1.5.2 Relevance of Product Life Cycle

The product life cycle is an important concept in marketing. It describes the stages a product goes through from when it was first thought of until it finally is removed from the market. Not all products reach this final stage. Some continue to grow and others rise and fall.

- **(a) Management Tool**: 'Product Life Cycle' concept may be used as a managerial tool. Marketing strategies must change as the product goes through the different life cycles. If the managers understand the product life cycle concept very clearly, they are in better position to forecast the future sales activities and plan marketing strategies accordingly.

- **(b) Planning the Entry of a New-Product**: The concept of 'Product Life Cycle' helps the marketer in pre-planning the entry of a new product in the market.

- **(c) Product Information**: The 'Product Life Cycle' indicates that the product is born or introduced, grows, attains maturity in a particular market and then sooner or later it is found to enter its declining stage.

1.5.3 Alternate Patterns of Product Life Cycle

Though the above graph is most common, not all products go through exactly the bell shaped product Life Cycle shown in Fig. 1.10 above. A few common alternate patterns of Product Life Cycle are depicted below:

- **(a) Growth-Slump-Maturity Pattern:** For some products that is a rapid growth in sales when the product is first introduced, but this sales curve then slumps or falls to a level. This level is then sustained because of consumers who are late adopters and buy it for the first time, much after its introduction and replacement of the product. Those who had purchased it when it was initially introduced were the early adopters.

Fig. 1.11: Growth-Slump-Maturity Pattern

(b) Cycle-Recycle Pattern: This type of a PLC pattern is seen when the initial promotion and advertising produces a first cycle of high sales growth. After some time the sales decline. This is when the organisation again tries to push the product through promotion and advertising. This is when the second cycle happens. However it is smaller than the first cycle.

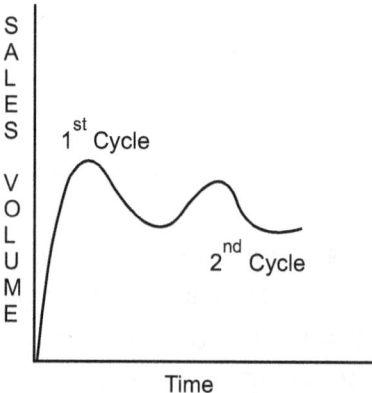

Fig. 1.12: Cycle-Recycle Pattern

(c) Scalloped pattern of the Product Life Cycle: This is observed when the sales volume passes through a succession of life cycles mainly due to discovery of new product characteristics or new uses or new users.

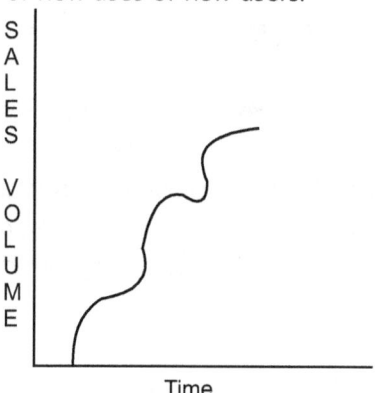

Fig. 1.13: Scalloped Pattern

1.5.4 Special Categories of Product Life Cycle

Apart from the common categories of product life cycles, we also need to look at some of the special categories of Product life Cycles. These are the Style, Fashion and Fad Life cycles.

Style: A style is a basic and very distinct way of expression appearing in human endeavours. It can last for generations and be the in-thing at times and be out of vogue at other times.

Fashion: A fashion is a currently accepted or a very popular style. Generally the pattern is similar to that of the classic product life cycle because like the Classic PLC, the fashion also passes through four stages. These are **Distinctiveness**- A stage where a particular product is new and distinct from others and hence becomes fashionable.

The second stage is **Emulation**, where many consumers start imitating by using the product;

The third stage is **Mass fashion** when the product gets accepted on a mass scale and lastly the **decline** stage when the product goes out of fashion.

Fad: Fads are fashions that peak very fast and decline equally fast. They are in vogue for a very short period of time.

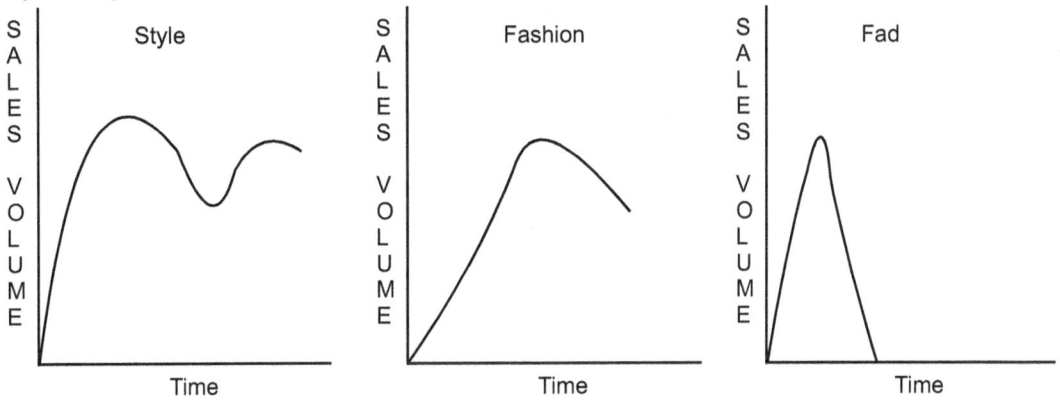

Fig. 1.14: Depicting Style, Fashion and Fad Life Cycles

1.5.5 Strategies Across Stages of the Product Life Cycle

As mentioned earlier, each of the stages of the product life cycle pose an opportunity and a challenge to the marketer. Let us now take a look at the various strategies that can be adopted by the marketer to ensure success in each stage of the Product Life Cycle. While discussing this, we shall first take a look at the characteristics of the stage and then understand the strategies that are needed.

(a) **Marketing Introduction Stage or pioneering stage**: In the introductory stage the marketer faces the challenge of launching the new product, ensuring a proper dealer network and creating consumer awareness and gaining their acceptance. Hence the pace at which sales moves is rather slow while promotional expenditures are peaking. As such it then becomes essential for the marketer to make a decision as to whether the organisation wants to be the first one to launch the product or be a follower in the market. Generally in a market where the rate of obsolescence is rather high, being an early bird is a good move. Most studies indicate that market leaders have the first advantage. However, there is a lot of risk involved and a lot of expenditure too.

Product strategy: While deciding strategies, the organisation needs to introduce the product in its basic or core avatar leaving room for further improvements or addition of features. (So that when the competition steps in with a product similar to the basic product, the pioneering organisation can introduce an improvised version).

Price Strategy: With regards to price, the marketer can adopt a cost plus pricing approach to ensure that it achieves its breakeven in the stipulated time.

Physical Distribution Strategy: The distribution has to be done in select areas through a network that is reliable. In the initial stages, it is essential that the marketer goes for selective distribution.

Promotional Strategy: With a lot of advertising to create awareness it is also necessary to use heavy sales promotion to lure the customer into trying the product for the first time.

(b) **Market Growth Stage:** In this stage, consumers who have already purchased the product will typically go in for repeat purchases and those who have not will now begin to purchase the product. This leads to a rapid increase in the sales. Attracted by the opportunities presented by the market, the competition enters at this stage.

Product Strategy: To strengthen the product by introducing additional features or newer extensions.

Price Strategy: Prices may remain the same or can be reduced slightly to create entry barriers for the competition.

Promotional Strategy: It is advisable for marketers to maintain the promotional expenditures and continue to dominate the consumers mind with advertisements.

Physical Distribution: In order to increase the profits, the organisation must expand its distribution and other untapped areas.

(c) **Market Maturity Stage:** In this stage the rate of sales starts to reduce. The maturity stage is generally divided into three phases and lasts for a while. The three phases are growth, stable and decay.

In the first phase, the sales growth rate reduces newer areas to expand the distribution and competition intensifies. In the second phase sales flatten because of the market saturation. In the third phase the absolute level of sales begins to drop and customers begin switching to other products.

Product Strategy: Increasing R&D budgets to develop product improvements and line extensions.

Pricing Strategy: As competition intensifies, frequent mark downs become necessary to sell the product.

Promotion: Increasing advertising works to a certain extent.

Distribution: The organisation now needs to look at intensifying the distribution to unknown areas and untapped markets.

Generally in this stage it is seen that weaker competitors leave the market and eventually a few dominant players are left in the market. These would typically be the cost leader, the quality leader and the service leader. Also some firms catering to the niche market and providing customisation are able to co-exist in this market.

(d) **Marketing Strategies - Decline stage:** The reasons for decline of a product in the market are many. The sales may decline due to technological advancement and the earlier technology becoming obsolete, or because of change in the consumer likes and tastes, also because of increased competition.

Product Strategy: As sales start to decline some firms feel it wiser to withdraw from the market and drop the products from their product line.

Price Strategy: A price cut serves to do away with the remaining stocks.

Distribution: In this stage the distribution is curtailed and unprofitable. Outlets are shut down or distribution to areas where sales is low is stopped.

Promotion: Some amount of advertising is continued, but all sales promotion activities are stopped.

Points to Remember

- **Product**
  A product is anything that can be offered to a customer to satisfy a want or a need.
- **Levels of a Product**
  (a) Core Benefit Level
  (b) Basic Product Level
  (c) Expected Product Level
  (d) Augmented Product Level
  (e) Potential Product Level
- **Product Hierarchy**
  There are seven levels in the product hierarchy.
  o Need Family
  o Product Family
  o Product Class
  o Product Line
  o Product type
  o Brand
  o Stock Keeping Unit (SKU)

- **Product Classification**

  The various bases used by marketers to classify products are:

  (a) On the basis of durability and tangibility of the product

  (b) On the basis of Consumer Shopping Habits. On the basis of use in industry

- **Product Mix**

  The product mix is part of the marketing mix. The various components of the product mix are:

  o Product Line Product Line Length Product Line Depth

  o Width or breadth of the product mix Length of the Product Mix

  o Depth of the Product Mix

- **Product Line Decisions**

  The various product line decisions are:

  (a) Line stretching – Upwards and Downwards

  (b) Line filling – Only in between

  (c) Line Modernization

  (d) Line Featuring

  (e) Line Pruning

- **New Product Development**

  Rationale for New Product Development

  There are several reasons as to why organisations launch new products.

  (a) Technological obsolescence

  (b) To fight competition

  (c) To fulfill consumer needs

  (d) Upgrading existing products

  (e) Minimizing risks

- **Types of New Products**

  Generally the new products are classified into three main categories, namely

  (a) Truly Innovative New Product

  (b) Replacements in the market that are significantly different from existing products

  (c) C. Imitative products new to organisation but not to market "ME TOO"

- **Booz Allen and Hamilton Classification Scheme for New Products**

  (a) Technological Breakthroughs/New to the world products

  (b) Significant improvements

  (c) Modified Products

  (d) Products new to company

  (e) Repositioning

  (f) Cost reductions

- **The New Product Development and Decision Process**

  The steps involved in the process are:
  1. Idea Generation
  2. Idea Screening
  3. Concept development and testing
  4. Marketing Strategy Development
  5. Business Analysis
  6. Product Development
  7. Market Testing
  8. Commercialisation

- **Brand**

  Business Goods Test Marketing

  The methods used for test marketing Business goods differ from those used for consumer goods.
  1. Alpha testing organization
  2. Beta testing organization
  3. Trade Shows organization
  4. Display in Distributor and Dealer showrooms organization

- **Brand and Branding**

  A Brand is a name, term, sign, symbol or design or a combination of them intended to identify the goods or services of one seller or group of sellers and to differentiate them from those of the competitors.

- **Levels of Meaning of a Brand**

  There are six levels of meaning conveyed by a brand. They are
  - Attributes
  - Benefits
  - Values
  - Culture
  - Personality
  - User

- **Packaging**

  Packaging includes all activities of designing and producing the container or wrapper for a product.

- **Purpose of Packaging**

    Packaging has various purposes. Some of these are mentioned below:
    (a) Product Protection
    (b) Product attractiveness
    (c) Product Identification
    (d) Product Convenience

- **Requirements of a good Package**

    A good package entails a good package design, use of proper packaging material and convenience of use

- **Labelling**

    Labelling is actually a part of packaging or can be termed as a subset of packaging.

- **Functions of Labels**

    (a) The label identifies the product and gives it a name that differentiates it from other products in the same category.
    (b) The Label describes the product as to who made it, where it was made and when it was made, what it contains, and how it is to be used.
    (c) The Label also promotes the product through attractive graphics.

- **Product Life Cycle**

    The product life cycle is the graphical representation of the various stages that a product goes through in its life. It comprises of 4 stages. They are

Questions for Discussion

(A) Long Answer Questions:
1. Define a product. Discuss the various levels of a product.
2. With the help of suitable examples explain the difference between goods and services.
3. Discuss in detail product hierarchy and its relevance to the Marketing Manager.
4. What do you understand by Product Classification? Describe in detail the various bases used to classify products? Give examples.
5. With the help of a suitable example explain the new product design and development process in detail.
6. Discuss the significance of the Product Development Stage. What are the common techniques for conducting consumer tests in this stage?
7. "Idea Generation is at the core of product development". Discuss this statement in light of the common methods used for idea generation.
8. "Test Marketing stage for a product is a very crucial stage". Comment explaining the objectives and the rationale of test marketing.
9. Compare the techniques for consumer test marketing vis-a-vis business goods test marketing.

10. Describe the procedure for test marketing. Use an example to substantiate your answer.
11. Define a brand. What are the common branding decisions that a brand manager needs to take while deciding the brand name for a new product?
12. "A package is a silent salesperson". Critically evaluate this statement.
13. With the help of suitable examples discuss the various types of co-branding techniques.
14. Discuss the various decisions that a product manager has to make with regards to the product lines of an organisation.
15. Discuss the concept of product life cycle. What are the factors affecting the product life cycle of a product?
16. Discuss the strategic importance of product life cycle from the point of view of managing the product in the various phases of the Product Life Cycle.
17. What are the various types of new products? With the help of suitable examples, explain the classification.

(B) Short Questions/Short Notes - Write Short Notes on:
1. Product mix.
2. Alternate patterns of product life cycle.
3. Special categories of product life cycle.
4. Rationale for new product development.
5. Booz Allen and Hamilton Classification scheme for new products.
6. Idea screening stage.
7. Concept development stage.
8. Product development Stage.
9. Consumer adoption process.
10. Test Marketing of new products.
11. Commercialisation stage.
12. Causes of failure of new products.
13. New trends in packaging.
14. Functions of labelling.
15. Classification of labels.
16. Purpose and significance of branding.
17. Marketing strategies in decline stage of a product.
18. Types of new products.
19. Advantages and disadvantages of branding.
20. Types of packaging.

(C) Multiple Choice Questions:

1. A product comprises of:
   (a) Only Physical goods
   (b) Only services
   (c) Physical goods, services and ideas
   (d) Only ideas
2. By nature services are:
   (a) Tangible
   (b) Intangible
   (c) Long Lasting
   (d) Separable
3. Product mix is also called as:
   (a) Product Depth
   (b) Product Assortment
   (c) Product Line
   (d) Product Length
4. Product line decisions include:
   (a) Line pruning
   (b) Line mixing
   (c) Line fixing
   (d) Line matching
5. Staples are goods that are purchased:
   (a) On a regular basis
   (b) Sometimes
   (c) Rarely
   (d) None of the options
6. Capital items are those items whose purchase amounts to:
   (a) Bad Debts
   (b) Capital expenditure
   (c) Losses
   (d) Minor expenses
7. One of the main reasons for an organisation to go for New Products Development is:
   (a) To do concept testing
   (b) To commercialise the new product
   (c) To do market testing
   (d) To reduce risk and take care of technological obsolescence
8. Various types of new products include:
   (a) Increasingly new product
   (b) "Me too" or imitative new products
   (c) New ideas
   (d) New markets
9. Idea generation stage includes:
   (a) Market testing
   (b) Concept development
   (c) Business analysis
   (d) Brainstorming
10. One of the techniques of concept development and testing is:
    (a) Morphological Analysis
    (b) Idea Generation
    (c) Conjoint Analysis
    (d) Idea Screening
11. A common technique to find out consumer preferences in the Product Development stage is:
    (a) Paired Comparison
    (b) Forced relationships
    (c) Brainstorming
    (d) Expert Opinion

12. One of the techniques to carry out consumer goods test marketing is:
    (a) Monadic rating method	(b) Simple rank order method
    (c) Sales Wave Research	(d) Attribute Listing
13. A common technique for test marketing Business Goods is:
    (a) Paired Comparison	(b) Alpha testing
    (c) Monadic rating method	(d) Brainstorming
14. An organisation that introduces additional brands in the same product category is said to be using:
    (a) Co-branding strategy	(b) Line extension
    (c) Multi-Brand strategy	(d) Umbrella brand strategy
15. Branding decision includes a decision about:
    (a) Brand strength	(b) Brand vitality
    (c) Brand share	(d) Brand name
16. One of the strategies used to choose a brand name is:
    (a) Brand-Sponsor Strategy
    (b) Brand Repositioning Strategy
    (c) Blanket family name for diverse product categories
    (d) Brand Health Strategy
17. Main purpose of packaging is:
    (a) Selling	(b) Pricing
    (c) Protection of the product	(d) Idea generation
18. The third stage is the Product Life Cycle is:
    (a) Growth	(b) Introduction
    (c) Decline	(d) Maturity
19. Special category of product life cycle includes:
    (a) Growth Cycles	(b) Fashion Cycles
    (c) Profit Cycles	(d) Introductory Cycles
20. When the sales volume of a product passes through a succession of life cycles mainly due to discovery of new product characteristics you get a:
    (a) Cycle-recycle pattern	(b) Scalloped Pattern
    (c) Growth Slump Maturity pattern	(d) Fad pattern
21. Factors affecting Product Life Cycle include:
    (a) Rate of acceptance of the product by the customer
    (b) Promotion mix
    (c) Profit Cycles
    (d) Product line

22. In the Introduction stage of the Product Life Cycle:
    (a) Expenses are very less
    (b) Expenses are very high
    (c) Profits are very high
    (d) Sales volume is very high
23. The Customers who adopt the product very late i.e. in the decline stage are
    (a) Innovators
    (b) Laggards
    (c) Early adopters
    (d) Middle Majority
24. Product Life Cycle is useful for:
    (a) Understanding new product
    (b) Understanding new markets
    (c) As a tool for forecasting
    (d) As a tool for studying competition
25. Maturity Stage of the Product Life Cycle is also known as:
    (a) Market Acceptance Stage
    (b) Plateau Stage
    (c) Pioneering Stage
    (d) Awareness Stage

Answers

1. (c)	2. (b)	3. (b)	4. (a)	5. (a)	6. (b)	7. (d)	8. (b)	9. (d)	10. (c)
11. (a)	12. (c)	13. (b)	14. (b)	15. (d)	16. (c)	17. (c)	18. (d)	19. (b)	20. (b)
21. (a)	22. (b)	23. (b)	24. (c)	25. (b)					

(D) Project Questions:

1. You are the owner of an organisation manufacturing a range of personal care products and your shampoo and moisturiser is a brand leader in the market. Your competitor is planning to launch an exclusive shampoo that is likely to affect your number one position. What elements of the product mix will you modify to handle the situation? Why?
2. Prepare a flowchart to explain product hierarchy. You may assume a suitable product for the same.
3. As a marketing manager in an organisation manufacturing office automation products, discuss the strategies that you will adopt for the introduction of a new range of photocopiers.
4. A latest fad amongst youngsters is Shirts that have cuts from the elbow to the wrist. This is very popular with the teenage and college going crowd. As a consultant to an organisation engaged in manufacturing and selling shirts, prepare a graphical representation of the probable Product Life Cycle for this product.
5. As a manager of an organisation manufacturing consumer white goods like refrigerators and washing machines, suggest a suitable and cost effective packaging technique.
6. You are the manufacturer of pumps. You have developed a new type of pump that has inbuilt sensors to operate depending upon the level if water. Explain how you would test market the same?

Case Study

New Product Development at Georgina's

Background Note:

Georgina's was started as Georgina's Home Service (GHS), a fast food home delivery business in March 1952 by the US based Melwin Georgina (Melwin). The primary motive for starting this venture was to help Melwin's family dairy business survive in the wake of unfavorable changes in the then regulatory set-up.

Focused efforts on the part of the family helped GHS grow rapidly. In 1965, Melwin started selling frozen pizza as well from the fast food home delivery trucks to expand his product portfolio. The frozen pizza business proved to be very successful and Melwin decided to further explore the possibilities in this area.

In 1969, GHS acquired a pizza factory in Kansas and started selling pizzas to retailers as well as to institutional buyers such as schools, universities and hospitals. Over the next three decades, the company grew largely through the acquisitions route.

The GHS label marketed frozen pizzas under the brand name Cheezee. The Cheezee range of Pizza's was introduced in 1976 as an umbrella brand to offer variety of Pizza's to the customers. Under this brand, the organisation included varieties of Pizza's like double Cheese, Thin Crust, Roasted Crust and many such varieties.

Case:

The Need for Product Innovation

The pizza business in the United States had grown at a healthy pace since its inception in the 1960s. In 1985, pizza was ranked as the fifth most popular food in the country and by the late 1990s, the industry was growing at 8% per annum with yearly sales of $2 billion.

In 1999, pizza became the most popular food in the US. Significantly, of the four broad segments in the Pizza Business i.e. dine-in, take-away, home-delivery and frozen, the last segment that is the frozen pizza segment was growing at the fastest pace. In fact, frozen pizza was growing the fastest within the entire US frozen food industry.

The reason behind the fast growth of the frozen pizza segment was attributed to the introduction of the 'rising crust' technology in the mid 1990s. By using this technology, it became possible for customers to get restaurant/take-away/home-delivery quality pizza at home.

The Cheezee Style of New Product Development

While it was true that competition made it important for Georgina to focus on developing new offerings, there was another factor that fuelled its decision to launch a truly innovative product. The company was quick to realize that the single-serve segment lacked a good quality, convenient and universally appealing product. It was this realization that lead to the development and introduction of Cheezee.

In this new product Development exercise, Georgina followed some exceptional practices that lead it to achieve greater success. This included some unique features in the new product development process.

To begin with Georgina started the entire new product development process after taking consistent feedback from customer's for a longer period of time. Introduction of the frozen Pizza was also the result of a similar feedback from the customers. Besides this they took painstaking efforts in modifying their pizzas and getting them to confirm to the taste of the customers.

With the increase in the variety that they offered to the customers Georgina was careful to evaluate each product variant and work on its modification process to suit the customer tastes.

An Effort Well-Rewarded

In October 2003, Georgina was declared as the winner of the '2003 Spirit of Innovation Awards.'

Georgina was given this award in the retail category for its newly launched product, cheezee frozen Pizza.

Another leading industry publication, *Stagnito's New Products Magazine* adjudged this product as the best new product of the year.

For the year 2002, Georgina also led the entire US food industry in terms of the maximum increase in the number of new products launched. The company was way ahead of seasoned food giants such as Kraft Foods, PepsiCo and Unilever

Interestingly, it was the only brand among the top nine rank holders that was not popular at the global level. These developments meant a lot to Georgina since it had reportedly been working hard for over two years towards introducing Cheezee Pizza.

Thanks to these awards and recognitions, the $3 billion, privately-held company established itself firmly as one of the most innovative players in the intensely competitive US frozen foods business.

In mid 2003, the company was the world's largest frozen pizza processor, and in terms of market shares, was next only to the country's largest food company, Kraft Foods.

Questions

1. Discuss the unique features of the new product development process adopted by Georgina's.
2. According to you what were the reasons for the success of the new product.
3. State the reasons why product development became a tool for deriving competitive advantages for players in this industry.

Questions from Previous Pune University Examinations

1. "Success of several consumer products in the Indian Market in the recent past was directly or indirectly related to packaging decisions". Critically evaluate the statement describing the nature and importance of packaging decisions. Give suitable illustrations from Indian Consumer Market. **[M.B.A. Dec. 2005]**
2. Discuss the Purpose, Types and New Trends in Packaging, Give examples. **[M.B.A. April 2007]**
3. Outline the New Product Decision Process. **[M.B.A. April 2007]**
4. What is Brand? Explain its Purpose and Significance in the Modern Marketing. **[M.B.A. Dec. 2007]**
5. Define Branding. State its Purpose and Importance. **[M.B.A. April 2010]**
6. Define Branding and Explain the Purpose and Significance of it in the Era of Cut-throat Competition. **[M.B.A. Dec. 2009]**
7. Define Packaging. Explain its Importance. Comment on the New Trends in Packaging by giving suitable examples. **[M.B.A. Dec. 2010]**
8. Write Short Notes:
   (a) Significance of Branding. **[M.B.A. Dec. 2005]**
   (b) Branding. **[M.B.A. April 2007, 2010, 2011 and Dec. 2010]**
   (c) Current Trends in Packaging. **[M.B.A. April 2009]**
   (d) New Trends in Packaging. **[M.B.A. April 2010]**
   (e) Packaging and Labelling. **[M.B.A. Dec. 2010, 2011]**
9. Explain in detail the Stages of New Product Development. **[M.B.A. Dec. 2011]**
10. What do you mean by the term Product Life Cycle (PLC)? **[M.B.A. Dec. 2011]**

■■■

Chapter 2...

Price

Contents ...
2.1 Introduction
2.2 Definitions and Meaning of Price
    2.2.1 Relationship between Price and Pricing
    2.2.2 Importance of Pricing
    2.2.3 The Changing Pricing Environment
    2.2.4 Factors Influencing Pricing Decisions
2.3 Setting the Price
    2.3.1 Setting Price Objectives
    2.3.2 Determining Demand
    2.3.3 Estimating Cost
    2.3.4 Analysing Competitor's Costs, Price and Offers
    2.3.5 Selecting a Pricing Method
    2.3.6 Selecting the Final Price
2.4 Adapting the Price
    2.4.1 Geographical Pricing
    2.4.2 Price Discounts and Allowances
    2.4.3 Promotional Pricing
    2.4.4 Discriminatory Pricing
2.5 Price Changes
- Points to Remember
- Questions for Discussion
- Case Study
- Questions from Previous Pune University Examinations

Learning Objectives ...
- To understand the meaning of pricing and its importance
- To study the various objectives of pricing
- To recognise the various factors influencing the pricing decisions
- To have an insight into the various approaches to setting price
- To learn the various strategies to adapt price
- To study the actual process of pricing and the various conditions therein
- To understand the situations of price change and managing price change

2.1 Introduction

Price is an important aspect of any product or service. It is not just a tag attached to a product. Price can be represented in many forms, and price performs a number of functions as well. Price is something that a consumer pays in return for the product or service and hence he would look at the product or service as value for the money that he/she pays. Price is also made up of a number of components. Thus learning about price and pricing strategies is very crucial from a marketer's point of view.

In the entire marketing mix, amongst all the P's Price is the only element which brings in revenue while all others generate costs. Any change in the price can affect all the other P's of the marketing mix.

2.2 Definitions and Meaning of Price

Price is something that is paid in return for obtaining a product or a service. In today's market, price is the amount of money and/or other items with utility needed to acquire a product, a service or an idea. In other words it can be said that price is what a consumer pays for what he gets. However, this is a narrow perception of price. Speaking of price in a broader sense, it can be said that price is the sum of all the values that the consumers exchange in return for the benefits that are offered by the usage of a product or the benefits that are obtained by availing a service.

Price

: is the amount of money that you pay for something or that something costs

: the amount of money given or set as consideration for the sale of a specified thing

Philip Kotler defines Price as *"the amount of money charged for a product or service"*.

Stanton defines Price as: *"Price is the amount of money or goods needed to acquire some combination of another goods and its companying services."*

There are various terms that are used to describe price for different products/services. Table 2.1 given below highlights some of these terms.

Table 2.1

Sr. No.	Product/Service to be availed by Consumer	What the Consumer pays
1.	Education	Tuition Fees
2.	Use of money (Loan)	Interest
3.	Use of space	Rent
4.	Use of Transportation Services	Fare
5.	Use of a roadway/highway	Toll
6.	Services of blue collared workers	Wages
7	Insurance	Premium

Product, distribution and promotion are all part of the process of providing something satisfying to the customer. Product activities conscern the design and packaging of the good or service itself, distribution involves getting the product to the customers and promotion involves communicating the product's existence and benefits to customers and potential customers. All three of these types of marketing activities contribute to the product being of value to customers. Pricing on the other, is not primarily concerned with creating value.

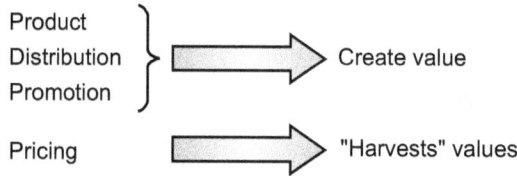

2.2.1 Relationship between Price and Pricing

Price and pricing are two different terms. While price is what the seller feels is worth of the product to the buyer and what the buyer pays for the product. Pricing is the process you need to go through to figure out what price to attach to each unit. Pricing, therefore, is a strategic process that you must learn, and use, for business success.

It involves:

- Establishing pricing objectives.
- Identifying the factors that govern the price.
- Deciding the product value in monetary terms.
- Formulating policies and strategies for pricing.
- Implementing and controlling the strategies.

2.2.2 Importance of Pricing

Traditionally, price has operated as the major determinant of buyer choice. Although recently there has been a shift in buyer behaviour with non-price factors also playing a role in the consumer decision process, price still remains the major factor that influences the buyer's decision. As mentioned earlier, price is the only element of the marketing mix that generates revenues while all other elements lead to costs.

Similarly, price is also the most flexible element of the marketing mix, as in, it can be changed quickly, unlike other elements such as product features, promotional campaigns or channel relationships.

Organisations are known to handle price in different ways. In small organisations, prices are often set by the top management, whereas in large organisations, it is seen that pricing is handled by Product Line Managers for those lines of products that they are responsible for. However, irrespective of the size of the organisation, the general pricing objectives and policies are laid down by the top management.

Price is an important element of the marketing mix for the following reasons:

(a) Price is the most important factor for a consumer when it comes to making a purchase decision. Rarely will it be otherwise. As such, the right kind of pricing strategy can help achieve organisational goals.

(b) Price can be easily changed and is flexible thereby helping the organisation to respond quickly to marketplace changes.

(c) Price can also be used as a differentiating factor to set aside the said product from other products in the same category.

(d) Price is also often used to target a particular segment of customers.

(e) And, last but not the least; price is the only element of the marketing mix that fetches revenue for the organisation.

2.2.3 The Changing Pricing Environment

While studying pricing, we need to look at the way, pricing practices have evolved over the years. Although the marketplace is becoming more competitive by the day, there are organisations which have been able to move consumers up to more expensive products by offering them value for money. The internet is also playing a crucial role in bringing out new trends in pricing practices. The Internet provides consumers with instant price comparisons at the click of a button, and also allows them to set the price through auction sites. On the other hand, Seller's and Marketers can monitor customer behaviour and make tailor made offers to individuals, give special offers to some customers and negotiate prices in online auctions

2.2.4 Factors Influencing Pricing Decisions

There are several factors that an organisation must take into consideration when setting the price. The pricing decision depends upon a number of factors. These factors are divided into two categories i.e. Internal factors and External factors. The table 2.2 below depicts the internal and the external factors that influence the pricing decisions.

Table 2.2: Factors influencing the pricing decisions

Internal Factors	External Factors
Organisational factors	Estimated Demand
Marketing Mix	Competitive Reactions
Product Differentiation	Suppliers
Cost of the Product	Economic Conditions
Objectives of the Organisation	Buyers
Product Life Cycle	Government Regulations
Functional Position	

Let us take a look at these factors.

(a) Internal Factors

(i) **Organisational Factors:** In any organisation, pricing decisions happen at two separate levels. The overall pricing strategy is decided at the top level. However the actual price setting is done at the operational level. As such the dynamics of these two levels do influence the pricing decisions.

(ii) **Other Marketing Mix Elements**: Price is a part of the marketing mix. In fact, it is the only element in the marketing mix that brings in the revenue and can be changed easily, and this is precisely the reason that other elements of the marketing mix must be considered while setting the price.

Any change in the product, whether in terms of components of the product, type of packaging, or branding, will be possible only at some cost to the organisation. As such, while setting the price, it is essential that the costs incurred in manufacturing the product and the future changes anticipated, be taken into consideration.

Similarly, the price will depend upon the channel of distribution and the margins to be paid to the channel members. These need to be incorporated in the price to ensure that the organisation does not run into losses on account of distribution of the product.

Promotion, another element of the marketing mix, is also an important one from the pricing point of view. At any given point, promotion is the main source of communication between the organisation and its customers. Whether it is advertising, personal selling, sales promotion or publicity and public relations, all these would have a considerable effect on the pricing of the product.

(iii) **Product Differentiation:** The price of the product is also largely influenced by the characteristics of the product. That is to say, that if the product has innovative features or superior quality that makes it unique when compared with competitive offerings, then this will definitely influence the pricing decision.

(iv) **Cost of the Product:** The cost of the product is a base line to guide the organisation regarding the price of the product. The cost incurred in manufacturing the product and the other overheads would naturally become a part of the price of the product.

Some organisations take to the reverse method of pricing the product. This method is called as "**Target Pricing**". Here the conventional process of first designing the product, determining its cost, estimating the price based on the costs and then finding out if the product can be sold at the said price, if not followed. Instead, the organisation begins the pricing process by determining a price that the customer is willing to pay and then targets the costs to ensure that the desired price can be achieved.

(v) Objectives of the organisation: Pricing is one way in which an organisation can fulfil its objectives. If the objective of the organisation is to position its product against another luxury brand in the said segment, it will have to charge a higher price. On the other hand if the objective of the organisation is to be a leader by grabbing maximum market share, it will have to lower the price. Similarly, an organisation seeking to maximise its sales revenue will have to higher the price to get maximum sales revenue.

Thus the objective of the organisation does play a crucial role in setting the price.

(vi) Product Life Cycle: As seen in chapter number one, the pricing will change depending upon the stage in the life cycle of the product. For example in the growth stage when there is market acceptance, the prices are increased.

(vii) Functional Position: The functional position of the manufacturer, the distributors and the retailers will impact the pricing decision. Longer channels tend to be more expensive, resulting in higher prices of the end product. However, in many cases this may be necessary to be able to reach the target consumers effectively.

(b) External Factors

(i) Estimated demand: An organisation will always estimate the potential for its product in the market. While doing so, it will estimate the demand for that product. This estimation will, to a very large extent, depend upon the size of the market and the expected sales.

Before setting the price, the organisation needs to understand the relationship between price and demand for its product. The price-demand relationship will vary in different types of markets. Similarly the perception of the buyer with regards to the price will also affect the pricing decision. Let us look at these two aspects in greater detail

(a) Pricing in different types of markets: Generally there are four types of situations making up the markets. These are,

(i) Pure Competition: Here the market comprises of many buyers and sellers trading in uniform commodities like rice, wheat etc. In such situations a single buyer or seller cannot bring about a change nor have any effect on the on going market price.

(ii) Monopolistic Competition: In such situations the market consist of many buyers and sellers who trade over a range of prices rather than over a single price. This range mainly depends on the different offers that the seller makes to different buyers depending upon the quality of the product, its features, allied services etc. Since there are many sellers in the market, each organisation is affected very little by the competitor's pricing strategies.

- **(iii) Oligopolistic Competition:** This market situation comprises few sellers who are highly sensitive to the competitor's pricing strategies. Here products can be either uniform or non-uniform.
- **(iv) Pure Monopoly:** In a purely monopolistic situation, market consists of only one seller. In absence of **competition** the seller can price the product as per his wish

(b) **Consumer perception about price:** No matter what the price, set by the seller, the buyer will take a final call on whether the price is appropriate or not. The consumer will buy the product or service if and only if he feels that the price justifies the value that the product or the service gives to the consumer. For this the organisation needs to adopt buyer-oriented pricing. This involves understanding the value that the buyer places on the benefits that he receives and sets a price corresponding to that value. This is however a difficult task.

(c) **The Price-Demand Relationship:** The demand for any product or service will change with a change in the price of that product or service. As such, each price that an organisation charges for a particular product or service will generate a different level of demand for that product or service.

In the case of normal goods the price and demand are inversely related; that is higher the price, lower the demand and similarly lower the price, higher the demand. However this does not hold true in case of prestige products or luxury goods. These are goods where the consumer perceives that higher price means better quality and vice versa. These goods are also called as goods with a "Snob Appeal"

(ii) **Competitive Reactions:** Competition is an inevitable part of the market. While setting the price, the organisation has to take into consideration competition in the form of other organisations manufacturing the same products as well as those manufacturing substitute products.

If the organisation sets a price that is high as compared to that of the competing organisations, the customers might find the product expensive and not buy it. On the other hand, if the price is set much below that of the competitor's price, the customer might equate this as a sign of poor quality or inferior quality and not buy the product. So the price has to be set in a way that is neither too high nor too low.

Again, the competitor may also react in a number of ways to the prices set by the organisation. If the price set is lower than the price of the competitor, then the competitor may also slash its price, or may enhance the value of the offering, keeping the price the same or may resort to increasing the price to create an image of a superior quality product.

All these reactions will have a bearing on the demand for the organisation's product.

(iii) Suppliers: Suppliers of raw materials can impact the pricing decisions significantly. If the cost of the raw material goes up, the supplier charges a higher cost to the manufacturer, who in turn has to increase the prices of his products.

(iv) Economic Conditions: The economic conditions of the market influence pricing decisions. In case of a recessionary trend, prices are lowered to ensure minimum level of sales is maintained.

(v) Buyers: Buyers of a particular product can affect the pricing decision when the volume of purchase is large. The pricing decision is also influenced by the strength of the buyer in terms of the reputation of the organisation, the volume of purchase, the need for the product and other such factors.

(vi) Government: Pricing decisions are also affected by the price control policies or regulations of the Government.

2.3 Setting the Price

2.3.1 Setting Pricing Objectives

It is generally assumed that the main objective of setting the price is to maximise profits. Although profit is one of the main objectives, there are several other objectives that have to be taken into consideration while pricing. These objectives would vary depending upon the situation the organisation is facing. Sometimes pricing is done from the point of survival, while at other times, pricing is done to maximise current revenues.

An organisation has to set the price for a product for the first time when it wants to launch a new product in the market (Either a product developed by the organisation or acquired by it). Similarly, when an organisation wants to introduce a product in a new geographical area, it has to set the price of the product.

While setting the price, an organisation must move through the six-step procedure.

The six steps in the process of setting the price are shown below:
(i) Selecting the Pricing Objective;
(ii) Determining Demand;
(iii) Estimating Costs;
(iv) Analysing competitors' costs, prices and offers;
(v) Selecting a method for pricing;
(vi) Selecting the final price;

(i) Pricing Objectives: The pricing objectives for each organisation will depend on a number of factors and hence will differ from organisation to organisation. Traditionally it is assumed that businesses operate to maximise profits and hence the sole objective of pricing is profit maximisation. However, profit maximisation as an objective does not give the Marketing Manager a single and exclusive guideline for selecting prices.

As such, pricing objectives should be ideally derived from the overall marketing objectives of the organisation, which, in turn, should be derived from the corporate objectives of the organisation. Clarity on the objective makes it easier to set the price.

Some of the objectives that the organisations may have are:

(a) **Survival:** In times of intense competition and continuously changing consumer wants, organisations often find themselves in the clutches of over-capacity and the task of keeping the plant running and the inventories turning over. At such times, the very survival of the organisation is at a risk and profits take a back seat. In such situations, the organisation will cut prices to the extent that prices cover variable and fixed costs, without giving much thought to profits.

However, one must also note that survival is a short-term objective and organisations cannot sustain for very long by cutting prices. In the long run, they must take some positive steps towards adding value.

(b) **Maximum current profit:** Most organisations try to set the price in such a way that it maximises the current profits of the organisation. Based on an estimation of the demand and the costs, the organisation sets a price that would lead to a maximum current profit cash flow or, in some cases, even maximum rate of return on investment.

(c) **Maximum current revenue:** Many organisations are sales driven and they believe in maximising the sales revenue. This calls for estimating only the demand function and ensuring that prices are set accordingly so as to fulfil the demand.

(d) **Maximum sales growth:** Another objective that many organisations adopt is maximising the sales. The thought behind this objective is that higher sales volume will lead to lower unit costs and result in higher long-run profit.

(e) **Maximum market skimming:** Many organisations adopt an objective of setting a high price to be able to skim the market. This objective is particularly applicable in the following situations:
- There is a high demand for the product;
- The unit cost of producing in small volumes does not nullify the advantage of charging the high price;
- The initial high price does not attract competitors to the market;
- High price creates a perception of superior quality or superior product in the minds of the target market.

(f) **Product quality leadership:** Organisations aiming to become product-quality leaders in the market may look at setting the price using premium pricing strategy. The rationale behind this is that premium quality calls for premium pricing and it is not possible to provide a quality product at a lower price.

(g) Some other pricing objectives: Other than the objectives mentioned above, organisations in the non-profit sector adopt other objectives. They would set the price to recover partial costs; similarly some organisations working in the social sector may set a social price to cater to the varying income situations of different clients.

2.3.2 Determining Demand

The demand that the organisation can expect will vary with the price. For every price change, the level of demand will change. In the normal case, price and demand are inversely related, that is, an increase in the price will lead to a decrease in the demand and vice-versa.

However, this may not hold true in case of prestige goods or goods that are said to have a snob appeal. In the case of such goods/products, a higher price is an indicator of better quality. As such, an increase in the price leads to a higher demand.

The increase or decrease in demand with the change in price is mainly due to the different price sensitivities of the target market. Therefore, the first step in determining the demand is to understand the factors that affect the buyer's price sensitivity. Marketers have identified nine factors that affect the price sensitivity of buyers. They are as follows:

(a) **Unique value effect:** Buyers are less price sensitive to products that are unique and more distinctive.

(b) **Substitute awareness effect:** Buyers are less price sensitive when they are less aware of substitute offerings. And in a reverse situation when buyers are aware of substitute products, their price sensitivity increases.

(c) **Difficult comparison effect:** Also buyers are less price sensitive when they find it difficult to draw a comparison between the substitute products.

(d) **Total expenditure effect:** Buyers are less price sensitive when the expenditure to be made is low in comparison to their total income.

(e) **End-benefit effect:** If the buyer of a product is an Original Equipment Manufacturer (OEM), who will incorporate the purchased product into his product, and if his product is a price sensitive product, it will definitely result in him being price sensitive while purchasing the product to be incorporated.

For e.g. An OEM of mobile phones buys the casing of the phone from another manufacturer and manufactures the mobile phone and assembles it using the casing. Now the mobile phone is a price sensitive product. If the price of the casing increases, the OEM will become sensitive to the price change and look for other options, because an increase in the price of the casing will result in an increase in the end product that is the mobile phone, due to which his phones may not find acceptance with his target market.

(f) **Shared cost effect:** Buyers are less price sensitive when the cost of the product is to be partially borne by another party.

(g) Sunk-investment effect: Buyers are less price sensitive when the product is used in conjunction with assets previously purchased.

(h) Price-quality effect: Buyers are less price sensitive when it is perceived that the product is of a better quality or is more prestigious.

(i) Inventory effect: Buyers are less price sensitive when the product cannot be stored.

Methods of Estimating Demand Curves

The relationship between the price and demand is depicted by a demand curve. Most organisations would want to measure their demand curves to understand the demand. There are three common methods used to measure the demand curves.

1. The first method entails statistically analysing existing data on past prices, quantities sold and other factors to estimate the relationship. The data can either be longitudinal (i.e. over a period of time) or cross sectional (i.e. spread over different geographies at the same time).
2. The second method calls for conducting price experiments. Here, the price of the product is systematically varied in an actual store or retail setting and the results and variations therein are recorded. Alternately, organisations charge different prices in similar territories and note the change in demand.
3. The third approach is to question buyers about their purchase intention at different proposed prices for the product. The problem with this method is that buyers tend to understate their purchase intentions at higher prices.

Price Elasticity of Demand

The responsiveness of demand to the change in price is termed as the price elasticity of demand. Basically it is the change in demand with respect to the change in price. When there is little or no change in demand with a change in the price, we say that the demand is inelastic and conversely, when demand changes considerably with a change in price, we say that the demand in elastic.

The figures given below depict inelastic and elastic demand.

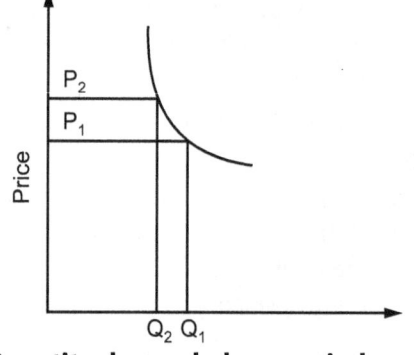

Fig. 2.1: Depiction of Inelastic Demand

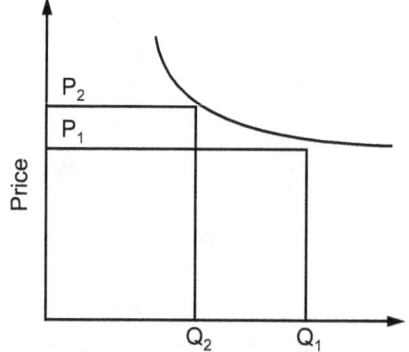

Fig. 2.2: Depiction of Elastic Demand

Fig. 2.1 depicts inelastic demand, that is, with change in price, there is very little change in the quantity demanded

Fig. 2.2 depicts elastic demand, that is, with change in price, there is a substantial change in the quantity demanded.

In this regard, it is necessary to understand what determines the price elasticity of demand. Demand is likely to be inelastic in the following situations:

(a) There are few or no substitutes or competitors;

(b) Buyers do not readily notice the higher price;

(c) Buyers are slow to change their buying habits;

(d) Buyers think that higher prices are due to quality improvements;

If the demand is elastic, sellers will consider lowering the prices to get better revenues through larger sales volumes.

2.3.3 Estimating Costs

An organisation can charge a price only as what the market accepts. In other words, the demand for the product will set a ceiling on the price. On the other hand, the costs incurred in manufacturing, distributing, promoting and selling the product will be the base for the organisation while setting the price.

Before we start with the estimation of costs, it will help to understand the different types of costs and how this understanding can help in price setting.

Generally, the costs that an organisation will incur in manufacturing, distributing, and promoting a product, can be divided into two types:

- the fixed cost, which is also known as the overhead, which does not vary with the level of production, and
- the variable cost, which varies with the level of production.

Total costs = Fixed costs + Variable costs.

The following aspects of cost need to be studied to enable the organisation to set the price properly.

(a) **Cost behaviour at different levels of production:** To be able to price in a correct manner, organisations need to understand the cost behaviour at different levels of production.

Suppose an organisation M/s ABC Inc. has built a plant for manufacturing of fans having a capacity of manufacturing 50 fans in a day. The cost per unit of fan produced is high if less than 50 fans are produced in a day. As the production approaches 50 fans in a day, the average cost falls as fixed costs get spread over more number of units with each unit bearing a smaller portion of the fixed cost.

However, the average cost increases beyond 50 units of production as the plant becomes inefficient, that is, it is not able to efficiently handle the excess capacity leading to breakdowns, queuing up for machines, etc.

(b) **Cost behaviour as a function of accumulated production:** As the organisation progresses, all functions start getting streamlined and initial teething troubles are done away with. There is a marked improvement in production methods, smoother flow of materials is seen, procurement costs are cut and so on, leading to a decrease in the average cost, that is, the average cost tends to fall with accumulated production experience.

(c) **Cost behaviour as a function of differentiated marketing offers:** Organisations today are flexible in terms of their dealings with their customers and offer different terms and conditions of business to different customers. For example, a manufacturer of pickles may supply pickles to one food retailer once a week, while another retailer may ask for delivery of the same quantity in two batches a week. In such a situation, the costs incurred in serving the other retailer are higher. At such times, the organisation needs to use activity based cost accounting methods. In this method, the real cost associated with serving the customer is accounted for and both variable and fixed costs are decomposed and tagged back to the customer.

(d) **Target Costing**: In this method of costing, the organisation first carries out a research activity to establish the desired functions that new products must perform to satisfy the customers. Then the organisation determines the price at which the product will sell, given its utility value to customers, its appeal to the customers and the competitors' prices. From this price, the profit margin that the organisation expects or desires to achieve is deducted. The cost that then remains, is the target cost which the organisation must achieve. To be able to manufacture and market the product at the target cost, the organisation then examines each cost element like design, engineering, sales, manufacturing, etc. and breaks it down into further components. Ways are worked out to re-engineer the product, eliminate unnecessary functions and achieve the target cost.

2.3.4 Analysing Competitors' Costs, Prices and Offers

Every organisation needs to benchmark its costs against competitors' costs mainly to be able to understand whether it is operating at a cost advantage or a cost disadvantage.

While operating in the market, it is also necessary for the organisation to understand what kind of offers the competitor is making to the customers.

This can be done by sending out comparison shoppers to assess competitors' prices and offers. This gives an orientation point to the organisation to set its prices.

2.3.5 Selecting a Pricing Method

While setting the price, the organisation has to price the product in such a way that the price is neither too high nor too low. The following pricing methods are available to set the price:

(a) **Mark-up pricing:** This is one of the most elementary methods of pricing. Here, a standard mark-up is added to the product's cost. For example, suppose for a calculators' manufacturer, the unit cost of each calculator is ₹ 500/- for an expected sales volume of 5,000 calculators. Assuming that the manufacturer wants to earn 20% mark-up on the sales, the mark-up price is then calculated as:

$$\text{Marked-up Price} = \frac{\text{Unit Cost}}{(1-\text{desired return on sales})} = \frac{500}{(1-0.2)} = ₹\,625$$

So the manufacturer will charge ₹ 625 per calculator and make a profit of ₹ 125/- per calculator.

Mark-ups are different for different types of goods. They are generally higher for seasonal goods and for items that are slow moving or with high storage and inventory costs.

(b) **Target return pricing:** This is also a cost based pricing approach. Here, the organisation decides on the price that would essentially get the organisation its target rate of Return on Investment (ROI) made.

Consider an example where a microwave oven manufacturer has invested ₹ 5,00,00,000 in his business and wants to set a price to ensure a 10% rate of return on investment. The organisation can set the price using the formula

$$\text{Target return price} = \text{Unit cost} + \frac{\text{Desired return} \times \text{Invested capital}}{\text{Unit Sales}}$$

Suppose the organisation estimates a sale of 50,000 units and the cost that it incurs for each microwave oven is ₹ 5,000; then, as per the above formula, the Target Return Price will be calculated as follows:

$$\text{Target Return Price} = 5000 + \frac{0.1 \times 50000000}{50000} = 5500$$

However, one needs to take into consideration that this rate of return will be achieved only when the estimated costs are maintained and the estimated sales level is achieved.

(c) **Perceived Value pricing:** Many organisations today are deciding their price based on the perceived value of the product, that is, the buyer's perception of the product's value is considered as a base to pricing rather than the seller's cost. While using this method of pricing, several non-price variables are used to enhance the perceived value of the product in the buyer's mind. The organisation tries to estimate the sales volume at the given price level and decides whether it can achieve its objectives at the estimated volume.

(d) Value pricing: Under this method of pricing, the organisation believes that the price should represent a high value offer to the buyers. As such, in spite of the product being of superior quality, the price set is fairly low.

(e) Going-rate pricing: Here, the organisation bases its price largely on the prevailing price in the market, that is, the price charged by the competitors. The organisation may charge slightly less or more than the competitors, or exactly the same as the competitors' price. Here, the organisation does not base its price on the demand situation or on the costs incurred.

(f) Sealed Bid pricing: Here again, the organisation looks at competitive pricing. The organisation estimates the price that the competitors are likely to quote and accordingly submits its bid with a view to winning the contract. However, in most cases, the organisation will price its products in a manner that ensures that it does not sell below its costs.

Approaches to pricing

There are two basic approaches to pricing:

1. Cost based approach to pricing,
2. Market based approach to pricing.

1. Cost based Approach:

As indicated by the name, the cost based approach assumes cost as the basis for pricing the product. Here, an organisation has a choice of various approaches:

(a) Total Cost plus Pricing: It involves selling the product at the total cost of one unit of the product plus the desired profit;

(b) Price based on Marginal Costs only: Here, the price is based on the marginal cost and not the total cost per unit;

(c) Break Even Point or B.E.P pricing method: Break Even Point is the volume of sales at which the total sales revenue is equal to the total cost. It is a point at which the organisation is neither having a profit nor making any losses. For calculating the price based on this method, the total costs are broken into Fixed Costs and Variable Costs.

$$\text{B.E.P (in Units)} = \frac{\text{Fixed Costs}}{\text{Selling price per unit} - \text{Variable cost per unit}}$$

$$\text{B.E.P (in ₹)} = \frac{\text{Fixed Costs} \times \text{Total Sales}}{\text{Total Sales} - \text{Total Variable Costs}}$$

(d) Rate of return or Target Pricing Method: Under this method, at first the desired rate of return is decided. The amount of profits desired by the organisation is calculated based on the desired rate of return. This amount is then added to the cost of production and thus the selling price is arrived at.

Merits and Demerits of Cost-oriented Pricing Approach

Let us look at the merits and de-merits of cost-oriented pricing:

(a) Merits:
  (i) **Simplicity:** The approach is fairly simple and internal to the firm.
  (ii) **Scientific and safe:** This method takes into consideration the actual costs making it safer for the organisation in terms of recovery.

(b) Demerits
  (i) **Ignores Demand and Competition:** The demerit of this method is that it ignores the demand and the competitive situation
  (ii) **Cost Irrelevance:** Very often prices based on costs are not always relevant to the pricing situation. For example when there is better opportunity, incremental costs are more relevant than full costs.

2. **Customer-Demand Oriented Pricing:**

   In this approach a lot of emphasis is laid on what the demand is in the market.

   (a) **What the Traffic can Bear:** This is not a scientific method of pricing. Here the pricing is based on what the traffic can bear or what the customers are willing to pay.

   (b) **Skimming Pricing:** Here the organisation sets a premium price to start with. Then it goes on reducing the price upto a particular level to skim the market. In adopting this type of pricing, the organisation's objective is to achieve an early break even and maximise profits in a shorter time span.

   (c) **Penetration Pricing:** As opposed to the skimming pricing, the objective of penetration pricing is to gain a foothold in a highly competitive market. As such in this methods the prices set are low.

3. **Competition based Pricing:**

   Here, the price is based on the market situations like demand, and the competitors' pricing is taken into consideration. Here again, the organisation can follow any one of the following two methods:

   (a) **Pricing above the competition:** When the organisation decides to set the price above that of the competition, it is using price as a differentiator to convey to customers that its product is of a superior quality and has unique features to which the high price can be attributed. However, the risk associated with this is that, if the customers are not convinced about the value that the product is offering them then they may find the value proposition as too expensive and refrain from buying the product.

(b) Pricing below the competition: When the organisation decides to price below the competition, the main aim is to eat into the competitors' market share and grab as much of the market as possible. However, the risk associated with this approach is that the customer may equate low price with low quality and hence not buy the product.

Price and non-price competition: Organisations often use pricing as a tool to deal with the competition. But competition can also be in other forms. Let us take a look at price and non-price competition:

(i) **Price Competition:** Organisations engage in price competition by regularly offering products priced as low as possible and typically accompanied by a few services. This is also called as value pricing.

(ii) **Non-price competition:** Here, sellers maintain stable prices and attempt to improve their market position by emphasising other aspects of their marketing programmes. The seller uses product differentiation and promotional activities to fight competition.

2.3.6 Selecting the Final Price

The above-mentioned pricing methods help the organisation to arrive at a price range for its products. However, while selecting the final price for the product, the organisation has to take into consideration some other factors that are likely to affect the price. These factors are:

(a) Psychological pricing: While setting prices, marketers often take into consideration the psychological effect of the price. For example, some marketers believe in setting an odd figure for the price rather than a round figure.

An example is the Bata footwear; the prices are always odd figures like ₹ 599 or ₹ 399. Here, the psychology of the consumer is that he sees the price in the range of ₹ 500 or ₹ 300 whereas actually the price is just one rupee less than ₹ 600 and ₹ 400 respectively.

Similarly, for products that are considered as having a snob appeal or as being ego sensitive, a high price indicates high quality. Examples are perfumes, diamonds, etc.

(b) Influence of other elements of the marketing mix on the price:
  (i) Brands having a good quality and very high advertising budgets are able to command price premiums in the market.
  (ii) Brands with exceptional quality and very high advertising budgets manage to charge maximum price for the product.

(c) Impact of price on other stakeholders: While setting the price, the organisation must take into consideration the reactions or impact that the price is likely to have on other parties like dealers and distributors. Similarly, competitors' reaction to price must also be taken into consideration.

2.4 Adapting the Price

After going through the process of setting the price, organisations generally arrive at a price structure that reflects variations in geographical demands, variations in the requirements of several market segments that they intend to cater to, and variations in cost as well.

Due to this, the organisation has to adapt the price to suit each of the variations that it encounters. As a result, the organisation works out discounts, allowances, and promotional support to ensure that the profit objectives are met irrespective of these variations. This is the process of adapting the price. Some of the common price-adaptation strategies are mentioned below:

2.4.1 Geographical Pricing

In this strategy, the organisation has to arrive at prices for different products in different geographic locations. The issue here is whether to charge the same price at different locations or different prices considering the shipping and transportation costs. When prices are varied according to the location, it is termed as geographical pricing.

Counter trade is another issue with regard to the different geographic locations in getting the payment. Many a time, buyers in other countries lack sufficient hard currency to pay for the products. At such times, they may want to offer other items as payment. This is known as counter trade.

Some of the well-known forms of counter trade are described below:
- **(i) Barter:** Barter is the direct exchange of goods with no money and no third party involved.
- **(ii) Compensation deal:** Here, the payment is partially in cash and partially in the form of products. However, a major percentage of the payment is in cash.
- **(iii) Buyback arrangement:** Here, the seller sells plants, equipment, etc. to another country and agrees for the partial payment in terms of products manufactured with the equipment supplied.
- **(iv) Offset:** The seller receives full payment in cash but agrees to spend a substantial amount of the payment received within the same country in a stipulated time span.

2.4.2 Price Discounts and Allowances

Organisations often reward or incentivise customers for early payments or volume purchases. These price adjustments are called as discounts or allowances.

Cash Discounts: A cash discount is a price reduction to buyers who make prompt payments. Here is a typical example; if the payment is due within 30 days and the buyer makes the payment within 10 to 15 days he is given a deduction of 2% or 3% on the bill amount.

Quantity Discounts: A quantity discount is a reduction in price to buyers who buy the product in large volumes.

Functional Discounts: Also known as trade discounts, these are discounts offered to the trade channel members like dealers, distributors and wholesalers for performing the trade functions such as selling, storing, record keeping, etc.

Seasonal Discounts: A seasonal discount is a price reduction to buyers, who buy products in off-season so as to boost the sales during that season.

Allowances: Allowances are reductions from the list price. For example, buyback allowances are allowances that are made when turning in an old item while buying a new one. This basically means that the consumer returns the old product and buys a new one and gets a price reduction in the new one which is approximately the buyback or current value of the old product.

2.4.3 Promotional Pricing

There are several types of promotional pricing that organisations resort to. Let us take a look at a few of them.

(i) **Loss-Leader Pricing:** Here, the retailers drop the prices of well-known brands to attract more customers and increase the number of footfalls to their outlets.

(ii) **Special Event Pricing:** Sellers establish special prices in some seasons to draw in more customers. For example, during Diwali, goods are sold at special prices.

(iii) **Cash Rebates:** Consumers purchasing certain products in a specified time frame are offered cash rebates. It helps manufacturers to clear inventories in time and make shelf space available for new items.

(iv) **Low Interest Financing:** Here, finance at very low rates is offered to customers to encourage them to buy products. This is typically seen in the automobile market as well as the white goods market.

(v) **Longer Payment Terms:** In this case, banks as well as sellers stretch their loans over longer periods to facilitate lower monthly instalments for the customers.

(vi) **Warranties:** Many organisations promote sales by offering a free warranty.

(vii) **Psychological Discounting:** This involves labelling the product with an artificially high price and then offering or announcing a discount on the same.

2.4.4 Discriminatory Pricing

Discriminatory pricing or price discrimination is said to happen when an organisation sells a product or a service at two or more different prices that are not due to proportional difference in costs. Some of the common forms of discriminatory pricing are:

(i) **Customer segment pricing:** Different customer groups are charged different prices for the same product or service. For example, the Railways charge a different price to students and a different price to other citizens for the same service.

(ii) **Product form pricing:** Different forms of the product are priced differently but not in proportion to their respective costs. For example, a sachet of Clinic Plus shampoo costs ₹ 1/- whereas a bottle of 100 ml costs ₹ 150/-.

(iii) **Image pricing:** Some organisations set different prices for the same products by projecting them at different image levels.

(iv) **Location pricing:** Many organisations price the same product differently at different locations even though the cost of the product remains the same.

(v) **Time pricing:** Prices are also changed or varied depending on the season (off season and peak season pricing), day (weekdays and weekends pricing), and hour (peak hour and non-peak hour pricing).

Product mix pricing

The logic used to set the price must be modified when the product being sold is a part of the product mix. There are six such occasions for product mix pricing. They are described below briefly:

(i) **Product line pricing:** Generally when an organisation develops a product line, it positions each product uniquely, and as the line progresses, each product in the line has some additional features and hence pricing is varied accordingly.

(ii) **Optional features pricing:** In this case, organisations leave it to the customer to select optional features or accessories along with the main product. In such cases, the price of the optional features of the product or optional accessories should be in line with that of the main product.

(iii) **Captive product pricing:** Some products are such that they require the presence of another product to be useful. In such cases, the price of the captive product should fall in line with that of the main product. For example, razor blades are captive products for razors and hence they must be priced accordingly.

(iv) **Two-part pricing:** Here, the organisation charges a fixed price for a particular product or service up to a particular use limit and beyond that, the rate of pricing varies. This can be seen in the pricing for electricity and telephone services.

(v) **By-product pricing:** Manufacturing of certain products often yields by-products. By-products should be priced depending upon their value to the customers rather than on the main product.

(vi) **Product-bundling pricing:** Organisations are known to bundle their products and sell them at a price that is lesser than the cost of purchase of individual products.

Some other strategies in Pricing

(i) **Market Entry Strategies:** Generally when new products are introduced in the market, the organisation is trying to gauge what kind of price the market is likely to accept. Skimming and Penetration pricing are two strategies that are generally used for new products.

(a) **Skimming Pricing:** Setting a relatively huge initial price for a new product is referred to as market skimming. Here, the price is high in comparison to the target market's expected price range so that the creamy layer of the market alone can afford it, and it is later reduced to include subsequent layers of the market.

Skimming is done because:
- It provides healthy profit margins;
- It is intended primarily to recover R&D costs as fast as possible;
- Lofty prices can be used to connote high quality.

Market skimming is suitable under the following conditions:
- The new product has distinctive features strongly desired by consumers;
- Demand is fairly inelastic;
- The new product is protected from competition through one or more entry barriers such as patent, copyright, etc.

(b) **Penetration Pricing:** Here, a relatively low initial price is established for the product. Price is low in relation to the target market's expected price range.
- Penetration pricing is done;
- To generate substantial sales volume and a large market share;
- Discourage other firms from introducing competing products.

Market penetration is suitable under the following conditions:
- A large market exists for the product;
- Demand is highly elastic;
- Economy of scale can be achieved;
- Fierce competition already exists.

(ii) **Geographic Pricing:** Point of Production – Here, the seller-quotes the price at the point of production and it is up to the buyer to select the mode of transport and bear the charges.

- **Uniform Delivered Pricing:** Here, the delivered or landed price is quoted to all buyers regardless of their location;
- **Zone Delivered Pricing:** Here, the market is divided into geographic zones and pricing for each zone is done;

(iii) **Special Pricing Strategies:** Some of the special pricing strategies are discussed below briefly.

- **One price or single price:** The organisation maintains the same price for all customers irrespective of the type of customer or the quantity purchased or other such factors.

- **Flexible/variable price:** The organisation sets different prices for different customers for the same product. This pricing is based on various factors like age of customers (senior citizens offered discounted prices), time of purchase (lower rates at non-peak hours), etc.
- **Flat rate pricing:** Pricing remains same irrespective of the quantity of the product consumed.
- **Single price:** All products sold by the organisation carry the same price. Example is the 1 Dollar Shops in the US.
- **Price lining:** In this case, the organisation sets a limited number of prices at which it will sell related products. (₹ 49, ₹ 99, ₹ 199)

2.5 Price Changes

Although the organisation does set the price for its various products, there will be situations when the organisation would have to raise or cut their prices. Some of the situations where price changes may have to be made are as follows:

(a) Initiating Price Cuts: Many a time, there will be situations which will require the organisation to cut its prices. Here is a list of some common situations.

  (i) Excess plant capacity necessitates additional business. When this requirement of additional business cannot be generated through increased sales or promotional efforts, product improvements or other similar measures, the organisation may resort to aggressive pricing and decide to initiate price cuts.

  (ii) Again, when the organisation is facing a decline in the market share, it may feel the need to initiate a price cut to regain the lost market share.

  (iii) Price cuts are also made to capture the market through lower costs. Here, the organisation relies on getting substantially larger volumes through lower prices.

Although price cuts are strategies that organisations often resort to, there are some risks or traps associated with this strategy. Let us discuss these in greater detail:

- **Low-quality trap:** In markets where consumers generally equate price with the quality of the product, it is possible that consumers may believe the product to be of an inferior quality when compared with high priced products of the competitors.
- **Fragile market share trap:** Consumers who buy the product simply because it is priced low, will not have any loyalty to the product. The moment a lower priced competitive product comes in the market; these very consumers will shift to that product.
- **Shallow pocket trap:** The higher priced competitors may follow suit when an organisation initiates price cuts, and if these competitors are stronger and have the power to sustain for a longer period with the price cut because of deeper cash reserves, the organisation initiating the price cut may not be able to remain in the market.

(b) Initiating Price Increases: As mentioned earlier, just as some situations demand a price cut, some situations demand a price increase.
- (i) Cost inflation is one major circumstance that would lead to a price increase for the product.
- (ii) Also, when the demand for a particular product is more than the supply (over demand), an organisation may resort to price increase to ration the supplies to the customers.

Organisations often resort to the following types of price adjustments:
- **Adoption of delayed quotation pricing:** This type of a pricing technique is used mainly in industrial products or heavy engineering or manufacturing items. Here, the final price is not set until and unless the product is finished or delivered. Since production lead times are rather long for these types of products, prices are increased considering all the costs that change as time passes.
- **Use of escalator clauses:** An escalator clause in the contract is based upon some price index, that is, if a particular price index increases, the price of the product is escalated.
- **Unbundling of goods and services:** Bundled prices offered earlier are discontinued and products that were sold at discounted or reduced prices earlier as a part of the bundled offer are now sold at their originally high prices individually.
- **Reduction of discounts:** The organisation refrains from offering normal cash or quantity discounts.

Some other methods for an organisation to manage high costs or demand without affecting the price are as follows:
- Shrinking the quantity of the product instead of raising the price;
- Substituting with cheaper materials or ingredients;
- Reducing or removing product features to reduce the cost;
- Discontinuing the offering of certain product services;
- Promoting larger sizes of packaging and refraining from using expensive packaging;
- Reducing the number of variants or models offered.

(c) Responding to price changes: When an organisation initiates price changes, it must be prepared for reactions to those price changes. Any kind of a price change will affect the customers of the organisation, the competitors and other stakeholders. However, the opinion of the customers and the competitors are more important for the organisation. As such, the organisation must be prepared for their reactions.
- **(i) Customers Reactions**: Customers will often try to find out the reasons behind price variations. In case of a price cut, the following reactions may be expected:
    - (a) Customers may feel that the existing product is about to be replaced by a new product.

(b) They may feel that the item is faulty and not selling in the market, hence the price cut.

(c) They may assume that the organisation is in financial trouble and hence may not sustain in the market for long. This may lead to a 'wait and watch' strategy on part of the customers.

Similarly a price increase will also have certain reactions:

(a) Customers might think that the product is selling very well and may soon be unobtainable.

(b) The product represents a really good value and must be purchased.

(ii) **Competitors' Reactions**: An organisation that is planning to introduce a price change must also keep in mind the competitors' reactions.

Competitors are likely to react in a number of ways to the price change. This depends largely upon the type of the market and the number of competitors in the market.

On one hand, the competition may chose to respond in a set manner whereas on the other hand, the competition may spring surprises.

(a) The competition may maintain its own price irrespective of the price change.

(b) It could maintain the price and enhance the value proposition to the customer so as to create a feeling of enhanced value at the same price.

(c) It may, in some cases, reduce the price to match that of the organisation due to the fear of losing market share.

(d) In some cases, the competition may increase the price and improve the quality using this to differentiate itself in the market.

(e) The competition, while keeping the price of the existing product in the market the same, may choose to launch a low-priced variant in the market to fight the organisation's move of reducing the price.

Points to Remember

1. Price is an important aspect of any product or service

    Meaning of Price: Price is something that is paid in return for obtaining a product or a service.

    Definition: As such Price can be defined as the sum of all the values that a consumer exchanges in return for the benefits that are offered by the usage of a product or the benefits that are obtained by availing a service

    Relationship between Price and Pricing: Price and pricing are two different terms. While price is what the seller feels is worth of the product to the buyer and what the buyer pays for the product, pricing is the process of setting that price.

2. Factors influencing Pricing Decisions

   There are several factors that an organisation must take into consideration when setting the price. These factors are divided into two categories i.e. Internal factors and external factors.

3. Setting the Price: This involves
   - Setting Pricing objectives
   - Determining demand
   - Estimating Costs
   - Analysing competitor's pricing
   - Selecting the pricing method
   - Selecting the final price.

   (i) Pricing Objectives: The pricing objectives for each organisation will depend on a number of factors and hence will differ from organisation to organisation.

   Some of the objectives that organisations may have are:
   (a) Survival
   (b) Maximum current profit
   (c) Maximum current revenue
   (d) Maximum sales growth
   (e) Maximum market skimming
   (f) Product quality leadership
   (g) Some other pricing objectives

   (ii) Determining Demand: The demand that the organisation can expect will vary with the price.

   (iii) Estimating Costs: An organisation can charge a price only as high as what the market accepts. In other words, the demand for the product will set a ceiling on the price. Different types of costs associated with setting the price are:
   (a) Cost behaviour at different levels of production
   (b) Cost behaviour as a function of accumulated production
   (c) Cost behaviour as a function of differentiated marketing offers
   (d) Target Costing

   (iv) Analysing Competitors' Costs, Prices and Offers – Every organisation needs to benchmark its costs against competitors' costs mainly to be able to understand whether it is operating at a cost advantage or a cost disadvantage.

   (v) Selecting a pricing method - While setting the price, the organisation has to price the product in such a way that the price is neither too high nor too low. The following pricing methods are available to set the price:
   (a) Mark-up pricing
   (b) Target return pricing
   (c) Value pricing
   (d) Going-rate pricing
   (e) Sealed Bid pricing

Approaches to pricing - There are two basic approaches to pricing.
(i) Cost based approach
(ii) Customer - Demand Oriented Pricing
(iii) Competition based pricing

Selecting the final price: The above-mentioned pricing methods help the organisation in arriving at a price range for its products.

3. **Adapting the price**

   After going through the process of setting the price, organisations generally arrive at a price structure that reflects variations in geographical demands, variations in the requirements of several market segments that they intend to cater to, and variations in cost as well.

4. **Price Changes**

   Although the organisation does set the price for its various products, there will be situations when the organisation would have to raise or cut their prices, that is, they may have to change their prices. Some of the main situations where price changes have to be made are as follows:
   (a) Initiating Price Cuts
   (b) Initiating Price Increases

Questions for Discussion

(A) Long Answer Questions:

1. Explain in detail the steps involved in the process of setting the price.
2. Define Price and discuss the importance of pricing with special reference to the Marketing Mix.
3. Write a detailed note on factors influencing pricing decisions.
4. Describe the relationship between price and demand. Explain the concept of Price Elasticity of demand.
5. Discuss in detail the various methods of estimating demand.
6. With the help of suitable examples discuss the various approaches to pricing.
7. "Adapting price is essential to some situations" Do you agree? Explain in light of various methods of adapting the price.
8. Discuss in detail the various strategies for pricing.
9. Describe the reasons for price changes and the methods for price changes.
10. Distinguish between price and non-price competition and the applications of the same.

(B) Short Notes: Write Short Notes on:

1. Relationship between price and pricing
2. Importance of pricing
3. Changing pricing scenario
4. Impact of internet on pricing
5. Factors influencing pricing decisions

6. Pricing objectives
7. Price sensitivity of buyers
8. Price elasticity of demand
9. Different types of costs associated with setting the price
10. Selecting a pricing method
11. Cost based approach to pricing
12. Demand oriented pricing
13. Adapting the price
14. Skimming pricing vis-a-vis penetration pricing
15. Geographic pricing

(C) Multiple Choice Questions:

1. Price is the only element of the marketing mix that:
   (a) Generates costs
   (b) Generates revenue
   (c) Generates demand
   (d) Generates interest in the product
2. In today's pricing environment, internet enables buyer to:
   (a) Get competitive information
   (b) Check out the product physically before purchase
   (c) Physically test samples of the product
   (d) Discuss the product features with the salesperson
3. The pricing objectives for an organisation may include:
   (a) Product advertising
   (b) Product development
   (c) Profit Maximisation
   (d) Price negotiation
4. One of the internal factors affecting pricing decisions is:
   (a) Changing external environment
   (b) Competition
   (c) Costs
   (d) Nature of the market
5. One of the external factors affecting pricing decisions is:
   (a) Objectives of the Organisation
   (b) Government policies and regulations
   (c) Cost of production
   (d) Promotional costs
6. In pure monopoly the market consists of:
   (a) Many sellers and many buyers
   (b) Few sellers and many buyers
   (c) Many Sellers and few buyers
   (d) One seller and many buyers
7. Under oligopolistic competition:
   (a) Seller's are highly sensitive to each other pricing strategies
   (b) Seller's are not sensitive to pricing strategies of competitors
   (c) Seller's are not sensitive to buyer's demand
   (d) Seller's are sensitive to price changes for non-competing products
8. In elastic demand:
   (a) As price increases demand increases
   (b) As price changes demand remains constant
   (c) As price increases demand decreases
   (d) None of the above

9. In case of prestige goods the demand:
   (a) Demand increases with decrease in price
   (b) Demand increases with increase in price
   (c) Demand does not change with increase in price
   (d) None of the above
10. Competition based pricing includes:
    (a) Break even pricing
    (b) Value based pricing
    (c) Going Rate pricing
    (d) Cost-Plus Pricing
11. Cost Based Pricing includes:
    (a) Skimming Pricing
    (b) Penetration Pricing
    (c) Pricing Above competition
    (d) Markup Pricing
12. New Product pricing strategies include:
    (a) Pricing below competition
    (b) Markup Pricing
    (c) Skimming Pricing
    (d) None of the above
13. Product mix pricing strategy includes:
    (a) Product Line pricing
    (b) Discounting
    (c) Giving allowances
    (d) None of the above
14. Geographical Pricing includes:
    (a) Going rate pricing
    (b) Discounting
    (c) Allowances
    (d) None of the above
15. Special Pricing includes:
    (a) Single price strategy
    (b) Discounting
    (c) Skimming
    (d) Optional product pricing
16. Discriminatory pricing includes:
    (a) Time based pricing
    (b) Competitive pricing
    (c) Break Even Pricing
    (d) All of the above
17. In case of price changes organisations often resort to:
    (a) Adoption of delayed quotation pricing
    (b) Use of escalator clauses
    (c) Unbundling of goods and services
    (d) All of the above
18. Special event pricing is a part of:
    (a) Discriminatory pricing
    (b) Geographical pricing
    (c) Promotional Pricing
    (d) New product Pricing
19. Market skimming is suitable when:
    (a) Demand is fairly inelastic
    (b) Demand is highly elastic
    (c) Demand is very low
    (d) None of the above
20. Market penetration is suitable when:
    (a) Demand is fairly inelastic
    (b) Demand is highly elastic
    (c) Demand is very low
    (d) None of the above

Answers

1. (b)	2. (a)	3. (c)	4. (c)	5. (b)	6. (d)	7. (a)	8. (c)	9. (c)	10. (b)
11. (d)	12. (c)	13. (a)	14. (d)	15. (a)	16. (a)	17. (d)	18. (c)	19. (a)	20. (b)

MARKETING MANAGEMENT   PRICE

(D) Project Questions
1. Jindal Steel, a major steel company, has developed a new process for galvanising steel sheets so that they can be painted and used in car body parts to avoid rusting. What factors should Jindal Steel take into consideration when pricing this product?
2. A major food and beverage retailer, Spencers, has reduced the prices of all its offerings by a flat 10%. What reactions can Spencers expect from the customers and the competitors?
3. Godrej, a manufacturer of consumer white goods, wants to introduce a new washing machine that can adjust the time depending upon the load of clothes to be washed. The organisation wants to understand the advantages of an introductory skimming approach vis-à-vis a penetration approach. Discuss the pros and cons of each strategy.
4. Discuss the importance of promotional pricing from the point of view of stimulating early purchases.
5. Explain with the help of suitable examples how cash discounts and allowances are used to adapt prices.
6. List down at least five examples of discriminatory pricing that are currently available
7. The Gold's Gymnasium has recently launched a Happy Hours Scheme wherein membership is available at half the normal price for workouts between 1 pm to 4 pm. Under which category of pricing will you place this strategy and why?
8. Wal-Mart is said to have a special pricing strategy. Get more information about this from the internet and list the salient features of their pricing strategy
9. Discuss the conditions suitable for Point of Purchase pricing.
10. List some examples/situations suitable for Break Even Pricing.

Case Study

A leading Gymnasium, Workout Fitness, has been in the health care business for several years. One of the oldest and reputed Gymnasiums in the city, it has been enjoying a market share of almost 55%. The Gymnasium is known for its state-of-the-art machinery. The trainers are well trained for helping the patrons with their workouts and are quite friendly and polite. Workout Fitness has 12 branches in various parts of the city.

The target audience of Workout Fitness comprises of the Upper Middle Class and the Upper class. Most patrons feel it as a matter of pride and prestige to be a member of Workout Fitness.

Workout Fitness provides various other services to its patrons as well. They provide counseling on diets, exercise regimen, personal trainers, yoga, aerobics, an all women's relaxation area and other activities on certain days of the week. They charge an annual membership fee of ₹ 48, 000/- .The membership fee though hefty includes all these services. For a six month period the fees are ₹ 28,000/- and the same for a quarter amounts to ₹ 18,000/-.They do not have an option for monthly membership.

Recently two more new Gymnasiums have opened up in the vicinity of Workout Fitness. Both these Gymnasiums have opened up branches wherever Workout Fitness has branches. Both these Gymnasiums are posing a huge competitive threat to Workout Fitness. The main issue here is that both the Gymnasiums have priced their annual membership at ₹ 30,000/-, their six monthly membership at ₹ 17,000/- and quarterly membership at ₹ 8,000/-. Besides, they also allow for a monthly membership at ₹ 3,000/- per month.

As a result of this, some of the patrons of Workout Fitness have left and joined the new Gymnasiums. Also because of the low pricing, the new Gymnasiums are getting customers from the Lower middleclass and lower class as well.

Q.1 As a Manager of the Workout Fitness your job is to retain the patrons and do something so that they do not leave your Gymnasium. Do you think that cutting prices will help?

Q.2 Suggest a pricing strategy for Workout Fitness to get more memberships from its target customer base.

Q.3 Suggest some ways of implementing discriminatory pricing strategy to ensure more customer traffic at Workout Fitness.

Questions from Previous Pune University Examinations

1. Define Pricing. Describe Various Factors influencing the pricing Decisions.
   [M.B.A. Dec. 2005]

2. Which Internal and External Factors influencing the Setting of the Price of a Product?
   [M.B.A. April 2007]

3. "Pricing Strategies have to be based on two Considerations, Performance in the present market and Survival in the future market." Present your view point.
   [M.B.A. Dec. 2007]

4. State the Factors influencing Pricing Decision. Discuss Different Approaches of Pricing. **[M.B.A. Dec. 2009]**

   OR

   What are the Factors influencing Pricing Decisions? Explain in detail.
   [M.B.A. April 2009]

5. "Price is the only element in the marketing mix that produces revenue". Justify.
   [M.B.A. April 2011]

6. Pricing is the most important P among all P's. Discuss. **[M.B.A. April 2010]**

7. Discuss the different pricing strategies. Give factors affecting pricing decisions.
   [M.B.A. Dec. 2010]

■■■

Chapter 3...
Place

Contents ...

3.1 Introduction

3.2 The Role of Marketing Channels
    3.2.1 Importance of Distribution Channels
    3.2.2 What are Marketing Channels?
    3.2.3 Rationale Behind Using Marketing Channels
    3.2.4 Functions of Marketing Channels
    3.2.5 Channel Levels
    3.2.6 Factors Determining the Length of the Channel

3.3 Channel Design Decisions
    3.3.1 Channel Management Decisions
    3.3.2 Channel Dynamics
    3.3.3 Managing Channel Conflicts

3.4 Channel Options: Introduction to Wholesaling, Retailing, Franchising and Direct Marketing
    3.4.1 Wholesaling
    3.4.2 Retailing
    3.4.3 Franchising
    3.4.4 Direct Marketing
    3.4.5 E-commerce Marketing Practices

3.5 Market Logistics Decisions
    3.5.1 Marketing Logistics
    3.5.2 Major Functions of Logistics System

- Points to Remember
- Questions for Discussion
- Case Study
- Questions from Previous Pune University Examinations

Learning Objectives ...

In this chapter, we shall focus on understanding the element of Place or Physical Distribution. Place or Physical Distribution is an important element in the marketing mix. The learning objectives of this chapter are:

- Understanding the importance of physical distribution and its relevance in the marketing mix.
- Studying the functions of the distribution channels and their role.
- Studying the various types of channels of distribution.
- Designing channels of distribution and understanding the criteria therein for the purpose of designing.
- Studying the wholesaling, retailing and franchising functions in distribution management;
- Understanding the concept of direct marketing.
- Gaining an insight into the impact of technology and internet in today's global scenario with respect to distribution.
- Understanding the Logistics function with respect to order processing, warehousing, Inventory and transportation.

3.1 Introduction

This topic will cover:

- The meaning and purpose of place (distribution).
- Different distribution channels.
- Factors to be considered when choosing distribution channels.
- The objective of PLACE (Distribution) is to make products available in the right place at the right time in the right quantities.
- A distribution channel moves a product from production to consumption.
- Each party in a distribution channel is called an intermediary.
- Retailer is the final step in the chain - deals directly with the customer. Retailers are focused on consumer markets. There are various kinds of retailers such as specialist chains, department stores, convenience stores, independents and franchises.
- Wholesales make money by buying at a lower price from the producer and adding a profit margin onto the price paid by the retailer.
- There are two types of channels: direct and indirect.

3.2 The Role of Marketing Channels

We do know, as a matter of fact, that most of the manufacturers do not sell their products directly to the end users or the final consumers. Intermediaries present between these two entities are the ones responsible for the movement of these products from the manufacturers to the end users. These intermediaries or middlemen, as they are commonly known, form the channels of distribution. Intermediaries perform a variety of functions for both the manufacturers as well as for the consumers. In fact, they are the link between the two.

Marketing channel decisions are amongst the most critical decisions that the organisation has to make. The decision of the channel, affects all other marketing decisions. As such, it is a key element of the marketing mix and has a bearing on all marketing decisions.

3.2.1 Importance of Distribution Channels

For any organisation, a distribution channel or a distribution system is a vital link between itself and its customers. Given this, organisations ought to realise that distribution channels and channel members are a key external resource. Usually it takes years to build a distribution channel, and once it has been built, it is quite a difficult task to change or replace it. This is because of the various functions performed by channel members and its linkages with the customers.

The importance of the distribution channel lies in the fact that it represents a corporate commitment to a large number of businesses and to the markets that the channels serve.

The effectiveness of most marketing activities of the organisation, to a very large extent, depends on the distribution channels. Any kind of marketing communication must have the channel support for its success.

Given the main function of distribution that is performed by channel members, distribution channels determine the reach of the organisation; hence it is of utmost importance to select and choose a channel with care in order to ensure maximum reach across target markets.

Last, but not the least, since channel members are the ones in touch with the actual end users, they provide feedback from them to the producers or manufacturers, thus making it possible for the organisation to feel the pulse of the market.

3.2.2 What are Marketing Channels?

A marketing channel consists of individuals and firms involved in the process of making a product or service available for use or consumption by consumers or industrial users.

Marketing channels are the ways that goods and services are made available for use by the consumers. All goods go through channels of distribution, and marketing depends on the way goods are distributed. The route that the product takes on its way from production to the consumer is important because a marketer must decide which route or channel is best for his particular product.

Stern & El-Ansary define marketing channels as *"sets of independent organisations involved in the process of making a product or service available for use or consumption."*

3.2.3 Rationale Behind Using Marketing Channels

(i) Many organisations lack the resources (financial as well as other resources), to carry out direct marketing and reach out to their many customers without the help of any intermediary. For this purpose, marketing channels are used to take the products from the manufacturing organisations to the final consumers.

(ii) For many smaller products, direct marketing may not be feasible considering that exclusive retail outlets for small products may not work, and having to stock other products might end up in having just another grocery or food outlet which would not serve the purpose. Setting up exclusive retail stores for marketing of small products like chocolates would not be a feasible idea.

(iii) Given the lower return on investments in the retail business, organisations would be better off investing their money in their main business rather than taking up retailing or other channel functions.

As such, the use of intermediaries is mainly to make the goods available and accessible to target markets. Intermediaries, because of their specialisation, experience, and scale of operations, are able to achieve more than what the organisation can in terms of reaching to the target markets.

3.2.4 Functions of Marketing Channels

A marketing channel mainly performs the task of moving goods from the producers or manufacturers to the final users. The channel is instrumental in overcoming the gaps between the producers and consumers in terms of time, place and possession or ownership. The functions of the distribution channels are:

(a) **Information:** The marketing channels perform the task of collecting and disseminating of marketing information about customers, competitors as well as potential customers and other market forces.

(b) **Promotion:** Persuasive communication is disseminated through the channels to the customers. The channels also often help in the design of these communication messages.

(c) **Negotiation:** The channel members are the ones who negotiate with other channel members and customers to facilitate the transfer of ownership.

(d) **Financing:** The marketing channels work towards the acquisition and allocation of funds required to finance inventories at different levels of the marketing channels.

(e) **Risk taking:** The channel members assume the risk for carrying out the channel work.

(f) **Physical possession:** The channel members also take the responsibility of storage of goods during the successive stages to the final consumers.

(g) **Ordering**: This function is with regards to the communication of channel members regarding the intention to purchase.

(h) **Payment:** The channel members also assume responsibility for the buyers honouring their payments to the sellers through banks and other financial instruments.

(i) **Title:** The channel members facilitate actual transfer of ownership from one organisation or person to the other.

The Fig. 3.1 shows one major source of cost savings affected by using intermediaries/distributors. The Fig. 3.1 (a) depicts three producers, each using direct marketing to reach three consumers. This system requires eight different contacts. On the other hand we can see in Fig. 3.1 (b) three producers contacting three consumers through one distributor. This requires six contacts. In this way we can see that intermediaries reduce the work of the producers.

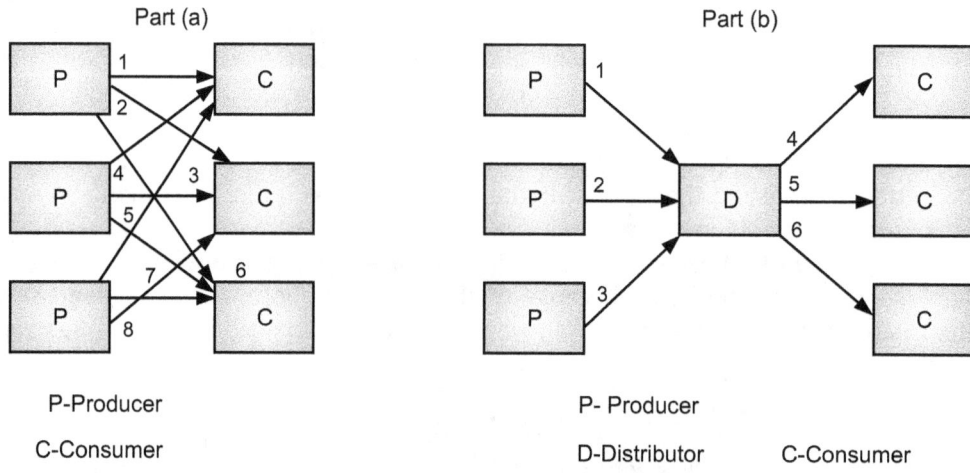

P-Producer
C-Consumer
D-Distributor

Fig. 3.1: Distributor as a Source of Cost Saving

3.2.5 Channel Levels

A channel comprises several intermediaries. Each intermediary moves the product one step further towards the final consumer, and as such, each intermediary forms a level of the channel. The producer/manufacturer and the final consumer form a part of the channel and are at both ends of the channel. There are channels with different number of levels.

(a) **A zero level channel:** As the name suggests, in this type of a channel, there are no intermediaries or zero level of intermediaries. Here, the manufacturer sells directly to the customer. This is also known as a **direct marketing channel**. Examples of this type of channel include door-to-door sales, mail order, telemarketing, TV selling, and manufacturer-owned stores.

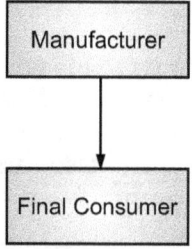

Fig. 3.2: Zero Level Channel

(b) One level channel: This type of a channel comprises of only one selling intermediary such as a retailer.

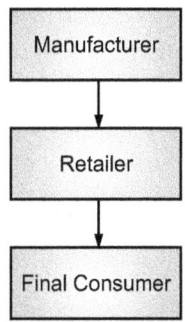

Fig. 3.3: One Level Channel

(c) Two level channel: This type of channel is mostly seen in the consumer goods markets. Here, there are two intermediaries in between the manufacturer and the final consumers; typically a wholesaler and a retailer.

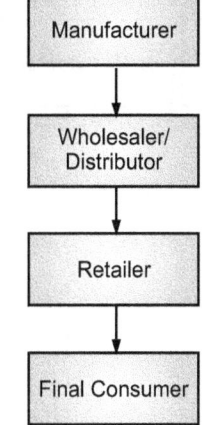

Fig. 3.4: Two Level Channel

(d) Three level channel: This type of channel consists of three levels of intermediaries in between the manufacturer and the final consumer.

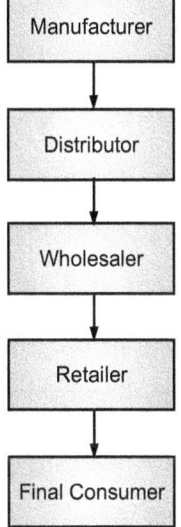

Fig. 3.5: Three Level Channel

(e) **More than three levels:** In some cases, one can observe longer marketing channels, that is, channels that have more than three intermediaries.

(f) **Channels used in consumer and industrial products:** The producer and the consumer are a part of every channel. Fig. 3.6 below shows indirect channels for various levels for consumer products and Fig. 3.7 depicts the same for industrial products.

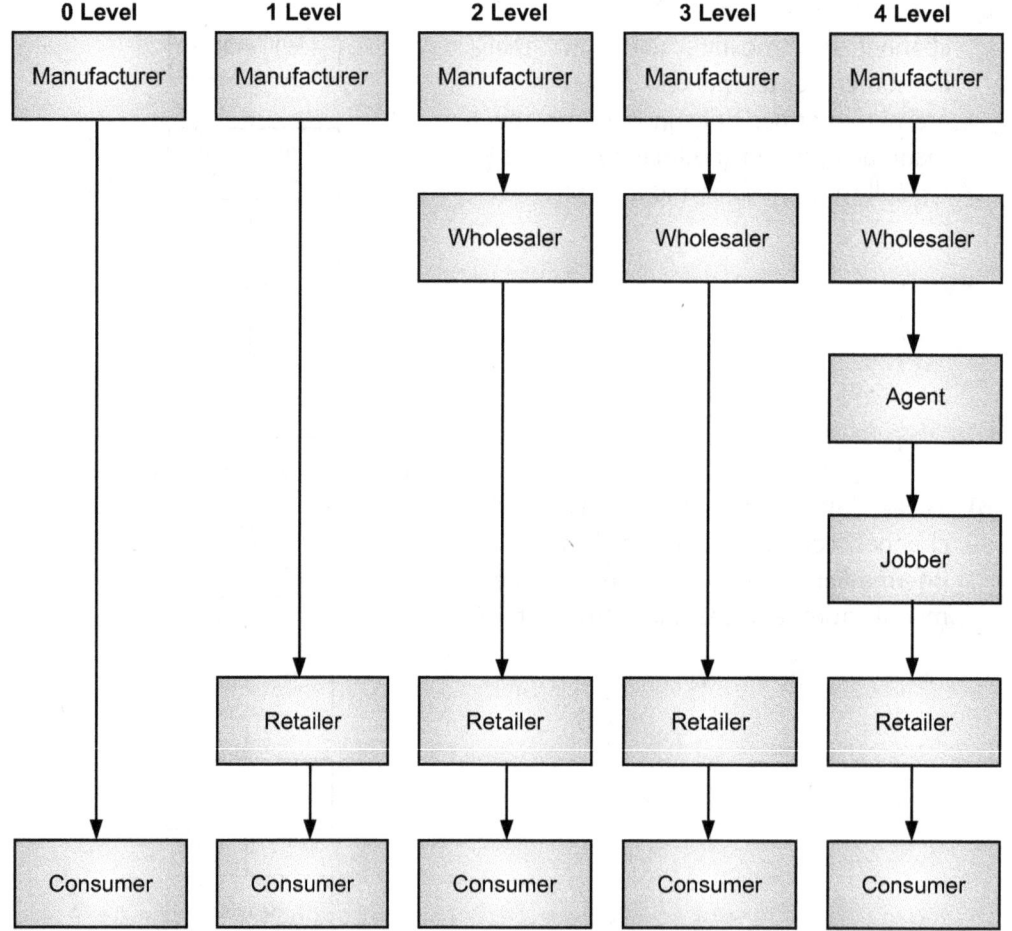

Fig. 3.6: Consumer Marketing Channels

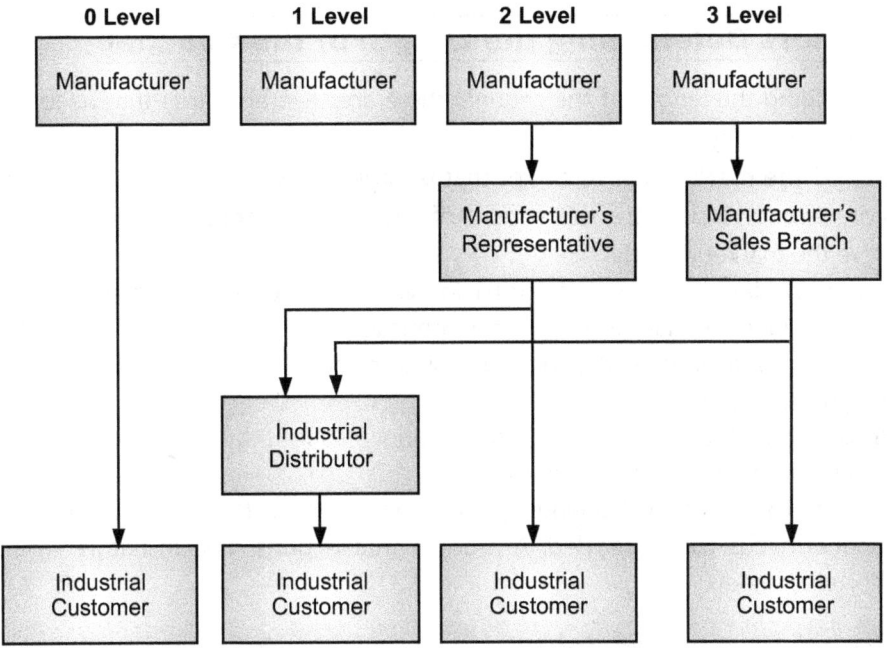

Fig. 3.7: Industrial Marketing Channels

(g) Channel of Distribution for Services: Generally services differ from physical goods in the sense that they are intangible and hence distribution of services poses special challenges. There are only two common channels used for services.

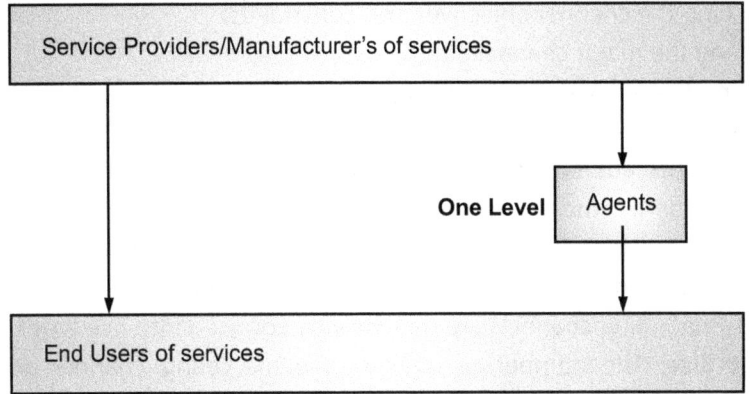

Fig. 3.8: Channels for Services

We have seen the levels of indirect channels as well as the various types of channels that are used in consumer and industrial goods and those for services. Let us now take a look at the factors determining the length of the channel.

3.2.6 Factors Determining the Length of the Channel

When deciding the length of the channel there are several factors that need to be taken into consideration. They are:

1. **Size of the market:** For a market that is large, use of indirect channels proves to be more economical. More the spread of the market, more expensive it becomes to serve the market directly.
2. **Order lot size:** If the average order lot size is smaller, transportation costs increase. Here the indirect channel is more economical.
3. **Service requirements:** A shorter channel is more useful when the level of service requirement is high.
4. **Product variety:** When the product variety sought by customers is high, selling through indirect channels is advisable.
5. **Type of the product:** Depending upon the nature of the product, the length of the channel needs to be decided. A product that is perishable in nature would need a shorter channel.

3.3 Channel Design Decisions

Designing the marketing channels is a task in which the manufacturer has to take into consideration several factors. An organisation needs to take into consideration what is desirable while not losing focus on what is feasible, affordable and available. The process of designing the marketing channels comprises four major steps. These are:

(a) Analysing the customers' desired service output levels;
(b) Establishing the channel objectives and constraints;
(c) Identifying the major channel alternatives;
(d) Evaluating the major channel alternatives.

Let us take a look at all these steps in detail:

(a) Analysing the customers' desired service output levels: Marketing begins with identifying the needs of the customers. The same holds true for marketing channels. Understanding how customers buy, why they buy a particular product, and what are their expectations when they buy, is the first step in designing a marketing channel. The service outputs given by marketing channels are generally categorised into five types.

  (i) **Lot Size**: The number of units that a marketing channel permits a typical customer to purchase on every occasion of purchase is referred to as the lot size. Basically, consumers prefer that the intermediaries permit them to buy the quantities that they desire. It may be a lot size of one for a household consumer purchasing a car, or a lot size of 20 for a corporate entity purchasing cars for its executives. The smaller the lot size, the greater is the expected level of service output.

(ii) Waiting Time: This is the time for which the customers would generally have to wait to get the delivery of goods. Customers expect and prefer faster delivery channels.

(iii) Spatial Convenience: One of the major functions of the marketing channel is to provide time and space convenience. Customers will prefer those channels that make it easy for them to purchase the products.

(iv) Product Variety: The breadth of the assortment offered by the channel member represents the variety of the products that the channel member offers to the customers. Most customers prefer a situation where more variety is available as it facilitates better choice.

(v) Service Backup: Service backup typically deals with added services like installation, repairs, credit card payment, free delivery and so on. More the service backup more is the preference for the channel.

Although higher service output levels are desirable by customers, one has to take into consideration the fact that higher service output levels translate into higher pricing for consumers. At times, consumers may be willing to accept lower service levels when it translates into lower prices.

(b) Establishing the channel objectives and constraints: As mentioned in point (a) above, some customer segments are, at times, willing to accept lower service output levels with regards to the channel if it translates into lower prices. Different customer segments would desire different levels of service output. Effective channel planning would require the organisation to determine which market segments to serve, and based on that, decide the most suitable channel.

Channel objectives will also vary in line with the product characteristics. Perishable products would require more of the direct marketing channels because of the risks associated with delays. Bulky products would require the channels that minimise the number of the handlings and also the shipping distance.

Channel design also needs to take into consideration the strengths and weaknesses of the different types of channel members. For example, a manufacturer's representatives are able to have a better rapport with the customers. However, the cost of visits to every individual customer is high, and the exercise of covering all customers is time-consuming too.

While designing the channel, the organisation must also take into consideration the competitors' channels. The channel design must also adapt to the larger environment in terms of economic conditions, legal regulations and restrictions.

(c) Identifying major channel alternatives: After having taken the decision on the target market and establishing the objectives, it is time for the organisation to decide on the channel alternatives. While selecting the channel alternatives, three elements must be taken into consideration:

(1) Types of available business intermediaries
(2) The number of intermediaries needed, and
(3) The terms and responsibilities of each channel member.

Let us take a detailed look at these elements:

(i) **Types of intermediaries:** The organisation must identify the types of intermediaries available to carry on its channel work. Some examples of channel alternatives can be:
- The organisation's own sales force.
- **Manufacturer's agency Industrial distributors:** Finding and appointing distributors in different regions who, in addition to selling the products, will also keep stocks to facilitate faster deliveries.
- **OEM markets:** Original Equipment Manufacturers (OEMs) are those organisations that buy products from other organisations, incorporate the same in their own products, and sell them further.
- **Dealers and distributors:** The organisation can also consider dealers and distributors as channel alternatives.

(ii) **Number of Intermediaries:** The organisation has to decide the number of intermediaries to be used at each channel level. There are three strategies an organisation can use to decide the number of intermediaries:
- **Exclusive Distribution**: Exclusive distribution involves limiting the number of intermediaries handling the organisation's goods and services to just one. This involves a contract in which the intermediary agrees not to carry competing brands.

    This is normally done when the organisation wants to exercise a greater control on the service level and the inputs offered by the channel members.
- **Selective Distribution**: This type of a channel structure deals with more intermediaries; however, the number is lesser than the maximum number of intermediaries willing to carry a particular product.

    The rationale is that the organisation can develop good working relations with a few select intermediaries and expect better results. It is a structure which enables the organisation to gain more coverage and control with lesser costs than in case of intensive distribution.
- **Intensive Distribution**: Here, the manufacturing organisation places its goods in as many outlets as possible. This is specially done for products where the consumer looks for a greater deal of convenience while buying, like in case of daily use items, snacks, toiletries, bakery items, etc.

(iii) Terms and responsibilities of channel members: The channel member is an important constituent of the entire marketing mix, and hence, it is necessary that the organisation establish a long term relationship with channel members. While developing a relationship, it is imperative for the organisation to define the rights and responsibilities of each channel member, and ensure that they are given opportunities to have a profitable business. This is the trade-relations mix. The major elements of the trade-relations mix are:

- **Price policy**: Here, the organisation has to establish a price list as well as an indicative list of discounts that are considered as fair and equitable by the channel member.
- **Distributor's territorial rights**: Demarcating the territory is the task that is of utmost importance in the trade-relations mix. It is only fair that organisations inform the intermediaries of the terms and conditions under which they would enfranchise other intermediaries, and allocate to them commissions or profits on sales in their territory, even if it is not done by them directly.
- **Mutual services and responsibilities**: These must be clearly and explicitly mentioned so as to avoid any ambiguity and conflicts at a later stage. The organisation's policy with regards to building, promotional support, training and recruitment of staff and other such areas of mutual co-operation must be mentioned.

(d) Evaluating major channel alternatives: Having identified the major channel alternatives, it is now essential that the organisation evaluate these alternatives. There are three major criteria which are used to evaluate the available alternatives:

- **Economic Criterion**: The economic criterion involves the comparison and evaluation of expected costs and expected sales under various alternatives. Suppose there are two alternatives, which are, selling through the organisation's own sales force as against selling through an external sales agency. At first, the organisation should determine whether the organisation's own sales force will be able to achieve better sales vis-à-vis an outside sales agency. The next step is to establish the cost of having the internal sales force carry out the entire selling job as against the same being done by the sales agency, and the final step involves the comparison of the sales and the costs under both alternatives in order to decide which one is more profitable.
- **Control Criterion**: Another important criterion that must be considered is that of control over the channel members. There is certainly a risk of loss of control when dealing with external agencies as against dealing with the organisation's own sales force.
- **Adaptive Criterion**: In a rapid and dynamic market scenario, the willingness of a channel member to adapt to changing policies and increased demands must be considered.

3.3.1 Channel Management Decisions

After having selected the channel alternative, it is time for the organisation to select individual channel members and motivate and evaluate them, and modify the channel arrangements over a period of time to provide better service to the end users.

(a) Selection of channel members: While selecting channel members, it is essential for the organisation to first establish the characteristics that it seeks in these members. The characteristics could be with regards to the number of years the channel members have been in business, their growth and profit record, their market reputation, and their capabilities to handle the product.

(b) Motivating channel members: To motivate channel members to perform, the organisation must ensure that they help the intermediaries with the training of the personnel, supervision and encouragement. They also need to be incentivised and rewarded from time to time for performances that exceed set targets.

(c) Evaluating channel members: The organisation must periodically evaluate the performance of the channel members against set parameters like the attainment of sales targets, the average inventory levels maintained, the delivery time to customers, and co-operation in promotional and other business aspects.

(d) Modifying channel arrangements: To meet the ever-changing conditions in the marketplace, the channel arrangements would require modifications over a period of time. Modifications become necessary when the channel is not working as planned or anticipated, when newer channels emerge, or even when the product passes through progressive stages in its life cycle.

3.3.2 Channel Dynamics

Distribution channels are also constantly evolving with time. They keep changing with regards to their structures, functions, and their business arenas. Given this, there is also a greater possibility of channel competition and conflict. In this section, we will look at the changing channel dynamics with regards to the recent channel developments like the Vertical, Horizontal and Multi-channel Marketing Systems.

(i) Types of channels

- **A Vertical Marketing System (VMS)** comprises of the manufacturer, wholesaler and retailer, all acting as a unified system as against the conventional marketing channel system in which each of the channel members are a separate entity. Here, one channel member either owns the others, or franchises them, or exercises enough control over the other members to ensure the functioning as one unified system.
  There are three types of VMS: Corporate, Administered and Contractual.

- **Corporate VMS** looks at having the successive stages of manufacturing and distribution under a single ownership.
- **Administered VMS** looks at the co-ordination of the successive stages of manufacturing and distribution through the power of one of the channel members who exercises control over the others.
- **Contractual VMS** involves independent organisations at different stages of manufacturing and distribution and integrates their efforts on a contractual basis to obtain more economies of scale than would be possible for them to do individually. There are three types of Contractual VMS:
  - **Wholesaler sponsored voluntary chains:** Here, wholesalers organise voluntary chains of independent retailers who help them compete with the larger chains.
  - **Retailer Co-operatives:** In this case, the retailers come together to take up the task of wholesaling or even manufacturing in some cases.
  - **Franchise Organisations:** Franchisers might also link the successive stages in the manufacturing and distribution process.
- **Horizontal Marketing System:** This is another marketing system emerging in which two or more unrelated organisations come together and pool their resources to exploit a marketing opportunity. This coming together may be on a temporary or permanent basis. Also, there is a mutual benefit to both organisations, which they are otherwise not likely to achieve. This is also called as symbiotic marketing.
- **Multi-channel Marketing System:** Gone are the days when organisations sold to a single target market through a single channel. Given the complex nature of multiple segments that are tapped, multi-channel marketing has become the order of the day. Multi-channel marketing occurs when a single organisation uses two or more marketing channels to reach the same or more than one market segment.

(ii) Channel co-operation, conflict and competition:

Marketing channels involve a number of channel intermediaries, and this is always likely to result in a conflict of interests.

- **Channel Conflicts**: Vertical channel conflicts exist when there is conflict between different levels within the same channel. For example, when automobile manufacturers try to enforce policies on their dealers, it leads to a conflict.
- **Horizontal channel conflicts** exist when there is conflict between the members at the same level within the channel. An example of this type of conflict is one auto dealer having a conflict with another auto dealer.
- **Multi-channel conflict** exists when the manufacturer establishes two or more channels that are competing with each other in selling to the same market. An example of this type of conflict is if an organisation appoints two agents for the same territory.

- **Causes of conflict:** Some of the major reasons for conflict are:
  - **Goal Incompatibility**: When there is a goal incompatibility issue between the manufacturer and the channel member, it can give rise to a channel conflict. For example, if the manufacturers prefer to have lower prices and larger volumes whereas the dealers want higher prices and medium volumes, it can lead to a conflict.
  - **Unclear Role and Rights:** A conflict may arise on account of unclear roles and rights. For example, if an organisation sells to customers that are within the territory of the agents, this can lead to a conflict.
  - **Differences in Perception**: Differences in perception about the market requirements and their responses may lead to conflict. An example of differences in perception is when the manufacturer is hoping for higher sales and expects the channel member to carry higher inventory, while the channel member perceives the market conditions to be otherwise.
  - **Greater Dependence**: Conflicts might arise if the channel member is highly dependent on the manufacturer. For example, if the channel member is an exclusive dealer, he may have to comply with all the manufacturer's terms, even if he does not want to.

3.3.3 Managing Channel Conflicts

Some amount of healthy competition is necessary to foster growth. However, when competition moves towards conflicts, it can be highly dysfunctional. Some of the important methods to manage channel conflicts are explained here:

- **Adoption of Super-ordinate goals**: The channel members somehow agree to work towards a fundamental goal that they jointly seek, and in doing so, resolve their conflicts.
- **Exchange of Persons**: Here, persons from the channel member's organisation work in the manufacturing organisation, while those from the manufacturing organisation work in the channel member's offices. This results in them appreciating each other's roles and constraints, and helps resolve conflicts.
- **Co-optation**: Here, one organisation gets the support of the other organisation by involving leaders of the other organisation on their advisory boards, councils, etc.
- **Joint Membership in and between Trade Associations**: Co-operation or joint membership of trade associations can help in arriving at common practices and codes that can help in resolving conflicts.
- **Diplomacy**: This happens when a conflicting side sends a representative to meet with a counterpart from the other organisation to resolve the conflict.
- **Mediation**: This involves referring the conflict to a neutral third party that helps reconcile the conflict between the two parties.
- **Arbitration:** This occurs when the two conflicting parties agree to present their arguments to an arbitrator (a third party) and abide by his decision.

3.4 Channel Options: Introduction to Wholesaling, Retailing, Franchising and Direct Marketing

Wholesaling, retailing and franchising are some of the major intermediaries in the marketing of goods and services. Each of them has specific roles to play in the marketing channel and form an important part of the distribution chain.

Let us study them one by one.

3.4.1 Wholesaling

Wholesaling includes all activities involved in selling goods and services to those who buy for resale or business use. Wholesaling excludes manufacturers and farmers because they are mainly involved in production, and similarly, it also excludes retailers.

Wholesalers perform a number of functions for the manufacturers as well as for the consumers. These are as given below.

- **Selling and promotion**: Wholesalers help manufacturers by providing a sales force thereby enabling them to reach many small business customers in smaller or distant areas at a relatively low price. In these areas, it is seen that buyers often trust the wholesaler more than they would trust a distant manufacturer.
- **Buying and assortment building**: Wholesalers are able to select and buy assortments that are specifically required by their customers, saving them the time and effort of building one themselves.
- **Bulk breaking**: Wholesalers also help their customers by buying in large quantities and breaking the bulk into smaller quantities to suit their customers.
- **Warehousing**: Wholesalers carry a lot of inventory thereby reducing the inventory costs and associated risks for the suppliers and customers.
- **Transportation**: Wholesalers often provide faster deliveries to buyers as they are closer to the buyer than the manufacturer, and thus reduce delays in transportation.
- **Financing**: Wholesalers finance their customers by offering credit, and also finance their suppliers by placing orders and paying bills on time.
- **Risk-bearing**: Since wholesalers buy goods from the manufacturers, they take title to the goods, and in doing so, bear the risk of damage, spoilage, and obsolescence of the goods.
- **Market information**: Wholesalers provide information to their manufacturers regarding the feedback from customers, activities of the competitors and also provide information to customers about new products, prices, and so on.
- Management services and counselling – Wholesalers are known to often help their retailers in improving their operations by providing training to their sales clerks, helping with store layouts, displays, etc. They may also help by offering technical services.

Types of Wholesalers

Having seen the functions of the wholesalers, let us now take a look at the various types of wholesalers. There are basically four types of wholesalers. They are:

(a) Merchant Wholesalers;

(b) Brokers and Agents;

(c) Manufacturers' and retailers' branches and offices;

(d) Miscellaneous Wholesalers;

All these types are further classified as shown below in Fig. 3.9 below:

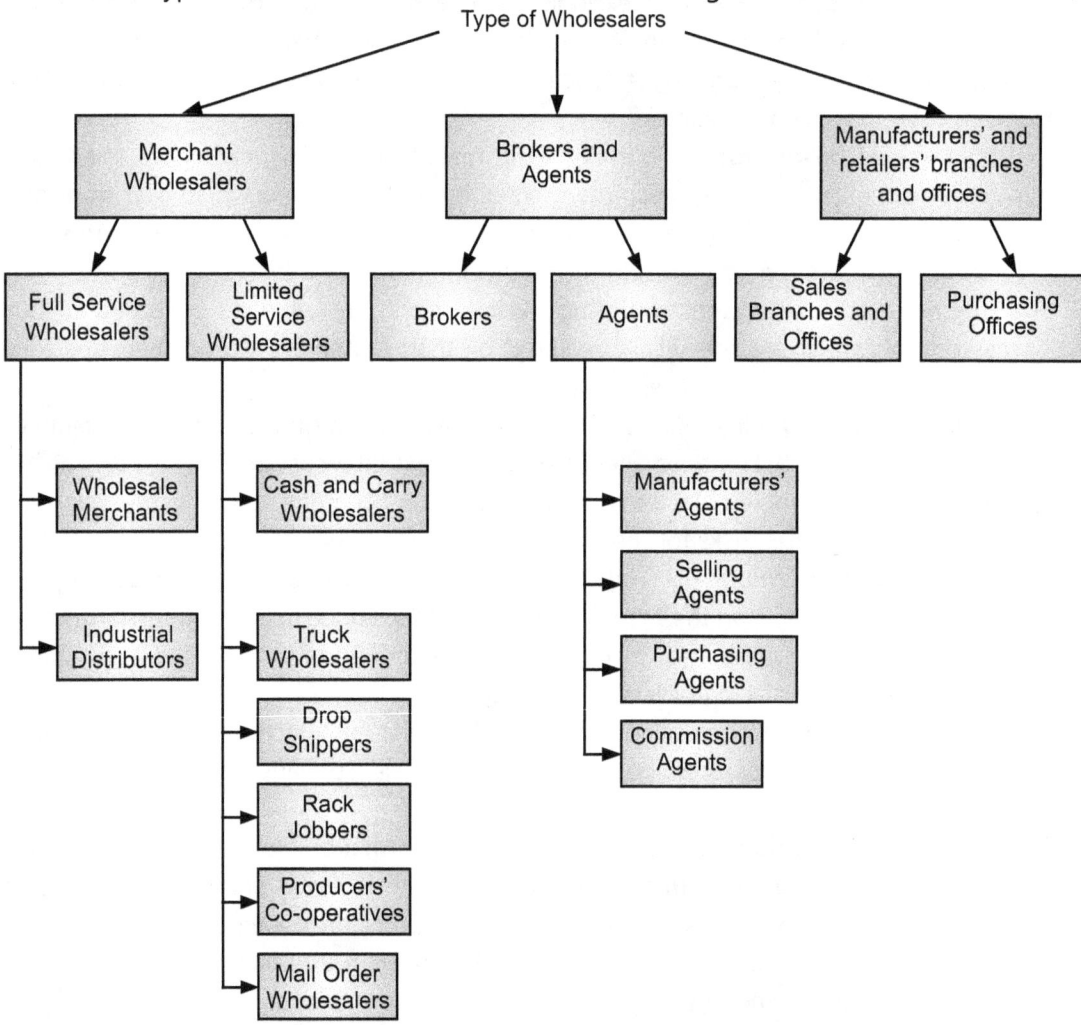

Fig. 3.9: Types of Wholesalers

Let us take a look at these various types of wholesalers in greater detail.

(A) Merchant Wholesalers:

These are independently owned businesses that take title to the merchandise they handle, that is they buy the merchandise that they are to handle. Different industries call them by different names - jobbers, distributors, or mill supply houses. The merchant wholesalers are further divided into two categories – Full Service Wholesalers and Limited Wholesalers.

- **(a) Full service wholesalers**: As the name suggests, these wholesalers provide a full line of services of carrying stock, maintaining a sales force, offering credit, making deliveries, and providing assistance. Full service wholesalers are further categorised into wholesale merchants and industrial distributors.

    - **(i) Wholesale merchants:** They are full service wholesalers who primarily sell to retailers. General merchandise wholesalers carry several merchandise lines while general line wholesalers carry one or two lines in greater depth. Speciality wholesalers specialise in carrying only part of a line.

    - **(ii) Industrial distributors:** These sell to manufacturers rather than to retailers. They provide the full range of services and may carry a broad range, or a general line, or a speciality line.

- **(b) Limited service wholesalers**: Again, as the name suggests, they provide limited services or fewer services, and do not provide the entire range of services like the full service wholesalers. There are several types like cash and carry wholesalers, truck wholesalers, drop shippers, rack jobbers, producers' co-operatives and mail-order wholesalers.

    - **(i) Cash and carry wholesalers:** They have a limited line of fast moving goods to sell to small retailers for cash. Normally they do not provide additional services like delivery, warehousing, etc.

    - **(ii) Truck wholesalers:** They primarily undertake the selling and delivery functions. They generally carry a limited line of semi-perishable merchandise, which they sell for cash to small retailers.

    - **(iii) Drop shippers:** These wholesalers operate in bulk industries such as coal, lumber and heavy equipment. They do not carry inventory. When they receive an order, they select a manufacturer who directly ships the merchandise to the customer. The title and risk is taken by the drop shipper from the time the order is accepted to the time it is delivered to the customer.

- **(iv) Rack jobbers:** They generally serve mostly non-food items to grocery and drug retailers. They price the goods, keep them fresh, and set up point of purchase displays, and keep inventory records. They maintain title to the goods and bill the retailers only for those goods that are sold to consumers.
- **(v) Producers' co-operatives:** These are owned by farmer members, who assemble to sell their farm produce in local markets. The profits made by these co-operatives are distributed to its members.

(B) Brokers and Agents:

These types of wholesalers typically do not take title to the goods and perform only a few functions. Their main function is to facilitate the buying and selling process for which they receive a commission. They generally specialise by product line or customer types.

- **(a) Brokers:** Their main function is bringing buyers and sellers together and assisting in the negotiation process. They are generally paid by the party who hires them. They are not responsible for carrying any inventory, do not assume financial risks, and do not take title to the goods. Some of the common examples are Real Estate Brokers and Security Brokers.
- **(b) Agents:** They represent either buyers or sellers on a more permanent basis than the brokers do. Let us look at some of the common types:
  - **(i) Manufacturers' agents:** They represent two or more manufacturers having complimentary product lines. Their businesses are governed by a written contract or agreement covering issues such as territories, order handling, pricing policies, and commission rates.
  - **(ii) Selling agents:** A selling agent has a contractual authority to sell a manufacturer's entire output. The manufacturer himself does not engage in the selling function. The selling agent serves as a sales department and has a significant influence over prices, and terms and conditions of sales. The selling agent normally does not have any territorial restrictions.
  - **(iii) Purchasing agents:** These are wholesalers who have a long-term relationship with buyers. They make purchases for the buyers and often take on the functions of inspection, warehousing and shipping for the buyers.
  - **(iv) Commission merchants:** They take physical possession of the products and negotiate sales. A commission merchant typically takes loads of material from the manufacturer to the central market place and sells it for the best price. He keeps a commission on the sales made and gives the balance amount to the manufacturer.

(C) Manufacturers' and retailers' branches and offices:

Here, the manufacturers conduct their own wholesaling activities and have branch offices and sales offices for the same.

- (a) **Sales branches and offices:** Sales branches and offices are set up by manufacturers to improve inventory control, selling, and promotion. Generally it is found that sales branches carry inventory whereas sales offices do not carry inventory.
- (b) **Purchasing offices:** These offices perform a role similar to that of brokers or agents, but are a part of the buyer's organisation.

3.4.2 Retailing

The word 'Retail' has been derived from the French word 'Retailer' which means to cut a piece off or to break bulk.

Who then is a Retailer?

A Retailer is any person, agency, a company or an organisation that is instrumental in reaching the goods, merchandise and services to the final consumer.

Retailing consists of all business activities involved in selling goods and services to consumers for their personal, family or household use. It includes every sale of goods and services to the final consumer.

Retailing is the last stage in the distribution process.

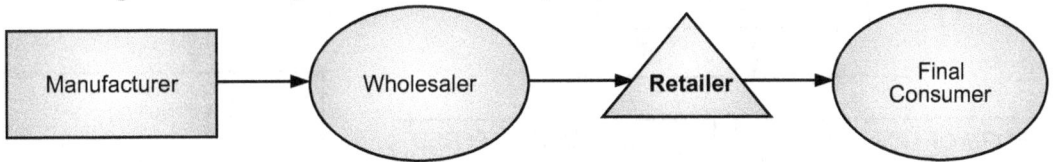

Fig. 3.10: Retailing in the Distribution Process

Retailers perform an array of functions for the manufacturers as well as the end users, that is, the consumers. Let us take a look at some of the major functions:

1. **Sorting:** Many manufacturers would like to make one basic type of item and sell their entire inventory to as few buyers as possible. Final consumers on the other hand, usually want to choose from a variety of options and purchase only a limited quantity. Here, the retailer plays the vital role of a link giving both the manufacturer and the consumer what they want. The retailer collects an assortment of goods and services from various manufacturers in large quantities and offers to sell them in small quantities to the consumers. This is known as the sorting process.

2. **Communication:** An important and significant function performed by the retailer is communicating with the customer, manufacturers, and the wholesalers. Shoppers learn about goods and services from the advertisements, store displays and sales

persons of the retail outlet, and at the same time, retailers provide information about sales forecasts, complaints, defective items, and inventory turnover to manufacturers and wholesalers.

3. **Transportation:** For small wholesalers and manufacturers, retailers provide assistance in transportation, storing, pre-packing and marking of merchandise.

4. **Completion of transactions:** Retailers also complete transactions with customers. This involves filling out orders, processing customers' credit, giving services such as gift wrapping, home delivery, and installations.

Types of retailers

Retailers range in size from small independent *kinara* shop owners to giant international category shops. The merchandise that they offer also varies from foodstuff to drugs to apparel to flowers. Hence, it is necessary to take a look at the formats that have evolved in the west and are now evolving in India.

Classification of Retailing

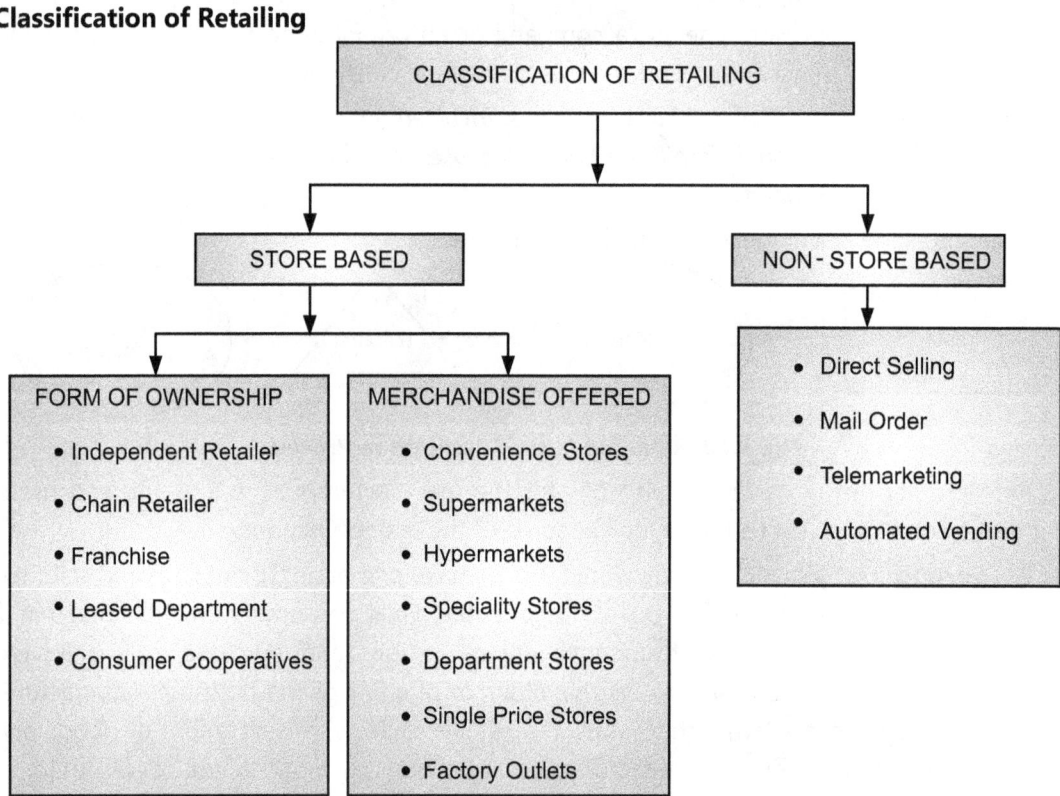

Fig. 3.11: Classification of Retailing

Retailing is basically classified into:
1. Store and
2. Non-Store based retailing.

In case of store-based retailing, the retailer operates from the store. This is a more common form of retailing.

In case of non-store retailing, the retailer does not operate from a store. This format, though known, is still an emerging format in many countries.

1. **Store-based retailing:**

   Store-based retailing is further classified on the basis of forms of ownership and merchandise offered.

   (a) **Classification on the basis of form of ownership**

   (i) **Independent Retailer:** An independent retailer is one who owns and operates only one retail outlet. Stores like the local *baniya* or *kirana* fall under this category (In the west, they are known as mom-n-pop stores). These have the owner or the proprietor with a few family members working as assistants.

   (ii) **A Chain Retailer:** A chain retailer is also known as a corporate retail chain. When two or more outlets are under a common ownership, it is called as a retail chain. These stores are characterised by similarity in merchandise offered, ambience, advertising, and promotion.

   (iii) **Franchising:** A franchise is a contractual agreement between the franchiser and the franchisee, which allows the franchisee to conduct business under an established name based on a particular business format for which the franchisee is compensated.

   Franchising may be for -
   - A product or a trademark or
   - A business format franchising

   (iv) **Leased Department -** These are also termed as shop-in-shops. When a section of a department in a retail store is leased/rented to an outside party, it is termed as a leased department.

   (v) **Consumer Co-operatives -** A consumer co-operative is a retail institution that is owned by its member customers.

   (b) **Classification on the basis of merchandise offered:**

   The following table gives a description of the format based on the merchandise offered.

   The categories under this classification are Convenience Store, Supermarkets, Hypermarkets, Departmental Stores, Single Price Stores and Factory Outlets to name a few.

Table 3.1: Classification of Retail outlets based on the merchandise offered

Format	Description	Merchandise offered
Convenience Stores	Usually located in residential areas, open for long hours.	Assortment of products including milk, eggs, bread, vegetables, etc.
Supermarkets	Self service, low cost, low margin and high volume stores.	These stores offer food, laundry, and household maintenance products.
Hypermarkets	Large self-service stores. Usually very big and low price types, low service level.	Offer almost all kinds of products like food, non-food items, CDs, DVDs, footwear, etc. with a depth in product mix.
Speciality Stores	Focuses on a brand or a particular category with high service level.	Offers a narrow product line but very good depth.
Department Stores	Large store selling several product lines with each operating as a department. High level of service.	Product mix is generally non-food like apparel, accessories, books, music, footwear.
Single Price Stores	Meant for the budget-conscious customer. Has goods having a typical price.	Offers an assortment of branded and unbranded merchandise.
Factory Outlets	These are generally factory outlets of particular brands. They sell merchandise at a discount. Situated away from main markets.	Stores that sell branded merchandise at prices less than the MRP.

2. **Non-Store Retailing**

    This is further classified into Direct Selling and Direct Response Marketing.

    (a) Direct selling: It involves the making of a personal contact with the end consumer at his home or place of work. Products such as cosmetics, food, nutritional products, etc. are often sold in this manner.

(b) Direct response marketing: This involves various non-personal methods of communicating with the customer. These include:

(i) **Mail Order/Catalogue Retailing:** Mailers, along with an order form, are sent to customers, giving information about the product. The customer needs to fill out the form marking the products he would like to purchase and sends it back to initiate delivery.

(ii) **Television Shopping:** Details and usage of the product are demonstrated on the television; the customer has to call a toll free number to place an order.

(iii) **Electronic Retailing:** This is done through information kiosks. These kiosks comprise computer terminals housed inside, and a touch-screen on the outside provides customers with product and company information and aids in purchases.

In addition to the above formats, some of the recent and emerging trends in retailing are:

- **Automated Vending Machines:** Here, automated machines are placed at railway stations, bus terminals, in libraries, hospitals, etc, where the customer inserts a coin (of the required denomination) into the machine and the machine dispenses the product.
- **Airport Retailing:** Retail is becoming increasingly important for airport operators. Airports are actually becoming shopping plazas for air travellers.
- **Cash-n-Carry Outlets:** The term cash-n-carry means that customers do their own order picking, pay in cash and carry the merchandise away. Cash-n-carry is also a kind of wholesale format that aids small retailers and businessmen.

3.4.3 Franchising

A franchise is a contractual agreement between the franchiser and the franchisee, which allows the franchisee to conduct a business under an established name, as per a particular business format, in return for which he receives compensation.

The dictionary meaning of the word Franchise is:

1. *A privilege or right granted to a person or a group by a Government, State, or Sovereign.*
2. *Authorisation granted by a manufacturer to a distributor or dealer to sell his products.*

According to the International Franchise Association, *a franchise is a continuous relationship in which the franchiser provides a licensed privilege to do business, plus offers assistance in organising, training, merchandising, and management in return for a consideration from the franchisee.*

The legal definition further adds that: *A franchise may also extend the right to use a predetermined method for marketing products or services through outlets that use a known name or trademark.* Franchising is not a business or an industry, but is a method used by businesses for the marketing and distribution of products or services.

In this, typically, we have two parties - one is the Franchiser, and the other, the Franchisee. The table below explains the roles of the Franchiser and the Franchisee. These may vary slightly depending upon the parties involved.

Table 3.2: Roles of the franchiser and franchisee with respect to several functions

Function	Franchiser	Franchisee
Site Selection	Oversees	Chooses with approval
Design	Provides prototype design	Incurs the cost
Employees	Training	Hires, Supervises, pays
Products to be sold	Decides	Can change only with approval
Prices	Sets/recommends	Follows
Advertising/Promotions	Determines at a national level	May suggest local requirements

3.4.3.1 Advantages and Limitations of Franchising

1. **Low Risk:** A franchise business eliminates the risk of learning from a completely new business. Therefore, the risk of failure is less as compared to a totally new business.

2. **Growth:** A franchise is a part of a network. As the network grows, the opportunities for the individual franchise to grow also increase.

3. **Ease of financing and operational support:** Many a time, a franchiser may assist the franchisee in obtaining finance for setting up the business. The franchiser also gives training, consultancy on the product, service and day-to-day handling of the same.

4. **Advertising:** Advertising costs are greatly reduced because these costs are shared by the franchisees. So the franchisee enjoys a national exposure at an affordable price.

3.4.3.2 Limitations or Disadvantages

Royalty/Fees: The fees or royalty payable by the franchisee may be pretty high in case of successful brands.

Lack of control: Franchising requires adherence to stipulated terms and conditions as laid down by the franchiser. The overall control mostly lies with the franchiser, and in some cases, the franchiser has the right to terminate the agreement if the policy and regulations prescribed are not observed.

3.4.3.3 Types of Franchising

(i) **Product or trademark franchising:** Here, the franchisee acquires identities of the franchiser, by agreeing to sell the latter's products and/or operate under the latter's name.

(ii) **Business format franchising:** The franchisee receives assistance on location, quality control, start-up, décor, management training, and trouble shooting from the franchiser. The franchisee has to adhere to stringent quality controls in all processes.

3.4.4 Direct Marketing

The **Direct Marketing Association** defines Direct Marketing as follows:

Definition: *"Direct Marketing is an interactive marketing system that uses one or more advertising media to affect a measurable response and/or transaction at any location'.*

As is evident from the definition, the emphasis is on a measurable response, which typically means an order from the customer.

Direct marketing makes use of a large number of channels for reaching to the prospects and customers. Let us take a look at some of these:

(a) **Face-to-face selling:** The oldest and most original form of direct marketing is the sales call. Here, the representative of the organisation calls on the prospect/customer and makes a personal presentation of the goods/services offered by the organisation, urging the prospect/customer to buy. This is commonly observed in the insurance industry, Consumer Goods Company, etc. Some successful organisations using this form of marketing are Amway, Avon, and Eureka Forbes.

(b) **Direct mail marketing:** This involves sending marketing communications (an offer, a reminder, or any other kind of communication) to a particular person at a particular address. Highly selective mailing lists are used for these purposes. The marketing communications are sent out in the form of letters, flyers, folders, etc. This is a popular medium because it permits high target market selectivity, can be personalised, and is flexible.

Until the electronic and internet revolution, all mail was paper based. However, the new forms of direct mailing that are now used are:

(i) **Fax mail:** Here, a fax machine is used by one party to send a paper based mail to another, over the telephone line.

(ii) **E-mail:** E-mail or electronic mail allows users to send a message or file directly from one computer to another without the use of paper. The receiving person can store the message/file electronically, or take a print and store it in a paper format.

(iii) **Voice mail:** Voice mail is a system for receiving and storing oral messages at a telephone address.

(c) **Catalogue marketing:** Catalogue marketing happens when an organisation mails a catalogue to the selected addressees, who have a high likelihood of purchasing the product/service.

(d) **Telemarketing:** Telemarketing is a major tool of direct marketing. Some telemarketing systems are fully automated. They have an automated dialling system, which then plays a pre-recorded advertising message and takes orders from interested customers on an answering machine, or by directing the call to an operator.

(e) **Television and other major media direct response marketing:** Television is used to market products directly to the consumers. Here, direct response marketers air television spots that persuasively describe a product and provide consumers with a toll free number to place their orders. Another approach is to have an entire channel dedicated to selling goods and services. Here, the products are offered at bargain prices. A third approach is a video-text service in which the consumers' TV sets are linked with the sellers' computer databanks by a cable or telephone line. The video text service consists of a computerised catalogue of products. Consumers can place orders by means of a special keyboard-like device connected by a two-way cable.

Magazines, newspapers and radio are also used as direct response selling channels.

(f) **Kiosk marketing:** Some organisations have designed customer order-placing machines, which are placed in stores, airports, and other locations. The customer can access the product range through the kiosk and place the order through the kiosk giving a credit card number.

3.4.5 E-commerce Marketing Practices

E-commerce involves buying and selling processes that are supported by electronic means, primarily the internet. **E-Markets** are virtual market spaces rather than physical market spaces. Organisations use e-markets to offer their products and services online to customers. **E-Purchasing** or buying comprises organisations purchasing goods, services as well as information from online suppliers. In business to business transactions often huge networks of e-marketers and e-buyers is formed leading to an online distribution channel.

E-commerce and the internet have revolutionised the way products and services are sold and purchased. The internet revolution has introduced an online channel for the purpose of distribution.

An online marketing or distribution channel is one that a person can reach via a computer and the use of the internet. The online channels provide an array of benefits to both the sellers (marketers) and the buyers (Consumers)

Benefits of online marketing channels

The main reason for the popularity of online marketing channels is the benefits that customers derive, as well as those that the marketer derives. These are:

Benefits to Customers

- **Convenience:** Customers can order products 24 X 7 from wherever they are. As long as they are able to access the internet, buying becomes an easy process.
- **Information:** The internet is a sea of information. At the click of a button, customers can acquire information about competitive product offerings and compare the same.
- **Hassle-free:** With online services, customers can do what they want, and how they want, without having to deal with persuasive sales people.

Benefits to Marketers

- **Quick adjustments to market conditions:** Organisations can very quickly add products, and delete products from their product line. Also, the online medium enables marketers to change prices and descriptions very quickly.
- **Lower costs:** Online marketers can do away with the costs associated with maintaining a store, paying rent, maintaining sales staff, insurance and other costs. They can also produce digital catalogues that cost much lesser than actual paper catalogues.
- **Relationship building:** Online marketers can talk with their customers and learn from them. They can upload useful information regarding the organisation, and offer free demonstrations online.
- **Audience sizing:** By counting the number of hits on their site, the marketers can get an idea of how many people visited their site, and can also find out how many people stopped at particular places on their site.

Some other ways of using the internet and technology for distribution purposes:

- **Creating an electronic store front:** Many organisations have created a home page on the internet. The homepage serves as an electronic storefront. It has a menu from which customers can view product categories, rates, or any other information about the store.
- **Placing ads online:** Advertisements or commercials can be placed online to increase the visibility of the organisation, to create awareness about its products, and offer a toll free number for placing orders.
- **Using email:** As mentioned earlier, email can be used to send useful communication to the customer. Here, one more important application of the email is to encourage customers to give feedback, ask questions, and give suggestions as well as to refer other customers.

E-Marketing Domains

There are four major e-marketing domains. They are:

- **B2C – Business to Consumer:** This involves the online selling of goods and services to the final consumer.
- **B2B – Business to Business:** This involves online trading of goods and services between two businesses. Here firms use B2B trading networks, auction sites, spot exchanges, online product catalogues and other online resources like barter sites to reach larger number of customers, offering product information, enabling customer purchasing and offering online customer support services.
- **C2C – Consumer to Consumer:** This involves online exchanges between two consumers (interested parties) for a wide range of products and services.
- **C2B – Consumer to Business:** Here consumers interact with organisations online. It may involve giving feedback, registering complaints, sending in suggestions etc.

3.5 Market Logistics Decisions

Organisations need to decide on the best way to ensure that their products reach their consumers at the right place and at the right time, in right quantities. This can be achieved only through effective marketing logistics.

3.5.1 Marketing Logistics

Marketing Logistics involves planning, implementing and controlling the physical flow of goods, services and related information from the point of origin to the point of consumption to meet the requirements of the customer. Marketing Logistics is also called as Physical Distribution.

Marketing logistics comprises not only outbound distribution (i.e. moving products from factory to resellers and then to consumers) and inbound distribution (i.e. moving products and raw materials from suppliers to the factory) but also reverse distribution (moving broken, unwanted or excess products returned by consumers or resellers). Thus it involves the entire supply chain management that includes upstream as well as downstream movement of materials, goods, services and related information among suppliers, the organisation, the resellers and the final consumers. This is shown in Fig. 3.12 given below

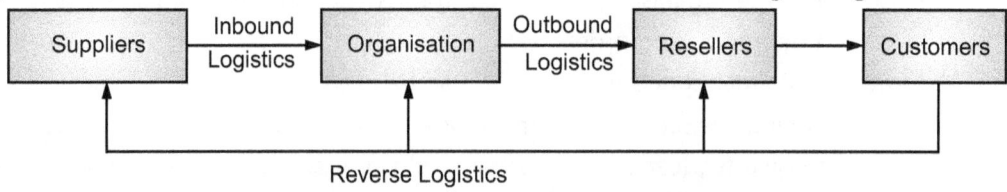

Fig. 3.12: Supply Chain Management

3.5.2 Major Functions of Logistics System

The major logistics functions include Warehousing, Inventory Management, transportation and logistics information management. Let us take a look at each of these functions in detail:

(a) Warehousing: In most cases, one can see that the production of goods happens much earlier than their consumption. That is goods are first manufactured, then transported, stored, sold through channel members and then consumed. As such the production and consumption cycles are not in synchronisation with each other. Owing to this it becomes necessary for the organisation to store the goods until the time that they are ready to be sold. Storage of goods helps organisations to overcome the differences in the needed quantity and the timing, ensuring that the products are available just when the consumers need them. It is here that organisations look at the warehousing function.

As a part of the warehousing function, organisations need to decide on how many and what type of warehouses it needs and where.

Types of warehouses: Generally organisations can opt for two types of warehouses. They are:

(i) **Storage Warehouses**: These are simple warehouses that engage only in storage of goods for moderate to long periods.

(ii) **Distribution Centres**: These are warehouses that are designed to move goods rather than only store them. They are highly automated. The warehouse has inbuilt automated systems to receive goods from various suppliers, take orders, fill the orders and deliver the goods. As such they perform functions other than just storage of goods.

(b) Inventory Management: Inventory management involves maintaining sufficient inventory or stocks to suit the customer requirements. Here there is a trade-off between maintaining too little and too much inventory. With too little stock, there is a risk that the organisation may not have the desired goods when the customer needs it. On the other hand too much stock results in very high inventory carrying costs and stock obsolescence. As such both these aspects need to be delicately balanced.

Many organisations today have reduced their inventory carrying costs by adopting just-in-time logistics systems which enable the organisation to carry stocks for as little as 3 to 5 days of operations. New stock arrives just when needed, rather than being in the warehouse for a long time. This system however, requires accurate forecasting along with fast, frequent and flexible delivery schedules.

Organisations today are trying to look at new ways of making the inventory management system more efficient by leveraging technology. Use of RFID tags or smart tags embedded in the products has made tracking products very easy. Soon the entire supply chain will be automated and at any given point in time the organisation would be able to know where exactly a product is located, "Smart shelves" would not only prompt the time for re-order but also do the reordering automatically.

(c) Transportation: This is yet another important aspect of the Marketing Logistics function. Choice of the transportation carrier not only affects the final price of the product, but also determines the delivery performance and the condition of the goods on arrival ultimately affecting the customer satisfaction. In shipping goods the main modes of transportation that are available to the organisations include:
- Road Transport
- Rail Transport
- Water Transport
- Air Transport.

Many organisations also use intermodal transport systems, which is a combination of two or more modes of transport. Piggyback is the use of rail and trucks, fishy back (the use of water and trucks), train ship (water and rail), and air truck (air and truck) are all used together. Combining modes of transport helps organisations to maximise on the benefits offered by both the modes. While choosing the mode of transportation the organisation needs to look at speed of delivery, dependability, cost and availability.

(d) Logistics Information Management: Information is a vital aspect of logistics management. Information can be shared as well as managed through a number of sources like the email, telephone or even through electronic data interchange (EDI) which is the computerised exchange of data between organisations. Here the organisation is connected to the Suppliers through computer networks and change in the inventory levels of the organisation can be checked by the supplier who can then replenish the stocks. Many organisations have their suppliers to generate orders and arrange deliveries for their customers. Such systems are also known as Vendor Managed Inventory (VMI) system or Continuous Inventory Replenishment System.

Points to Remember

- For any organisation, a distribution channel or a distribution system is a vital link between itself and its customers. The importance of the distribution channel is mainly because
- It represents a corporate commitment to a large number of businesses and to the markets that the channels serve.
- The effectiveness of most marketing activities of the organisation, to a very large extent, depends on the distribution channels.
- Marketing Channels are sets of independent organisations involved in the process of making a product or service available for use or consumption.

- **Functions of Distribution Channels:**
  Members of the marketing channel perform a number of key functions:
  (a) Information
  (b) Promotion
  (c) Negotiation
  (d) Financing
  (e) Risk taking
  (f) Physical possession
  (g) Ordering
  (h) Payment
  (i) Title

- **Channel Levels:**
  A channel comprises of several intermediaries. Each intermediary moves the product further towards the final consumer, and as such, each intermediary forms a level of the channel. The producer/manufacturer and the final consumer form a part of the channel and are at both ends of the channel. There are channels with different number of levels.
  (a) A zero level channel
  (b) One level channel
  (c) Two level channel
  (d) Three level channel
  (e) More than three levels

- **When deciding the length of the channel there are several factors that need to be taken into consideration. They are:**
  1. Size of the market
  2. Order lot size
  3. Service requirements
  4. Product variety
  5. Type of the product

- **The process of designing the marketing channels comprises of four major steps. These are:**
  (a) Analysing the customers' desired service output levels;
  (b) Establishing the channel objectives and constraints;
  (c) Identifying the major channel alternatives;
  (d) Evaluating the major channel alternatives;

- **Various aspects of channel management decisions include**
    - (a) Selection of channel members
    - (b) Motivating channel members
    - (c) Evaluating channel members
    - (d) Modifying channel arrangements
- **Causes of conflict**

    Some of the major reasons for conflict are:
    - (a) Goal Incompatibility
    - (b) Unclear Role and Rights
    - (c) Differences in Perception
    - (d) Greater Dependence
- **Managing Channel Conflict:**

    Some of the important methods to manage channel conflicts are:
    - Adoption of Super-ordinate goals
    - Exchange of Persons
    - Co-optation
    - Joint Membership in and between Trade Associations
    - Diplomacy
    - Mediation
    - Arbitration

Channel Options:

- **Wholesaling**

    Wholesaling includes all activities involved in selling goods and services to those who buy for resale or business use. Wholesaling excludes manufacturers and farmers because they are mainly involved in production, and similarly, it also excludes retailers.

    Functions performed by wholesalers: Wholesalers perform a number of functions for the manufacturers as well as for the consumers. These are -
    - Selling and promotion
    - Buying and assortment building
    - Bulk breaking
    - Warehousing
    - Transportation
    - Financing
    - Risk-bearing
    - Market information
    - Management services and counselling

- **Retailing:** A Retailer is any person, agency, a company or an organisation that is instrumental in reaching the goods, merchandise and services to the final consumer.
- **Franchising:** A franchise is a contractual agreement between the franchiser and the franchisee, which allows the franchisee to conduct business under an established name, as per a particular business format, in return for which he receives compensation.
- **Direct marketing:** The **Direct Marketing Association** defines Direct Marketing as follows:
- **Definition**: Direct Marketing is an Interactive Marketing System that uses one or more advertising media to affect a measurable response and/or transaction at any location.
- **E-commerce** involves buying and selling processes that are supported by electronic means, primarily the internet.
- **E-Markets** are virtual market spaces rather than physical market spaces. Organisations use e-markets to offer their products and services online to customers.
- **E-Purchasing** or buying comprises organisations purchasing goods, services as well as information from online suppliers.

Questions for Discussion

(A) Long Answer Questions:

1. Discuss with suitable examples the need for distribution channels and functions performed by the marketing channels.
2. Design a marketing channel for an organisation that is entering into the manufacturing of consumer white goods like refrigerators, washing machines, microwave ovens, etc. Justify your design.
3. Explain in detail the steps involved in the process of designing the marketing channel.
4. Discuss the dilemma faced by the management in taking channel decisions with reference to the selection, motivation and evaluation of channel members, and modifying channel arrangements.
5. Newer channels have been emerging, considering the changing market scenario. Compare and contrast the vertical marketing system vis-à-vis the horizontal marketing system, and multi-channel marketing system.
6. List down the causes for channel conflict, and as a manager of the physical distribution process, what would be your solution to resolve such conflicts?
7. How does the length of the channel affect the price of the product being moved through the channel? What are the factors involved in deciding the length of the channel?
8. With the help of suitable examples discuss the classification of retailers.
9. Discuss the various types of wholesalers and the functions performed by them.
10. With the help of suitable examples, discuss the various types of franchising.

(B) Short Notes – Write Short Notes on:
1. Nature and importance of marketing channels
2. Channel design for industrial products and consumer goods
3. Channel Conflict
4. Vertical Marketing Systems
5. Multichannel Distribution System
6. Importance of Marketing Logistics
7. Warehousing
8. Inventory Management
9. Transportation
10. Use of technology in Marketing Logistics
11. Direct Marketing
12. E-commerce

(C) Multiple Choice Questions:
1. Marketing channels are:
   (a) Meant only for promotion
   (b) Meant as a vital link between the organisation and its consumers
   (c) Meant for direct marketing
   (d) Meant for supplying only to end users
2. Marketing channels are used because:
   (a) Many smaller organisations find it difficult to perform the functions of intermediaries
   (b) Distribution is a very easy function
   (c) Organisations want to spend money on Marketing channels
   (d) None of the above
3. One of the functions of the distribution channels is:
   (a) Pricing (b) Product design
   (c) Product Modification (d) Product Promotion
4. A zero level channel has:
   (a) One intermediary (b) Two intermediaries
   (c) Three intermediaries (d) None of the above
5. A three level channel has:
   (a) One intermediary (b) Two intermediaries
   (c) Three intermediaries (d) None of the above
6. Distribution channels for consumer goods can have:
   (a) One Level (b) Two Levels
   (c) More than three levels (d) All of the above
7. Distribution channels for services are generally:
   (a) One Level (b) Multi Level
   (c) More than three level (d) None of the above

8. Length of the channel depends upon:
   (a) Reputation of channel members
   (b) Type of the product being moved through the channel
   (c) Influence of the channel members
   (d) Conflict between channel members
9. One of the major steps in designing the marketing channels is:
   (a) Analysing the financial position of the channel member
   (b) Analysing the relationships of the channel members
   (c) Analysing the customers' desired service output levels
   (d) Analysing the conflicts the channel member has had in the past
10. One of the categories of service outputs given by marketing channels includes:
    (a) Price
    (b) Physical evidence
    (c) Promotion
    (d) Spatial Convenience
11. One of the three elements that must be taken into consideration by an organisation while identifying major channel alternatives is:
    (a) Types of available Business Intermediaries
    (b) Types of products
    (c) Convenience
    (d) All of the above
12. Limiting the number of intermediaries handling the organisation's goods and services to just one is:
    (a) Selective Distribution
    (b) Exclusive Distribution
    (c) Intensive Distribution
    (d) None of the above
13. When the manufacturing organisation places its goods in as many outlets as possible, it is:
    (a) Selective Distribution
    (b) Exclusive Distribution
    (c) Intensive Distribution
    (d) None of the above
14. One of the major elements of trade-relations mix is:
    (a) Distributor's Alternatives
    (b) Distributor's Conflict
    (c) Distributor's Behaviour
    (d) Distributor's Territorial Rights
15. Economic Criterion, Control Criterion and Adaptive Criterion are used for:
    (a) Analysing Customer Requirements
    (b) Evaluating Product Requirements
    (c) Evaluating available channel alternatives
    (d) Analysing channel relationships
16. Channel management decisions include:
    (a) Finding channel alternatives
    (b) Modifying channel arrangement
    (c) Evaluating Product Requirements
    (d) Analysing Customer Requirements

17. Three types of VMS are:
    (a) Corporate, Behavioural and Organisational
    (b) Corporate, Contractual and Organisational
    (c) Organisational, Behavioural and Contractual
    (d) Corporate, Contractual and Administered
18. Horizontal Marketing System is also called as:
    (a) Biological Marketing
    (b) Symbiotic Marketing
    (c) Organic Marketing
    (d) None of the above
19. Multi-Channel Marketing system is said to be used when an organisation uses
    (a) One single marketing channel
    (b) Two or more levels of marketing channels
    (c) Two or more marketing channels
    (d) All of the above
20. One of the reasons for channel conflict are:
    (a) Good relationships between channel members
    (b) Common goals
    (c) Unclear role and rights
    (d) Common perception
21. Methods to manage channel conflict includes:
    (a) Goal incompatibility
    (b) Unclear Role and Rights
    (c) Mediation
    (d) Dependence on each other
22. Which of the following are types of wholesalers?
    (a) Merchant Wholesalers
    (b) Brokers and Agents
    (c) Mail order Wholesalers
    (d) All of the above
23. Retailing includes sale of goods to:
    (a) Resellers
    (b) Wholesalers
    (c) End User or final consumer
    (d) Middlemen
24. Retailers are classified as:
    (a) Global and international
    (b) Middlemen and intermediaries
    (c) Store based and non-store based
    (d) Wholesalers and franchisees
25. Non-store based retailing includes:
    (a) Hypermarket
    (b) Convenience Store
    (c) Direct response marketing
    (d) Airport Retailing
26. Types of franchising includes:
    (a) Product or trademark franchising
    (b) Convenience Franchising
    (c) Direct Response Franchising
    (d) Wholesale franchising

Answers

1. (b)	2. (a)	3. (d)	4. (d)	5. (c)	6. (d)	7. (a)	8. (b)	9. (c)	10. (d)
11. (a)	12. (b)	13. (c)	14. (d)	15. (c)	16. (b)	17. (d)	18. (b)	19. (c)	20. (c)
21. (c)	22. (d)	23. (c)	24. (c)	25. (c)	26. (a)				

(D) Project Questions:

Q.1 A popular pizza chain is considering introducing breakfast pizzas, in order to increase its market share and tap newer markets. The pizza would be offered in traditional breakfast varieties like egg pizza, jam pizza, sausage pizza, bacon pizza, etc. Find out alternative channels to the existing ones (The existing channels are the pizza store and home delivery).

Q.2 Conduct a class activity on finding retail outlets in your vicinity as per the various classifications discussed in class for store-based format. Each student will have to visit at least 5 outlets. The findings have to be recorded in the following table:

Name of the Outlet	Ownership Type	Merchandise Offered

Q.3 Describe two types of marketing channels that you will use for distribution of a new type of mobile phone that has to be launched in the market.

Q.4 List down at least five products, that according to you will require multi-channel distribution. Justify your answers.

Q.5 As a Manufacturer of Pumps you are required to supply pumps regularly in some remote areas of the country. What kind of channel design will you employ and why?

Case Studies

The McDonalds – The Story of Fast Food Retailing in India

Background Note

Looking around for a quick and hassle free meal, you are most likely to spot the Yellow "M", synonymous with McDonalds. McDonalds Corporation is a leading fast food restaurant, in the quick service restaurant segment with a presence in almost every country in the world.

McDonalds Corporation was started in 1955 by Ray Kroc when he opened the first restaurant in Des Plaines, Illinois. He very soon replicated his success across the United States and beyond. In the year 1957, the company adopted the Quality, Service, Cleanliness and Value as its motto

Case

The Indian Fast Food Market: A nation as diverse as India is a challenging market in terms of food habits of the consumers. This is mainly because each region has its own traditional food habits as well as food specialties.

As per the Images India Retail report 2005, the Indian fast food market which is a part of the food service retail also known as the catering services market, is estimated to be worth ₹ 35,000 Crores, of which only 7% is accounted for under the organised retail market. Also according to an AC Nielsen survey, India is one of the top 10 countries amongst the 28 countries surveyed in terms of fast food consumption.

The report also states that fast food consumption is now more a part of everyday life than once-in-a-while impulse purchase.

The results of these surveys are a reflection of the changing lifestyles and food consumption habits.

McDonald's India Operations

In India McDonald's is a joint venture between McDonald's Corporation USA and two Indian partners' namely Hard Castle Restaurants and Connaught Plaza Restaurants Pvt. Ltd. The focus is on serving a quality meal in a friendly environment, in a clean place and at an affordable price.

As mentioned earlier, serving the Indian palate was a tough task. Six years prior to opening the first restaurant in India, Mc Donald's and its associates worked with the local Indian companies to develop products that met the stringent quality requirements of McDonald's.

Further McDonald's keeping in mind the Indian traditions and cultural values chose to offer a menu that had no beef or pork or any of their flavourings. Also all the vegetarian offerings of McDonald's in India included 100% vegetarian ingredients, including mayonnaise which was egg-less.

Some of the new product innovation that McDonald's made to suit the Indian palate are McVeggie, McAlooTikki, Veg Pizza McPuff, Chicken McGrill, Chatpatey Potato wedges, Chicken Maharaja Mac, Paneer Salsa Wrap, Shahi Paneer McCurry to name a few.

The value Proposition

Mc Donald's products aim at providing value to the customer. The value is in terms of the total package offered. That is fast food, in a clean and friendly environment and at extremely affordable prices. After conducting price sensitivity studies McDonald's has launched a variety of options grouped under the umbrella of a "Value Meal". The value meal includes a la carte items like the burgers, wraps and nuggets along with small drink and fries to make up a small value meal.

The "Happy Price Menu" aims to make the affordability of the meals visible to the target audience.

Location

Location is of prime importance to any retail outlet. McDonald's is known for being located at a place that is convenient for people.

Generally before finalising any location, the company studies certain parameters such as residences, shops, offices, entertainment, education institutes and transit points in that area.

In terms of space the requirement is around 3000 sq.feet on the ground floor, with a height of 11 feet and a frontage of 35 to 40 feet at a minimum. Once the location is finalised, the premises are either purchased or taken on a long term lease. The joint venture company makes majority of the investments. A McDonald's in-house team aided by architects, interior designers then works to create the outlet.

People and Training

Ray Kroc believed that if you take care of people (customers), the business will take care of itself. Service is the key element of the McDonald's operations. Each and every employee at McDonald's strives to perform to 100% level to satisfy customers and keep them happy.

Training at McDonald's is a combination of on-the-floor and classroom training, provided by the learning and development department with exposure to all other departments.

Those recruits displaying potential are given an opportunity for overseas training. Restaurant managers are sent to the Restaurant Leadership Program conducted at the prestigious Hamburger University. Similarly employees from other departments are also sent abroad for relevant trainings.

Supply Chain Challenges

The kind of products that McDonald's provide called for a premium quality and no less. This requires expensive, meticulous and stringent quality control. This was an uphill task in a country where a large quantity of food produced was wasted every year due to lack of proper infrastructure, transportation and storage facilities.

Under these conditions McDonald's Indian created cold chains for servicing its restaurants. The cold chain involved procurement, warehousing, transportation and retailing of all perishable food items under controlled temperature conditions. The process of building the cold chain took more than six years and an investment exceeding ₹ 450 crores.

McDonald's identified Indian businesses that shared its dedication and level of commitment to customers. These Indian Businesses were introduced to state-of-the art technology ad world class manufacturing standards making them competent.

Identifying and Developing Key Suppliers

For sourcing the right kind of potatoes for its French fries, McDonald's along with its supplier McCain Foods Pvt. ltd. began to work closely with farmers in Gujarat and Maharashtra to develop process grade potatoes.

Trikaya agriculture, supplier of lettuce was also provided with exposure to better agricultural management practices and agricultural technology and also know how on producing the crop round the year.

Vista Foods Pvt. Ltd received technical and financial support from McDonald's India and OSI industries USA, to set up world class infrastructure for manufacturing of frozen foods.

The Road Ahead

In the near future the company plans to focus on core markets, establish a strong base in these markets and then move ahead with terms to expansion.

Questions
1. What according to you are the challenges that McDonald's faced when it launched operations in India?
2. Internationally, McDonald's works on the franchising model. What are the issues that McDonald's will have to keep in mind if it has to develop a similar model in India?

Questions from Previous Pune University Examinations

1. Write a critical note on the Emerging Role of a Conventional Retailer in the context of the rise of Super-markets and Super Mall. **[M.B.A. April 2007]**
2. Describe Various Factors influencing Design of Distribution Channels.
[M.B.A. April 2009]
3. Write Short Notes :
   (a) Wholesaling. **[M.B.A. April 2010]**
   (b) Franchising. **[M.B.A. April 2009, 2011]**
   (c) Wholesalers. **[M.B.A. Dec. 2010]**
   (d) Direct Marketing. **[M.B.A. Dec. 2010]**

■■■

Chapter 4...

Promotion

Contents ...

4.1 Introduction
    4.1.1 Definitions
    4.1.2 Role of Marketing Communication
    4.1.3 Objectives of Marketing Communication/Promotion
4.2 Communication Mix Elements
    4.2.1 Advertising
        4.2.1.1 Main Objectives of Advertising
        4.2.1.2 Scope of Advertising
        4.2.1.3 Role of Advertising
        4.2.1.4 Types of Advertising
        4.2.1.5 Developing and Managing the Advertising Programme
        4.2.1.6 Advantages and Disadvantages of Advertising
    4.2.2 Media
        4.2.2.1 Categories of Media used in Advertising
    4.2.3 Sales Promotion
        4.2.3.1 Major Decisions in Sales Promotion
        4.2.3.2 Objectives of Sales Promotion
        4.2.3.3 Selecting the Sales Promotion Tools
        4.2.3.4 Types of Sales Promotional Tools used for Consumers
        4.2.3.5 Types of Sales Promotion Tools for Traders
    4.2.4 Personal Selling
        4.2.4.1 Objectives of Personal Selling
        4.2.4.2 Types of Personal Selling
        4.2.4.3 Advantages of Personal Selling
        4.2.4.4 Disadvantages of Personal Selling
    4.2.5 Publicity and Public Relations
        4.2.5.1 Objectives of Publicity and Public Relations
        4.2.5.2 Advantages of Publicity and Public Relations
        4.2.5.3 Disadvantages of Publicity and Public Relations
    4.2.6 Direct Marketing
        4.2.6.1 Forms of Direct Marketing
        4.2.6.2 Advantages and Disadvantages of Direct Marketing

4.2.7 The concept of Integrated Marketing Communication
    4.2.7.1 The Changing Communication Environment
    4.2.7.2 The Need for Integrated Marketing Communication
    4.2.7.3 Definition of Integrated Marketing Communication (IMC)
    4.2.7.4 The Role of Integrated Marketing Communication
4.3 Developing Effective Communication
4.4 Deciding the Marketing Communication Mix
    4.4.1 Factors in Setting the Marketing Communication or Promotion Mix
    4.4.2 Measuring Communication Results
- Points to Remember
- Questions for Discussion
- Project Questions
- Case Study
- Questions from Previous Pune University Examinations

Learning Objectives ...

- To understand the concept of promotion and the role of promotion in the marketing mix
- To understand the promotional mix
- To study in detail the various elements of the promotion mix
- To study the objectives of advertising, and the advantages and disadvantages of advertising as compared to the other elements
- To understand the objectives of sales promotion, types of sales promotion, and the advantages and disadvantages of sales promotion as compared to the other elements
- To study the objectives of personal selling, and the advantages and disadvantages of personal selling as compared to the other elements
- To understand the objectives of public relations, and the advantages and disadvantages of public relations as compared to the other elements
- To understand the impact of technology and internet on promotion
- To study the factors in setting the marketing communication mix and methods for measuring the communication results

4.1 Introduction

Marketing today is more than just having a good product, pricing it attractively, and making it available to consumers through a distribution channel. It is essential that organisations communicate with their present as well as potential customers, retailers, suppliers, and all other stakeholders. For most organisations, the question is what to communicate, with whom to communicate, and how often to communicate. The answer to these questions lies in the communication mix, also known as the promotion mix.

4.1.1 Definitions

An organisation's total marketing communication mix – also called as the promotion mix - comprises of the specific blend of advertising, sales promotion, public relations, personal selling and direct marketing tools that the organisation uses to pursue its marketing objectives.

According to **Philip Kotler**, *"Promotion compasses all the tools in the marketing mix whose major role is persuasive communications."*

Stanston's defines Promotion as *"Promotion includes, advertising, personal selling, sales promotion and other selling tools".*

4.1.2 Role of Marketing Communication

Communicating with your customers enables you to deliver your message to them so that they will react to it. Communication reaches the consumer. Think of it this way: communication is the message that is delivered to the client; marketing is the means of getting it there. Therefore communication is not just part of the marketing mix but also should be integrated into your customer service process.

Marketing Communications also known as promotion is one of the elements of the marketing mix or the 4 P's.

It is defined as all the personal and impersonal efforts by a seller, or the seller's representative, to inform, persuade or remind the target audience about the product or the firm.

Promotion helps marketers to communicate information to potential customers. This information could be about the Product existence (awareness), value and benefits offered by the product (utility). A well designed promotion mix is extremely crucial for brand building and positioning. In fact communication or promotional mix is at the centre stage in brand positioning and brand building activities. Promotional mix help marketers to attract, persuade, urge and remind customers of the companies brand. Effective promotion prove helpful in product differentiation and also help to counter competition.

Marketing communication or Promotion serves various purposes. It helps the marketer to communicate with the customer for the following purposes:

- To provide information to customers;
- To differentiate the product from that of the competitors' products;
- To generate more demand for the company's products;
- To make a product more attractive to an organisation's prospective buyers;
- To position a product, that is, to create a positive image of the product/firm.

4.1.3 Objectives of Marketing Communication/Promotion

Marketing Communication has several objectives. These objectives are:

- **Lead to behaviour modification**: Promotion aims to modify the behaviour of the consumer. For e.g. if the consumer regularly buys a particular brand of detergent say Surf, then to try and induce him to buy another brand such as Ariel. By using promotion the marketer hopes to create a favourable image in the consumer's mind that will motivate him to purchase the product.
- **Objective to inform**: In the early stages of the product, it is necessary to create awareness about the product in the target market. For this informing the target market about the product, its usage and benefits is required. Promotion is used for this purpose
- **Objective to persuade**: In the growth stage of a product, the marketer seeks to persuade consumers to buy the product repeatedly and in larger quantities. Here promotion is used to persuade the consumers.
- **Objective to remind**: The marketer has this objective in mind when the product reaches the maturity stage of the product life cycle. Here the marketer tries to ensure that consumers remembers the product and are not carried away by competing products in the market.

4.2 Communication Mix Elements

The marketing communication mix, also known as the promotion mix, consists of five major modes of communication/promotion. These are also known as the elements of the promotion mix:

(a) Advertising
(b) Sales Promotion
(c) Public Relations
(d) Personal Selling
(e) Direct Marketing

We will take a detailed look at all these in the chapter.

4.2.1 Advertising

Advertising is nothing but a paid form of non-personal presentation or promotion of ideas, goods or services by an identified sponsor with a view to disseminate information concerning an idea, product or service. The message which is presented or disseminated is called advertisement. In the present day marketing activities hardly there is any business in the modern world which does not advertise. However, the form of advertisement differs from business to business.

Advertisement has been defined differently by different persons. A few definitions are being reproduced below:
- According to **Wood**, "*Advertising is causing to know to remember, to do.*"
- According to **Wheeler**, "*Advertising is any form of paid non-personal presentation of ideas, goods or services for the purpose of inducting people to buy.*"
- According to **Richard Buskirk**, "*Advertising is a paid form of non-personal presentation of ideas, goods or services by an identified sponsor.*"
- According to **William J. Stanton**, "*Advertising consists of all the activities involves in presenting to a group, a non-personal, oral or visual, openly sponsored message regarding disseminated through one or more media and is paid for by an identified sponsor.*"
- According to **Philip Kotler**, "*Advertising is any paid form of nonpersonal presentation and promotion of ideas, goods, or services by an identified sponsor.*"

In simple words, "*Advertising is a means of informing and communicating essential information.*"

The above definitions clearly reveal the nature of advertisement. This is a powerful element of the promotion mix. Essentially advertising means spreading of information about the characteristics of the product to the prospective customers with a view to sell the product or increase the sale volume.

The main features of advertise are as under:
- It is directed towards increasing the sales of business.
- Advertising is a paid form of publicity.
- It is non-personal. They are directed at a mass audience and not at the individual as is in the case of personal selling.
- Advertisements are identifiable with their sponsor of originator which is not always the case with publicity or propaganda.

The purpose of advertising is nothing but to sell something -a product, a service or an idea. The real objective of advertising is effective communication between producers and consumers.

4.2.1.1 Main Objectives of Advertising

- **Preparing Ground for New Product:** New product needs introduction because potential customers have never used such product earlier and the advertisement prepare a ground for that new product.
- **Creation of Demand:** The main objective of the advertisement is to create a favourable climate for maintaining of improving sales. Customers are to be reminded about the product and the brand. It may induce new customers to buy the product by informing them its qualities since it is possible that some of the customers may change their brands.

- **Facing the Competition:** Another important objective of the advertisement is to face the competition. Under competitive conditions, advertisement helps to build up brand image and brand loyalty and when customers have developed brand loyalty, becomes difficult for the middlemen to change it.
- **Creating or Enhancing Goodwill:** Large scale advertising is often undertaken with the objective of creating or enhancing the goodwill of the advertising company. This, in turn, increases the market receptiveness of the company's product and helps the salesmen to win customers easily.
- **Informing the Changes to the Customers:** Whenever changes are made in the prices, channels of distribution or in the product by way of any improvement in quality, size, weight, brand, packing, etc., they must be informed to the public by the producer through advertisement.
- **Neutralising Competitor's Advertising:** Advertising is unavoidable to complete with or neutralise competitor's advertising. When competitors are adopting intensive advertising as their promotional strategy, it is reasonable to follow similar practices to neutralise their effects. In such cases, it is essential for the manufacturer to create a different image of his product.
- **Barring New Entrants:** From the advertiser's point of view, a strongly built image through long advertising helps to keep new entrants away. The advertisement builds up a certain monopoly and for the product in which new entrants find it difficult to enter.

In short, advertising aims at benefiting the producer, educating the consumer and supplementing the salesmen. Above all it is a link between the producer and the consumer.

4.2.1.2 Scope of Advertising

Advertising has a wide scope in marketing. Here we will discuss the scope of advertising based on the activities included under it and its objectives and functions.

- **Messages:** Advertising carries the message of the product. The message can be visual, oral and it is designed to influence the prospective consumer based on the objectives of the organisation.
- **Media:** Advertising involves the use of a medium to communicate the message to the target audience. Depending upon the product and the objective the media type has to be decided.
- **Merchandise:** Advertising is used to demonstrate the attributes or features of the product or service.
- **Advertising Functions:** Advertising helps to create demand, persuade consumers to buy the product, reminds consumers about the brand and helps to create a positive image in the minds of the consumer.

4.2.1.3 Role of Advertising

Advertising is widely used and influences consumers by informing and persuading them. The following are the basic roles that advertising plays:

- **Communication with Consumers:** Providing information about a wide variety of products, advertising is a strong medium to reach out to consumers. It aims at reminding existing consumers about the products and also at persuading prospective consumers to buy the product.
- **Contribution to economic growth:** Advertising contributes to the economic growth by helping to develop new market segments, thereby expanding to new markets.
- **Catalyst for change:** Advertising plays a major role in changing the image of an organisation in the minds of the consumers. Several recent examples have shown how advertising has been effectively used to clean tarnished images of organisations.

4.2.1.4 Types of Advertising

Advertising is mainly classified into two categories - Promotional Advertising and Institutional Advertising.

1. **Promotional Advertising**

   Promotional advertising is advertising that is designed to increase sales by:
   - creating an interest in products;
   - introducing new products and businesses;
   - explaining a product;
   - supporting personal selling efforts;
   - creating new markets;

2. **Institutional Advertising**

   Institutional advertising attempts to create a favourable impression (image) and goodwill for a business or an organisation.

   The purpose is to develop a positive image by presenting information about a company's role in the community, important public issues, and topics of general interest.

4.2.1.5 Developing and Managing the Advertising Programme

Developing and managing the advertising programme is a five-step process comprising of the 5 Ms. These 5 Ms are:

1. **Mission:** What are the objectives of advertising?
2. **Money:** How much can be spent on advertising?
3. **Message:** What message should be sent?
4. **Media:** What media should be used?
5. **Measurement:** How should the advertising be done and evaluated?

Setting the advertising objectives: This is the first step in developing the advertising programme. Colley has outlined a method for turning advertising objectives into measurable goals. This method is known as DAGMAR, that is, Defining Advertising Goals for Measured Advertising Results.

1. **Objectives of Advertising**

   Advertising is not done with the same objectives. There are various objectives for which advertising is done. Let us take a look at these objectives:
   - **Short term sales increase:** Advertising helps to increase the sales by making customers aware about the product and any offer that the manufacturer might want to make to the customer to boost the sales over a short period of time.
   - **Greater customer traffic:** Advertising also helps to increase the customer traffic to a store, or for a particular product, by attracting and persuading the customers to consider the said product/store in their choice set.
   - **Creating awareness about new products:** Advertising is a very effective medium to create awareness about new products. Creative teasers and advertisements go a long way in grabbing the attention of customers and increasing their curiosity towards the product being advertised.
   - **Developing and/or reinforcing the organisation's image:** Maintaining a positive image in the minds of the consumer is something that an organisation cannot afford to overlook. Customers are becoming increasingly conscious of organisations behaving ethically. In order to ensure customers about this and to instil a positive image of the organisation, advertising campaigns are used. Even when the image of the organisation has taken a beating due to some adverse events, advertising can be used very effectively to resurrect that image.

   For example, Cadbury India used advertising very effectively to reinstate the faith of the customers after worms were found in some of the company's chocolates.
   - **Providing information to customers:** Informing customers about goods and services and/or company attributes is another objective that can be fulfilled through advertising.
   - **Easing the job for sales personnel:** Since advertising is used to inform the customer and make him aware about the features of the product, this usually eases the job of the sales person.
   - **Developing demand for existing as well as new brands:** Organisations are known to create loyal customers for their existing as well as new brands.

2. **Deciding on the Advertising Budget**

   An organisation must take into consideration five factors while deciding the advertising budget. These are:
   - **Stage in the product life cycle:** New products would typically receive larger advertising budgets as compared to established products.

- **Market share and consumer base:** Product brands with a high market share will require lesser advertising expenditure as a percentage of sales to maintain their share. To increase or expand the market size, larger marketing expenditures will be required.
- **Competition and clutter:** In markets with a large number of competitors, a product needs to advertise more heavily to be heard in the noise of the competitors.
- **Advertising frequency:** The frequency of advertising repetitions should be made in order to clearly send across the message of the advertisement to its target customers.
- **Product substitutability:** Brands that have a higher number of substitutes in the market (typically commodity class) require higher advertising expenditures.

3. **Choosing the Advertising Message**

    Developing a creative advertising strategy is a four-step process. It includes:

    - **Message generation:** Basically, the product's message, that is, the benefit that it offers, is decided at the product development stage itself. However, within the given concept, a marketer can use a number of relevant messages. Over a period of time, the marketer might want to change the message, keeping the product same, especially if the consumers are seeking new or different benefits from the product.
    - Some of the common methods used by creative people to generate advertising appeals are:
    - **Inductive framework:** Here, the creative team develops a framework for the message by talking to consumers, dealers, experts, and competitors. Consumers generally are an important source of good ideas.
    - **Deductive framework:** Maloney proposed this framework in which four types of rewards that buyers expect from the product are combined with three types of experiences that the product is expected to generate, making it a total of twelve types of advertising messages. The four types of rewards that buyers expect from the product are rational, sensory, social, or ego satisfaction. The three types of experiences are result-of-use experience, product-in-use experience and incidental-to-use experience.

    More the number of creatives prepared, higher is the probability of finding an excellent message.

    - **Message evaluation and selection:** Having created several messages, the task now is to select a good and relevant message. A good advertisement will focus on one core selling proposition. Messages are rated on parameters like desirability, exclusiveness, and believability.

- **Message execution:** The impact created by the message depends not only upon what is said but also on how it is said. Advertisements use either rational positioning or emotional positioning to send across the messages. The message must also have a proper style, tone, image and format.
- **Social responsibility review:** Advertisers must ensure that their creative advertising does not go beyond the framework of social and legal norms.

4. **Deciding on the Media**

   The steps involved in deciding on the media include -
   - **Deciding the reach, frequency and impact of the media:** Media selection involves finding the most cost effective media to deliver the desired number of exposures to the target audience.
     - **Reach (R)** is the number of persons or households exposed to a particular media schedule at least once during the specified time period.
     - **Frequency (F):** The number of times within a specified time period that an average person or household is exposed to the message.
     - **Impact (I):** The qualitative value of exposure through a given medium.
   - Choosing among major media types – While choosing among the media types, marketers will consider the following variables:

   Target audience media habits, product, message, and cost.
   - **Selecting specific media vehicles:** The media planner will have to work on estimates of audience size, composition, and media cost.
   - **Deciding on media timing:** Here, the marketer has to deal with issues of macro and micro scheduling. Macro scheduling calls for deciding how to schedule the advertising in relation to seasonal and business cycle trends whereas micro scheduling deals with allocation of advertising expenditure within a short period of time to gain maximum impact.
   - **Deciding on geographical media allocation:** An organisation has to decide how to allocate its advertising budget over space as well as over time.

5. **Evaluating advertising effectiveness**

   Most organisations try to measure the effectiveness of the advertisement by measuring its effect on awareness, knowledge, or preference.

4.2.1.6 Advantages and Disadvantages of Advertising

Let us now see the advantages and disadvantages of advertising:

Advantages of Advertising

Some of the advantages of advertising are listed below:
- **A large audience is attracted:** Being a mass medium, advertising attracts a large audience. Each advertisement covers a large section of the target audience.
- **The cost per viewer, listener or reader is low:** Since the number of viewers, listeners or readers is very high, the cost per viewer, listener or reader turns out to be very low.

- A large number of alternative media is available, and therefore, an advertiser has control over the message content, graphics, timing and size.
- Wherever print media is used, the message can be studied and restricted.
- Editorial content (a TV show, a news story) often surrounds an advertisement. This may increase its credibility and the probability that it will be read.
- Reduced service operations are possible since a customer can become aware of the organisation and its offering before shopping.

Disadvantages of Advertising

Since the message is standardised and remitted through a mass medium, the advertiser cannot focus on the needs of individual customers.

- Some advertising requires large investments. This reduces the access of small firms to certain media.
- Media may reach a larger geographic area leading to inefficient use of funds for the organisation.
- Some media require a long lead-time for placing advertisements. This reduces an organisation's ability to advertise fad items or to react to some current event themes.
- Some media have a high throwaway rate. For instance, circulars and mail advertisements may be discarded without being read.
- Advertisements are often very brief and don't offer details.

Below are the print advertisements of some famous brands:

COCA COLA – Being an environmentally conscious marketer

Fig. 4.1: Coca-Cola: Recycle

Use your imagination and recycle. Our future depends on it.
Source: www.dirjournal.com/.../the-visual-tour-into-**Coca-Cola-print-advertising**

Fig. 4.2: Samsung is Mocking iPhone 4 Reception Issues...
Advertiser: Samsung Galaxy
Source:http://mastercom.over-blog.com/article-hello-samsung-galaxy-print-ad-mocking-iphone-4-reception-54363638.html

4.2.2 Media

What is Media?

Media are the agencies, means or instruments used to convey messages.

Advertising is done through a mass medium. Before we proceed further, it is necessary to take a look at the various types of media used for advertising.

4.2.2.1 Categories of Media used in Advertising

- Print media
- Broadcast media
- Speciality media

Print Media: Print media can include any of the following:

(a) Newspapers:

The advantages of using newspaper as a medium for advertising are:
- Large readership;
- Known circulation (easy to target);
- Low cost;
- Timely and flexible.

The disadvantages are:
- Wasted circulation;
- Disposable (short lifespan);
- Poor print quality.

(b) Direct Mail:

The advantages of direct mail are:
- The advertiser can be highly selective;
- Flexible and secretive;
- Wide choice of formats;
- Can use coupons or other incentives;
- Can directly make the sale.

The disadvantages of direct mail are:
- Low level of response;
- High costs;
- Poor image (junk mail) and often not read.

(c) Magazines:

Magazines can be classified as Local, Regional, National weeklies, Monthlies and Quarterlies. Another classification is based on where they are categorised - for example, consumer magazines (Reader's Digest, Femina, etc.) or business magazines (Fortune, Business World, etc.)

Advantages of using magazines for advertising are:
- Easy to reach the target audience;
- Read slowly and thoroughly;
- Good print quality.
- Longer life span because they are kept for an extended period of time.

The disadvantages are:
- Less mass appeal within a geographic area;
- More expensive than newspapers;
- Not timely or flexible (long lead times).

(d) Outdoor Advertising:

It comprises of three types of outdoor signs:
- Posters - Pre-printed sheets put up like wallpaper on outdoor billboards;
- Painted bulletins - Painted billboards that are changed every 6 months to a year;
- Spectaculars - Outdoor signs using lights and moving parts, and are situated in high traffic areas or cities.

Advantages are:
- Highly visible;
- Relatively inexpensive;
- Permits easy repetition of message;
- Can be geographically tailored for the target market.

Disadvantages are:
- Short message due to limited viewing time;
- Unknown audience;
- Government regulations.

(e) Directory Advertising:

This is not a very popular medium for advertising.

The main advantage is:
- Alphabetical listing of businesses;
- Relatively inexpensive;
- Found in 98% of households - all demographics;
- Kept for at least a year - not thrown away.

Disadvantages are:
- Very inflexible due to being printed yearly;
- Wasted advertising (to non-target market).

(f) Transit Advertising:

It involves using public facilities such as subways, buses, advertising in railway stations, etc.

Advantages are:
- Reaches a wide and captive audience;
- Economical;
- Defined market (usually urban).

Disadvantages are:
- Unavailable in smaller towns;
- Subject to defacement;
- Restricted to certain travel destinations.

(g) Broadcast Media:

It comprises of radio and television.

Advantages of radio advertising are:
- Can select the target audience;
- Flexible - can change quickly and easily;
- Mobile (can be taken anywhere - shopping, jogging, hiking or driving).

Disadvantages of radio advertising are:
- Short life span;
- Sometimes there are many stations and the advertiser will need to choose among them. If the advertiser decides to use all of them, it may be more expensive.

Advantages of television advertising are:
- All elements for creative message;
- Believability;
- More personal and effective;
- Can reach the masses or target specific interests;
- Adaptable to special needs.

Disadvantages of television advertising are:
- Expensive - the highest production costs - too high for small businesses;
- Audience size is not assured;
- Nuisance - channel surfing - leave during commercials.

(h) Speciality Media:

It comprises of inexpensive, useful items with an advertiser's name printed on them – these are usually given away for free.

4.2.3 Sales Promotion

Definition - *It is a sponsor-funded demand stimulating activity, designed to supplement advertising and facilitate personal selling.*

It frequently consists of a temporary incentive to encourage a sale or a purchase. Sales promotion may be directed at the consumer or the retailer/trader.

Sales promotion uses many tools like coupons, premiums, etc. Although these tools are diverse in nature, they offer three basic benefits to the marketer.

1. **Communications:** They gain attention and usually provide information that may lead the consumer to the product.
2. **Incentive:** They incorporate some concession, inducement, or contribution that gives value to the customer.
3. **Invitation:** The tools of sales promotion include a distinct invitation to engage in the transaction at that time.

4.2.3.1 Major Decisions in Sales Promotion

Some of the major decisions in sales promotion include:
- Establishing the sales promotion objectives;
- Selecting the tools;
- Developing the programme;
- Pre-testing the programme;
- Implementing and controlling the programme;
- Evaluating the results.

4.2.3.2 Objectives of Sales Promotion

Just like in advertising, there are various objectives for doing sales promotion. Let us look at some of these major objectives:

- **Increase in short term sales volume:** Sales promotion generally involves offering an incentive to the prospective customer for a short period of time in order to motivate him to buy. This results in a short term increase in the sales volume.
- **Maintaining customer loyalty:** In an era of ever-increasing competition, sales promotion gives loyal customers a reason to buy the product/brand and not switch from it. Thus, it helps to maintain customer loyalty.
- **Emphasising novelty:** Sales promotion, while incentivising the customer, is often used to urge customers to buy and try out newer products. Thus, it is often used with the objective of emphasising the novel aspect of the product.
- **Complementing other promotional tools:** Sales promotion blends well with the other elements of the marketing mix, and hence can be used as a complementing promotional tool for personal selling and direct marketing as well.

4.2.3.3 Selecting the Sales Promotion Tools

Many sales promotion tools are available. The marketer must take into account the type of the market, sales promotion objectives, competitive conditions, and the cost-effectiveness of the tool while selecting the tool.

Two categories of sales promotions tools

There are two categories of sales promotions:

(i) **Consumer promotions:** These are the promotions that are targeted at the consumers where they are offered an incentive to buy a product or a service.

(ii) **Trade promotions:** These are sales promotions targeted at the middlemen or traders. Here, the promotion is based on them buying from the manufacturer and reselling to the final consumer.

4.2.3.4 Types of Sales Promotional Tools used for Consumers

Sales promotional campaigns assume various forms. Some of the common types of sales promotions are:

- **Coupon:** In this type, a coupon is placed in the newspapers or in the packet of the product to be promoted. The customer is required to fill out this coupon and then redeem it at the retail outlet, or in some cases, there is a prize attached to the coupon.
- **Bonus packs:** Here, there is more of the product in the same pack than what the customer would usually find, for the same price, or a marginally higher price.

- **In pack and on pack:** Here, an additional product is given free on purchase of a pack, or as a compliment inside the pack.
- **Speciality container:** Here, the product is supplied in the form of a container that is not regularly or usually used for packaging. The design, shape and material of the container may lure the customers to buy the product.
- **Continuity programme / loyalty cards:** These are cards which are swiped with every purchase. The customer gains points for every purchase, which can be redeemed. There are also some special privileges for card holders.
- **Refund:** In this case, the consumer is induced to try the product by giving a guarantee that if the product does not perform, the money will be refunded.
- **Sweepstakes:** This is like a lottery, where the consumer is either given a ticket with a number on it, or has to fill a form with a number on it. Through a lottery system, a lucky winner is chosen.
- **Contest:** Some form of contest is held and winners are given prices.
- **Sampling:** Free samples of the product are distributed to entice the consumer to try the product.
- **Price off:** Here, a discount is offered on the MRP of the product in order to entice the consumer to buy the product.

4.2.3.5 Types of Sales Promotion Tools for Traders

Sales promotions done for traders comprise of:
- **Volume:** Here, the trader is asked to buy a particular volume of goods, and gets some more of it for free, which he can sell. For example: buy 10 crates of Coke and get one crate free.
- **Prompt payment:** If the trader makes an immediate payment, he gets a discount.
- **Free goods:** Here, the manufacturer provides goods to the retailer as free goods for giving away as promotional items. These are generally new products or slow-moving items.

Pre-testing the sales promotion programme: To ensure the success of the sales promotion programme, it is necessary to pre-test the programme. The pre-testing would help the marketer to decide if the tool used is appropriate, if the size of the incentive is adequate, and if the presentation method is effective.

Implementing and controlling the sales promotion programme: Marketers need to prepare an implementation and control plan for each promotion. A lead time is generally taken into consideration prior to launching the programme. Lead time helps undertake initial planning, design and changes, mailing of the material to be distributed, preparation of the advertising and point-of-sale material, notification to the field sales staff, and establishment of allocations for various distributors, etc. The selling time begins with the promotional launch and ends with the end of the campaign.

Evaluating the sales promotion results: Analysing and evaluating the result of the sales promotion campaign is very important. Generally marketers use one or a combination of the following three methods to evaluate the sales promotion effectiveness:
1. sales data,
2. consumer surveys or
3. experiments.

Advantages of Sales Promotion

Sales promotion has several advantages. Some of them are listed below:

- **Eye-catching appeal:** Sales promotions, being incentive-based, have an eye-catching appeal, and attract the attention of the audience, who would often have not noticed the product in a cluttered environment.
- **Themes and tools can be distinctive:** Sales promotion can be done with specific themes like festive themes, and the tools used can also be distinct to the purpose.
- **It helps draw customer traffic and retain loyalty to the organisation:** Sales promotion, by nature, incentivises customers and as such, provides new customers with a reason to buy the product, and existing customers to continue with their loyalty to the product.
- **Impulse purchases are increased:** Sales promotion may help to increase impulse purchases. Generally, if the promotional offer is tempting, the customer may go ahead and buy the product, even though he has not planned the purchase in the first place.
- **Customers can have fun with contests and demonstrations:** Often sales promotions are conducted through exciting contests and demonstrations. This leads to a lot of fun for the customers.

Disadvantages of Sales Promotion

- **It may be difficult to terminate certain promotions without adverse customer reactions:** Often customers get accustomed to sales promotions activities and start expecting the same during every purchase. In such a situation, it becomes difficult to terminate the promotion.
- **Retailers' image can get hurt if the right kind of promotion is not used:** Sales promotion has to be very carefully planned and meticulously executed. Besides, the promotion tools used must be in line with the organisation's overall objectives and goals. If this does not happen, it can end up hurting the image of the organisation.
- **Most sales promotions have only short-term effects:** Sales promotions are supposed to be run for a short period of time. As a result, the effect is not long lasting.

4.2.4 Personal Selling

It is defined as a direct presentation of a product to the prospective customer by a representative of the organisation selling it.

It takes place face-to-face or over the phone, and it may be directed to a business, person or a final consumer. Basically it emphasises on a personal interaction between the buyer and the seller.

4.2.4.1 Objectives of Personal Selling

All the tools or elements of the promotion mix are designed and used to fulfil certain objectives. Let us take a look at the objectives of personal selling:

- **To create a positive image of the organisation and the product in the minds of prospective customers:** Personal selling is often used to imprint upon the mind of the customer the image of the organisation and its products.
- **To explain the technical aspects of the product that cannot be done through advertising:** Often, it has been observed that for technical products, advertising cannot be used to communicate the technical aspects of the product. In such cases, personal selling is found to be immensely useful. One of the main advantages here is that the person promoting the product can get an immediate feedback from the customer and solve his queries regarding the same.
- **To create confidence in the minds of the customers:** When a product's features are explained, it creates confidence in the minds of the customers about the product.

4.2.4.2 Types of Personal Selling

Personal selling comprises of the following three basic types:
1. Direct Selling
2. Distribution Selling
3. Outlet Selling

1. **Direct selling:** Direct selling, as the name suggests, involves selling of the products/services directly by the manufacturer to the customer without any intermediary. In personal selling, direct selling has the following features:
    - Uses the human capital resource;
    - Offers high earnings to those who do not have businesses;
    - Home based;
    - People get people strategy- In other words people who purchase get other people to buy;
    - Very sound business model.

2. **Distribution selling:** Another form of personal selling is distribution selling. This involves:
   - Sales efforts to cover geographic region;
   - Covers relevant distribution channels.
3. **Outlet selling:** This is also a form of personal selling. It involves:
   - Sales efforts by a salesperson to customers who come to a specific outlet;
   - It is generally seen at all retail outlets.

4.2.4.3 Advantages of Personal Selling

Some of the major advantages of personal selling are:

- **Feedback is immediate:** By nature, personal selling involves an interaction with the seller either face-to-face or over the phone. In either case, the marketer can get an immediate feedback from the buyer with regards to the product or service that he is selling. He does not have to wait to see the effect the consumer feedback has on the sales.
- **Since there is a direct contact with the consumer, the seller is able to overcome objections immediately:** In case of all other tools of promotion, there is no direct contact between the marketer and the buyer. As such, even if the buyer has any objections, he may not be able to voice them, and instead, may choose to buy the other products. However, in case of personal selling, the buyer can voice his objections and the same can be immediately overcome by the marketer, and the buyer can be convinced to choose the product.
- **A personal rapport often helps in creating brand loyalty for the firm and the product:** Many a time, if the representative of the organisation is able to create a good rapport with the customer, the customer is likely to remain loyal to the brand.

4.2.4.4 Disadvantages of Personal Selling

Some of the disadvantages of personal selling are:

- **It is an expensive form of promotion:** Having a face-to-face contact or even a telephonic one with all the customers is quite an expensive way of promoting the product. It calls for a lot of investment in terms of time, money, and human resources.
- **It is time consuming:** In case of advertising or other forms of promotion that are generally targeted towards a mass audience, the message is sent across hundreds and thousands of customers at the same time through a mass medium. However, in case of personal selling, every customer is contacted individually, and this becomes a time-consuming task.
- **The reach is restricted as compared to advertising:** Since advertising is done through a mass medium, it has a wider reach than personal selling.

The next element of the promotion mix is publicity. Publicity and public relations are closely associated. Let us take a look at these.

4.2.5 Publicity and Public Relations

This encompasses a wide variety of communication efforts to create generally favourable attitudes and options towards an organisation and its products. Publicity is a special form of public relations that involves news stories about an organisation or its products.

4.2.5.1 Objectives of Publicity and Public Relations

There are several objectives of publicity and public relations.

- **To create a positive image:** Just having a good product is not enough in today's world. It is essential that the customers of the organisation as well as all other stakeholders have a positive image about the organisation. One of the major objectives of publicity and public relations is to create that positive image in the minds of customers and all stakeholders.
- **To defend the image of the organisation against competition:** To sustain in the competitive situation, it has become imperative for organisations to defend their image against the competitors. Since most organisations will have products and services of the same quality, customers will generally favour products and services of those organisations that have created a positive image vis-à-vis the competitors.
- **In case of any mishaps, to recover lost ground:** Many a time, the organisation finds itself in the eye of the storm due to certain controversies. The media, being very active, blows up many small issues into major ones. In such a situation, one of the objectives of publicity and public relations is to salvage the situation by clarifying the issues and creating confidence in the minds of the target audience.
- **To be a constant reminder to the target audience:** It is often said that - "Out of sight is out of mind." Publicity and public relations are often used to remain in the news and remind the target audience about the existence of the firm and its offerings.

4.2.5.2 Advantages of Publicity and Public Relations

- **Since it is not done by a known sponsor, it carries more weightage in the eyes of the consumer:** In case of advertising, sales promotion or personal selling, the sponsor is the organisation itself, and as such, it is assumed that it would project its own image and its products and services in a good light. However, in case of publicity, it is a neutral source (like the press) that writes about the organisation and its products and services, and therefore, it carries more weightage in the consumers' mind.
- **Creates a positive image in the minds of the customer:** Publicity and public relations create a positive image in the minds of the customer.

4.2.5.3 Disadvantages of Publicity and Public Relations

- **It can create a negative image:** It may also create some controversies and thereby lead to a negative image.
- **Customers might consider it as a ploy to hard-sell the products:** Customers might find an organisation as pushing hard for selling the products by undertaking more publicity.

4.2.6 Direct Marketing

As mentioned in chapter number 3, Direct marketing is an interactive marketing system that uses one or more advertising media to effect a measurable response and/or transaction at any location.

Direct Marketing consists of direct connection with carefully targeted individual consumers to obtain an immediate response as well as cultivate lasting customer relationships.

Previously we discussed Direct Marketing as direct distribution that is, as a marketing channel that contained no intermediaries. However, Direct Marketing is also an element of the communication mix, as an approach for communicating with the consumers directly.

4.2.6.1 Forms of Direct Marketing

The major forms of Direct Marketing include:
- Personal selling,
- Telephone marketing,
- Direct mail marketing,
- Catalogue marketing,
- Direct response television marketing,
- Kiosk marketing, and
- Online Marketing.

Fig. 4.3: Various forms of Direct Marketing

- **Telephone Marketing:** This involves using the telephone to sell directly to customers.
- **Direct-Mail Marketing:** This involves sending an offer, announcement, reminder or any other item to a person at a particular address.
- **Catalogue Marketing:** This involves direct marketing through print, video or electronic catalogues that are mailed to select customers made available in stores or presented online.
- **Direct Response Television Marketing:** Direct Marketing via television including direct response television advertising or infomercials and home shopping channels.
- **Kiosk Marketing:** Placing information and ordering machines called as kiosks at select locations to enable customers to place orders directly.

4.2.6.2 Advantages and Disadvantages of Direct Marketing

Advantages of Direct Marketing

Direct marketing provides a host of advantages to both the buyer and the seller.

For buyers Direct Marketing is:
- Convenient
- Easy to use
- Private
- Can be used from home
- At a convenient time
- Immediate and interactive.

For sellers:
- Powerful tool to build customer relationships
- Helps target smaller groups or even individual customers
- Helps send personalised communications
- Can be timed rightly
- Low cost communication tool.

Disadvantages of Direct Marketing

Some of the disadvantages of Direct Marketing are:
- **Invasion of privacy of the buyer:** Many a times buyers are upset at receiving mails/ phone calls or mailers that they have not solicited and can sue the organisation for invasion of privacy.
- **Irritation:** Buyers often get irritated with direct marketing phone calls/ mailers and other direct communications.
- **High throwaway rate:** Many buyers will simply throw away print communication sent as a direct mailer without even reading it.

Let us now look at a comparative table of all the elements of the Promotional Mix.

Table 4.1: Comparative characteristics of the elements of the Promotional Mix

Parameter	Advertising	Sales Promotion	Personal Selling	Publicity	Direct Marketing
Audience	Mass	Either mass or limited	Most of the times one-to-one	Mass	Mass or individual
Message	Uniform	Either a uniform or varied message	Highly specific and customised	Uniform	Either uniform or specific
Cost	Low per viewer or reader	Moderate per customer	High per customer	Free for media space and time, moderate for press releases and promotional material	Low cosy per customer
Sponsor	Organisation	Organisation	Organisation	No formal sponsor	Organisation
Flexibility	Low	High	High	None (Controlled entirely by the media)	Low
Control over content and placement	High	High	High	None (Controlled entirely by the media)	High
Credibility	Moderate	Moderate	Moderate	High	Low

4.2.7 The Concept of Integrated Marketing Communication

Each of the tools of the marketing communication mix has various elements that the marketer can blend depending upon the response that the organisation is seeking from its customers.

For example, advertising includes print, broadcast, indoor, outdoor and other forms of advertisements. If the objective of the organisation is to increase the awareness about a particular product, they may resort to outdoor hoardings rather than going for a print advertisement.

However, the new era of marketing is ushering in some unprecedented changes in the marketing environment. These changes would very naturally affect the marketing communication mix as well. We will now take a look at the changing communications environment.

4.2.7.1 The Changing Communication Environment

The two major factors that are changing the communications environment are:
1. Emergence of micro markets (narrowly defined markets that are fragments of the earlier mass markets) which seek specialised products and not mass products.
2. Vast improvements in information technology (Moving towards segmented marketing).

This shift from mass marketing towards segmented marketing is also bringing in a change in the communications mix. Just as earlier the mass marketing had led to a rise in mass media communications, segmented marketing is giving rise to specialised and targeted communication efforts.

Although mass media promotion tools like Television and magazines are still around their importance is on the decline. Organisations now look at other tools of communication like Internet catalogues, Web Coupons, Airports kiosks etc.

4.2.7.2 The Need for Integrated Marketing Communication

The shift from mass marketing to targeted marketing and the corresponding shift in the Communications mix do create a problem for the marketing organisation.

Organisations often send out different messages through different media of communication. However, the consumers look at these as a part of a single message about the organisation. As such conflicting messages from different sources create confusion in the consumers mind. The main cause for this is that Organisations more often than not, fail to integrate the communication sent through various communication channels. The problem lies in the fact that communications often comes from different departments of the organisation. For example advertising messages are planned and implemented by the advertising department, personal selling communications are developed by the sales management department, and similarly Public relations communications are developed by the Public Relations Office and so on. This is where the need for integrating all marketing communications comes into the picture.

4.2.7.3 Definition of Integrated Marketing Communication (IMC)

It is the concept under which an Organisation carefully integrates and coordinates its many communication channels, to deliver a clear, consistent and compelling message about the organisation and its products.

Under this concept, the organisation builds its brand identity and a strong relation with the customer by coordinating and integrating all its communication messages across all communication activities as well as all media. This calls for recognising all customer contact points where the customer is likely to encounter or interact with the organisation and its bran. At all such points the communication messages have to be consistent. Fig. 4.4 depicts the carefully blended mix of all promotional tools

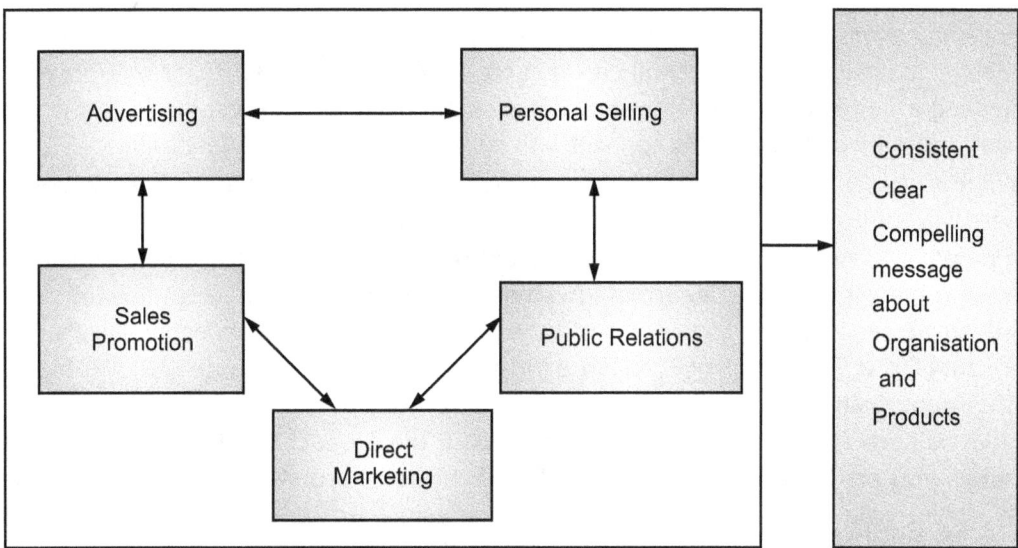

Fig. 4.4: Blended Mix of Promotional Tools

4.2.7.4 The Role of Integrated Marketing Communications

The role of the integrated marketing mix is to help the organisation achieve the objectives of marketing communications by:

- **Creating a Consistent Message:** A consistent message will help consumers identify with the organisation and its products without creating any confusion in their minds.
- **Clarity:** Integrated communications will not conflict with each other when being spread across various media since they are integrated and come from the same source. This will bring clarity in the message being sent across to customers.
- **Building Loyalty:** A consistent and clear message also works as an assurance to the consumers and builds greater Brand Loyalty.
- **Meeting all the Marketing Objectives:** Increase in brand loyalty and a larger customer base achieved through integrated marketing communications will help the organisation to achieve its marketing objectives.

Here is an interview by **Tim Bourne**: Chief Executive of Exposure highlighting the importance of Integrated Marketing Communications:

Nike, Snickers and Fosters have created powerful integrated campaigns – so what's their secret?

For an increasing number of campaigns, integration across a large number of media is essential. Tim Bourne, chief executive of Exposure, explains how it should be done.

Integration – campaigns that work equally well across online media, TV, print and outdoor – is something every agency claims to offer. But while brands crave it and it is often discussed, it is rarely achieved.

A common mistake is to imagine that having the same look and feel across different channels – "matching luggage" – will create successful integration. But that's a terrible basis for creating an integrated campaign. Just because the press ad and website have the same look and copy, it won't necessarily connect with consumers. It may just get boring.

What is crucial is a strong insight with a meaningful big idea that you can express in different ways. It is about connecting a brand truth with a real human emotion.

A powerful example is **Nike's Find Your Greatness** campaign, launched to tie in with this year's Olympics. It uses the idea that greatness is not reserved for elite athletes, but is something we can all aspire to in our own way. It is a clever way of connecting Nike's brand truth – **Just Do It** – to real people taking part in amateur sports. A strong idea like that can be used in any channel you chose, whether TV advertising, print or online.

Snickers have also created a strong platform with the product insight that **"you are not you when you are hungry"**. The campaign linked this to a consumer emotion: that you feel tetchy when you haven't eaten, making it possible to create a multidimensional communication campaign. It then got celebrities, including Katie Price and Rio Ferdinand, to tweet messages that were out of character, demonstrating the versatility of the idea across channels.

So remember: integration isn't about saying the same thing in different channels. But it is about taking a unique aspect of the brand and tying it to a consumer insight that is powerful and engaging – and which comes to life whether through Twitter, a TV ad or a piece of merchandise.

Source: www.theguardian.com › News › The Best Awards 2014

4.3 Developing Effective Communication

Having seen the importance of Integrated Marketing Communications, let us now look at the steps involved in developing effective marketing communication. Developing effective marketing communication involves:
- Identifying the Target Audience
- Determining the Communication Objective
- Designing a Message
- Choosing Media
- Selecting the Message Source
- Collecting Feedback.

1. **Identifying the Target Audience:**

   Identifying and knowing the target audience is one of the most important and primary steps in the process of developing effective communication. The target audience may be a niche market, special public, individuals, groups, buyers, or even prospects. Who the target audience is will determine the way the communication objective is fulfilled. That is, the Target audience will be the determinant of what will be said, how it will be said, who will say it, through which media the message will be communicated and when the message will be communicated.

   For example, If the communication objective of an organisation is to create an awareness for its ready-to-use range of spice mixes and their target audience are working women, then the communication message would have to portray a working woman using the ready-to-use spice mix, explaining its usage and convenience, and its benefits. The advertisement would be communicated through a number of media including the television. The advertisement would have to be broadcast during the prime slots in the evening between 8:00 p.m. to 9:30 p.m. as that would be the time that working women are most likely to watch the television.

2. **Determining Communication Objectives:**

   Once the target audience had been identified, the organisation must now clearly state the communication objective. Consumers generally go through a six phase consumer decision making process before they purchase any product. It is necessary for the organisation to be able to identify the stage in which the consumers currently are and to what stage they need to be moved. These stages include awareness, knowledge, liking, preference, conviction and finally purchase.

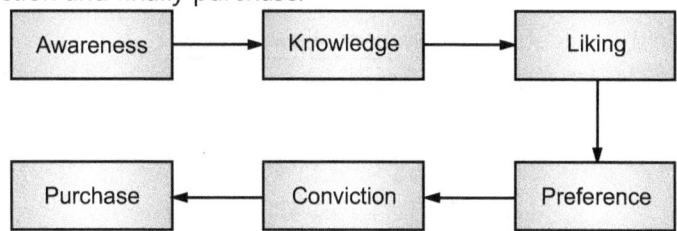

Fig. 4.5: Buyer Readiness Stages

In case the target market is totally unaware of the product, the communication's objective would be to create awareness and build knowledge. Many organisations start off with extensive teaser campaigns to launch new products and create awareness and curiosity about the said products.

Once the target audience is aware and has knowledge about the product, the next objective is to create a liking for the product and ensure that the consumer prefers the specific product over other competing offers. Organisations often use celebrities as brand ambassadors to create a liking for the product.

Thus the communication objective has to be based on the Buyer –readiness stage.

3. Designing the Communication Message

This is the most crucial step of the process of developing effective communication. Once the objective has been defined the organisation has to now look into creating the right message. To determine the effectiveness of the message, one of the frameworks or models followed by many organisations is AIDA. According to AIDA the message should:

- **A**- Get   **A**ttention
- **I**-Hold   **I**nterest
- **D**-Arouse   **D**esire
- **A**-Obtain   **A**ction

In putting the message together, the key components that need to be looked into, comprise of Message Content and Message Structure. This essentially means what to say and how to say it.

Message Content: The communicator needs to develop an appeal or a theme that will enable the organisation to get the desired response from the consumer.

There are three types of appeals that are generally used. They are:

- **Rational:** Rational Appeals relate to the audience's self interest. They give the consumer a valid reason to buy that product. The appeal shows how the product will deliver the desired benefits to the consumer. The functional benefit of the product is highlighted.

For example the Colgate advertisement shown below:

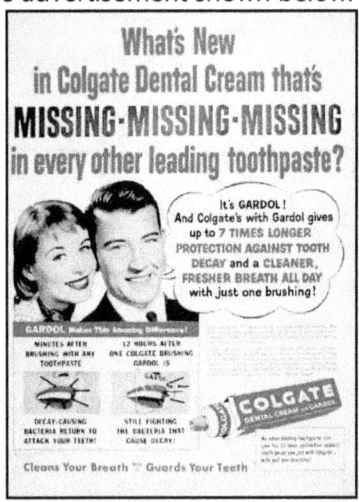

Fig. 4.6: Example of Rational Appeal

- **Emotional:** This is related to an individual's psychological and social need for purchasing certain products or services. These can be either negative or positive emotions. Positive emotions such as love, pride, and joy are used to motivate consumers, probing the desire to be different or the desire to confirm by using the product or service. Negative emotions like fear, guilt, and shame are used to get consumers to buy the product or service.

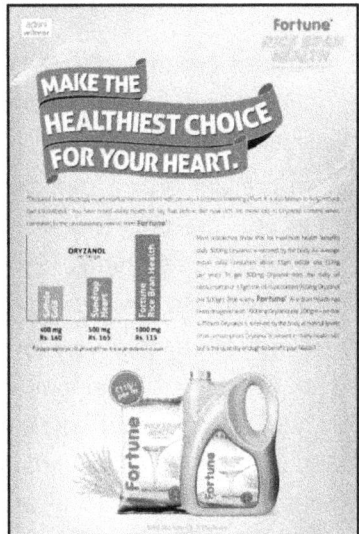

Fig. 4.7: Example of Emotional Appeal Using Fear

- Moral –These appeals try to bring out the moral values of the consumer as to what is right and what is wrong.

Fig. 4.8: Example of Moral Appeal

4. **Message Structure**

There are three major issues that the communicator or the marketer needs to decide in case of the message structure. These are:
1. Whether the message should draw a conclusion or leave it to the audience to draw their own conclusion by simply raising the questions. Research suggests that the latter option is a better one, when you leave it up to the audience to draw their own conclusions
2. Whether to present the strongest argument at the beginning or at the end. While presenting the strongest arguments in the beginning often helps in grabbing attention, it may lead to an anticlimax ending.
3. The third issue is whether to present only a one-sided argument (highlighting only the product's strengths) or to present two-sided argument (highlighting the strengths but also presenting the shortcomings). Two-sided messages are known to enhance the credibility of the advertiser; however they can also be risky.
4. **Message Format:** The message format to a very large extent will depend upon the media it is being carried in. In case of a print advertisement, the decision about headline, copy, illustration and colour would be responsible for making the format strong. Over the radio, the choice of words, sounds and voices would be important. In a television advertisement, in additional to all above elements, body language, dresses and costumes, have to be planned.

   The next step is to choose the channel of communication or in other words the media for communication

5. **Selecting communication Channels /Choosing Media:** Channels of communication are divided into two broad categories. They are personal and non-personal

   In personal communication channels, two or more people communicate with each other, either face to face, over telephone, through internet chat etc. Personal channels may or may not be controlled by the organisation. Channels like sales person of the organisation are controlled by the organisation. However, there are also channels that may not be directly controlled by the organisation. For example, personal communication about the product may reach the buyers through their friends, relatives, neighbours or other acquaintances. This channel is called as Word-Of–Mouth influence. This channel cannot be controlled by the organisation.

   Organisations often request opinion leaders to help them by giving favourable word-of-mouth opinion for their products.

   Personal Communication channels are media that carry messages without personal contact or feedback. They include major media, events etc. Major media include Print media like newspapers and magazines, Broadcast media like radio and television, display media like billboards, hoardings, signs and postersand online media like emails, websites etc).

Selecting the Message Source: In Marketing Communications, simply designing a good message is not sufficient to create an impact. The impact of the message on the target audience also depends on how the audiences view the communicator/organisation giving the message. Messages given through highly credible sources are more persuasive.

For example: Toothpaste producers use dentists in the advertisements to endorse the toothpaste. Similarly sports products use sportspersons in the advertisements to endorse the products.

Many organisations also use celebrities to endorse the product to increase the credibility and impact of the message

Fig. 4.9: Celebrity Endorsements

6. **Collecting Feedback:** The organisation does spend a sizeable amount on all marketing communications. After the message has been sent, it is necessary to find out, if the desired result has been achieved and what the effect the communication has, on the target market .This involves asking the target audience members whether they remember the message, what do they recall from the message, how they felt after seeing the message etc.

The communicator/organisation would like to also find out if the communication has impacted the behaviour of the consumer and whether the consumer is willing to buy the product, advise others to buy it, or at least visit the store selling it.

Feedback helps to improve the communication programme and make suitable changes in it.

4.4 Deciding the Marketing Communication Mix

After developing an effective communication, it is time to decide on the overall marketing communication mix. According to Integrated Marketing Communication, the organisation must blend all the tools of promotion to get a coordinated promotion mix.

4.4.1 Factors in Setting the Marketing Communication or Promotion Mix

While developing the promotion mix, it is necessary that the organisation should consider several factors. These factors include:
- Type of the Product Market
- Use of Push or Pull Strategy
- Consumer readiness to make the purchase
- The product's stage in the Product Life Cycle
- The organisations market rank.

1. Type of Product Market

The utilisation of various promotional tools would vary depending upon the market that is being catered to. That is to say that the utilisation will be different for consumer markets when compared with the industrial markets.

Spending in the consumer markets would be high on sales promotion, followed by advertising, personal selling and public relations respectively.

On the other hand, in Business Markets maximum spending would be on personal selling followed by sales promotion, advertising and public relations respectively.

The Fig. 4.10 given below represents the same

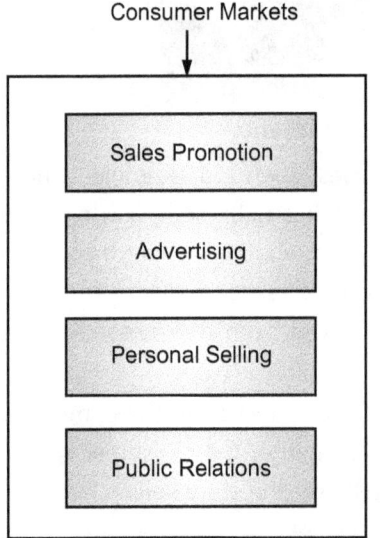
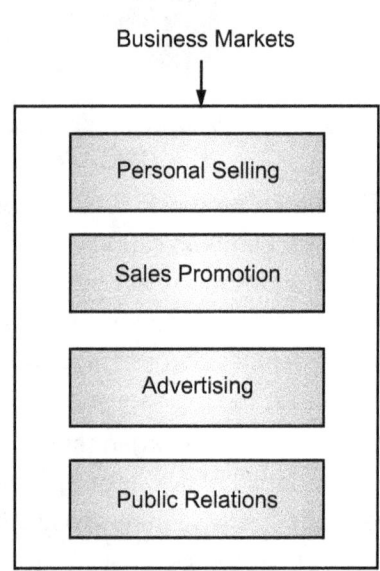

(a) Proportionate Spending for Consumer Goods   (b) Proportionate Spending for Business Goods

Fig. 4.10

2. Use of Push or Pull Strategy

As mentioned earlier organisations need to decide on the strategy that will be used for promotion. There are two basic strategies that most marketers would use. These are Push Promotion or Pull Promotion.

(a) **Push Strategy:** A push strategy involves pushing the product through the various channels of distribution, to reach the final consumer. All marketing activities aim to induce the channel members to carry the product and to promote it to the final consumers.

(b) **Pull Strategy:** In the pull strategy the organisation directs all its marketing activities towards inducing the final consumer to buy the product. An effective pull strategy would result in the consumer demanding for the product from the channel members.

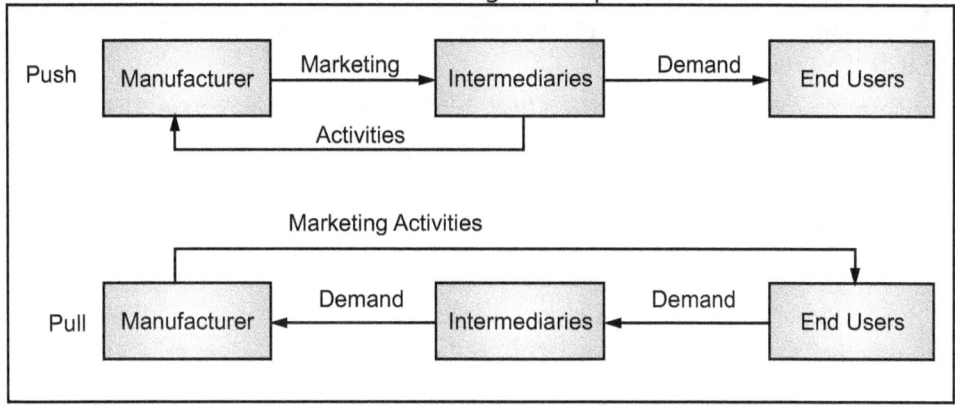

Fig. 4.11: Push and Pull Strategies

3. Buyer Readiness Stage

Just as the utilisation of promotional tools would vary with regards to the type of product market, so also the use and effectiveness of promotional tools will vary with regards to the buyer readiness stage.

For example, advertising and publicity will play the most important role in the first stage that is the Awareness stage. The second, third and fourth stage that is the Knowledge, liking and preference stages, are primarily affected by advertising and personal selling. In the fifth stage that is conviction, personal selling works the most and the last stage that is purchase is affected by personal selling and sales promotion.

Fig. 4.12 below is a graphical representation of Effectiveness of different promotional tools during different buyer readiness stages

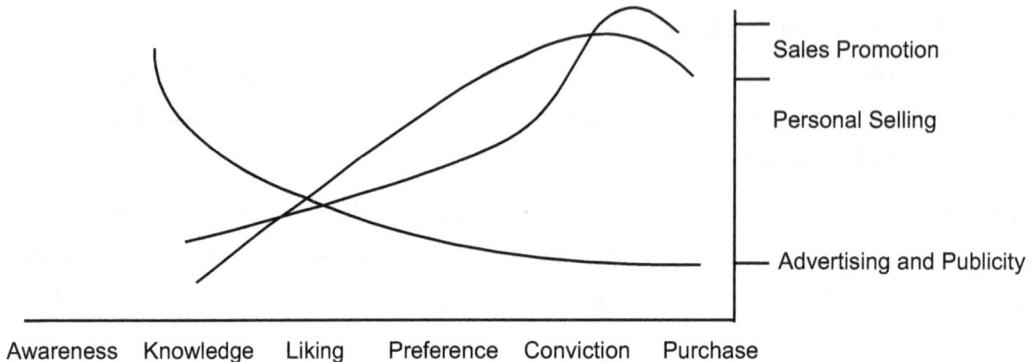

Awareness   Knowledge   Liking   Preference   Conviction   Purchase

Fig. 4.12: Effectiveness of different promotional tools during different buyer readiness stages

4. **Product Life Cycle Stage**

Promotional tools also vary in their effectiveness, depending upon the stage of the life cycle that the product is in.

In the Introductory stage, advertising and publicity are more effective. They are followed by Personal selling which is followed by sales promotion that helps by inducing the consumer to try the product.

In the growth stage all tools are more or less equally effective and not very extensively used. This is because the product has gained acceptance and there is enough demand.

In the maturity stage sales promotion followed by advertising and personal selling becomes effective.

In the decline stage sales promotion continues to be effective while other promotional tools are rarely used.

Fig. 4.13 below is a graphical representation of the same.

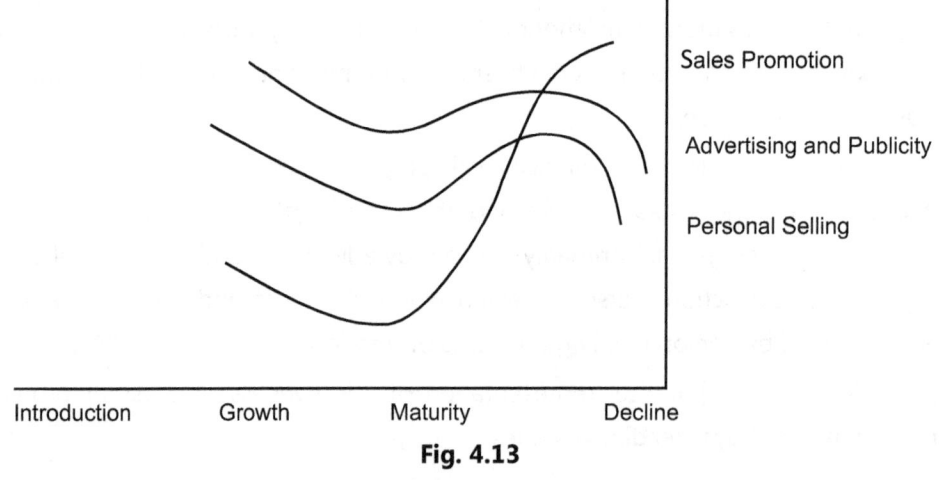

Fig. 4.13

5. Market Rank

It is generally observed that top ranking brands derive more benefit from advertising than from sales promotion. For the organisations that are ranked first three, their return on investment (ROI) has been found to rise with increase in the amount spent on advertising.

4.4.2 Measuring Communication Results

After implementation of the communication plan, the organisation needs to measure the effectiveness of the plan. It needs to monitor the impact of the communication on the target audience and check if the desired results have been achieved.

This involves getting feedback from the target audience. This can be done by conducting recognition and recall tests. It is also necessary to find out if the communication message has influenced the behaviour of the target audience in terms of purchase, repurchase or recommendation to friends, relatives and acquaintances.

Points to Remember

Marketing today is more than just having a good product, pricing it attractively, and making it available to consumers through a distribution channel. It is essential that organisations communicate with their present as well as potential customers, retailers, suppliers, and all other stakeholders. For this the organisation requires a communication mix, also known as the promotion mix.

Definition: An organisation's total marketing communication mix – also called as the promotion mix-comprises of the specific blend of advertising, sales promotion, public relations, personal selling and direct marketing tools that the organisation uses to pursue its marketing objectives.

Role of Marketing Communication

Marketing communication or Promotion serves the following purposes:
- To provide information to customers;
- To differentiate the product from that of the competitors' products;
- To generate more demand for the company's products;
- To make a product more attractive to an organisation's prospective buyers;
- To position a product, that is, to create a positive image of the product/firm.

Objectives of Marketing Communications/Promotion

Lead to behaviour modification
- Objective to inform
- Objective to persuade
- Objective to remind.

Communication Mix Elements
(a) Advertising
(b) Sales Promotion
(c) Public Relations
(d) Personal Selling
(e) Direct Marketing

Advertising

Advertising is a non-personal form of communication, paid for by a clearly identified sponsor promoting ideas, organisations or products through a mass medium.

Advantages and Disadvantages of Advertising

Let us now see the advantages and disadvantages of advertising:

Advantages of Advertising

- A large audience is attracted.
- The cost per viewer, listener or reader is low.
- Advertiser has control over message content, graphics, timing and size.
- Wherever print media is used, the message can be studied and restricted.
- Editorial content (a TV show, a news story) often surrounds an advertisement. This may increase its credibility and the probability that it will be read.
- Reduced service operations are possible since a customer can become aware of the organisation and its offering before shopping.

Disadvantages of Advertising

- Since the message is standardised and remitted through a mass medium, the advertiser cannot focus on the needs of individual customers.
- Some advertising requires large investments. This reduces the access of small firms to certain media.
- Media may reach a large geographic area leading to inefficient use of funds for the organisation.
- Some media require a long lead-time for placing advertisements. This reduces an organisation's ability to advertise fad items or to react to some current event themes.
- Some media have a high throwaway rate. For instance, circulars and mail advertisements may be discarded without being read.
- Advertisements are often very brief and don't offer details.

Sales Promotion

It is a sponsor-funded demand stimulating activity, designed to supplement advertising and facilitate personal selling.

Sales promotion uses many tools like coupons, premiums, etc. Although these tools are diverse in nature, they offer three basic benefits to the marketer.
- Communications
- Incentive
- Invitation

Major Decisions in Sales Promotion

Some of the major decisions in sales promotion include:
- Establishing the sales promotion objectives;
- Selecting the tools;
- Developing the programme;
- Pre-testing the programme;
- Implementing and controlling the programme;
- Evaluating the results.

Personal selling

It is defined as a direct presentation of a product to a prospective customer by a representative of the organisation selling it.

Objectives of Personal Selling
- To create a positive image of the organisation and the product in the minds of prospective customers
- To explain the technical aspects of the product that cannot be done through advertising
- To create confidence in the minds of the customers.

Direct Selling

In personal selling, direct selling has the following features:
- Uses the human capital resource;
- Offers high earnings to those who do not have businesses;
- Home based;
- People get people strategy- In other words people who purchase get other people to buy
- Very sound business model.

Distribution Selling

Another form of personal selling is distribution selling. This involves:
- Sales efforts to cover geographic region;
- Covers relevant distribution channels.

Outlet Selling

This is also a form of personal selling. It involves
- Sales efforts by a salesperson to customers who come to a specific outlet
- It is generally seen at all retail outlets.

Publicity and Public Relations

This encompasses a wide variety of communication efforts to create generally favourable attitudes and options towards an organisation and its products. Publicity is a special form of public relations that involves news stories about an organisation or its products.

Direct Marketing: Direct marketing is an interactive marketing system that uses one or more advertising media to affect a measurable response and/or transaction at any location.

Previously we discussed Direct Marketing as direct distribution that is, as a marketing channel that contained no intermediaries. However, Direct Marketing is also an element of the communication mix, as an approach for communicating with the consumers directly.

Forms of Direct Marketing: The major forms of Direct Marketing include:

- Personal selling
- Telephone marketing
- Direct mail marketing
- Catalogue marketing
- Direct response television marketing
- Kiosk marketing and
- Online Marketing.

The Concept of Integrated Marketing Communications

Each of the tools of the marketing communication mix has various elements that the marketer can blend depending upon the response that the organisation is seeking from its customers.

The Changing Communications Environment

The two major factors that are changing the communications environment are:
1. Emergence of micro markets (narrowly defined markets that are fragments of the earlier mass markets) which seek specialized products and not mass products
2. Vast improvements in information technology (Moving towards segmented marketing)

Definition of Integrated Marketing Communications (IMC)

It is the concept under which an Organisation carefully integrates and coordinates its many communication channels, to deliver a clear, consistent and compelling message about the organisation and its products.

The Role of Integrated Marketing Communications

The role of the integrated marketing mix is to help the organisation achieve the objectives of marketing communications by:

- Creating a Consistent Message
- Clarity
- Building Loyalty
- Meeting all the marketing Objectives.

Questions for Discussion

(A) Long Answer Questions:
1. What is integrated marketing communication? Discuss the need for integrated marketing communication.
2. "Integrated Marketing Communication plays a very important role in the Marketing Mix". Comment on this statement.
3. Discuss in brief the various elements of the communication mix.
4. Describe the various types of media used for advertising.
5. Compare and Contrast between advertising and sales promotion.
6. Write a note on advertising, its scope, role, objectives and types.
7. Discuss the various factors that an organisation must consider when deciding on the advertising budget.
8. What do you understand by the term "Sales Promotion"? Discuss the various categories of sales promotional tools.
9. Personal selling is an important aspect of the communication mix. Discuss this in light of the Objectives and types of personal selling.
10. With the help of suitable example, discuss the various objectives of sales promotion.
11. What is direct marketing? Describe the various forms of direct marketing.
12. Describe in detail the steps involved in developing effective marketing communication.
13. Discuss in detail the factors that are considered in setting the communication mix.
14. What are the major considerations that a marketer must make while deciding on the media?
15. Describe the five step process in developing and managing the advertising program.

(B) Short Notes – Write Short Notes on:
1. Role of marketing communication
2. Advantages and disadvantages of advertising
3. 5 M's of advertising
4. Advantages and disadvantages of personal selling
5. Advantages and disadvantages of Sales Promotion
6. Advantages and disadvantages of Publicity and Public Relations
7. Advantages and disadvantages of Direct Marketing
8. Direct Marketing as a channel of distribution and as an element of communication mix
9. Determining the communication objectives
10. Need for Integrated Marketing Communications
11. Factors in deciding promotion mix

12. Types of personal selling
13. Major decisions in sales promotions
14. Push and Pull Strategy
15. AIDA for designing a message

(C) Multiple Choice Questions:
1. Promotion Mix is the same as:
   (a) Marketing Mix (b) Pricing Mix
   (c) Communication mix (d) Product Mix
2. Some of the elements of the communication mix are:
   (a) Advertising, Sales Promotion and Messaging
   (b) Advertising, Personal Selling and Mobile applications
   (c) Advertising, Direct Marketing and Messaging
   (d) Advertising, Sales Promotion and Personal Selling
3. One of the purposes of marketing communication is:
   (a) To provide information to the customers
   (b) To design the product
   (c) To set the price of the product
   (d) To prepare a product strategy
4. Objectives of promotion include:
   (a) To remind the target audience (b) To design a product
   (c) To price a product (d) To prepare a product
5. Factors to be considered while deciding promotion mix are:
   (a) Type of costs (b) Type of Product Markets
   (c) Type of messages (d) Type of people
6. Various types of advertising include:
   (a) Educational and entertainment (b) Institutional and educational
   (c) Promotional and Institutional (d) Promotional and entertainment
7. Objectives of advertising include:
   (a) Creating awareness about new products
   (b) Pricing Products
   (c) Distribution of products
   (d) None of the above
8. Two frameworks used for message generation are:
   (a) Inductive and progressive (b) Inductive and deductive
   (c) Inductive and distributive (d) Inductive and subjective
9. Media Selection involves deciding:
   (a) Reach, position and type (b) Reach, frequency and type
   (c) Reach, frequency and impact (d) Reach, type and impact

10. Categories of media used in advertising include:
    (a) Print, paper and pencil
    (b) Print, Outdoor and indoor
    (c) Print, Paper and Outdoor
    (d) Print, Broadcast and Speciality
11. Newspapers and magazines are a part of:
    (a) Print media
    (b) Broadcast Media
    (c) Information Media
    (d) Outdoor Media
12. Transit Advertising involves use of:
    (a) Radio
    (b) Television
    (c) Subways, Buses and trains
    (d) Information Media
13. Major decisions in sales promotion include:
    (a) Selling
    (b) Buying
    (c) Exploring
    (d) Establishing sales promotion objectives
14. Two categories of sales promotion are:
    (a) Consumer and Substitute promotion
    (b) Consumer and Trade Promotion
    (c) Consumer and Impact Promotion
    (d) Consumer and buyer promotion
15. Tools of sales promotion include:
    (a) Coupons, Bonus packs and sweepstakes
    (b) Coupons, purchase and pricing
    (c) Coupons, Bonus and Purchase
    (d) All of the above
16. Types of personal selling include:
    (a) Direct Selling, indirect selling and outdoor selling
    (b) Direct Selling, Distribution selling and outlet selling
    (c) Direct Selling and advertising
    (d) Direct Selling and Outdoor selling
17. As compared to advertising:
    (a) Personal selling is cheaper
    (b) Personal selling is neither expensive nor cheaper
    (c) Personal selling is expensive
    (d) None of the above
18. AIDA stands for:
    (a) Attention, Impact, Distribution and Action
    (b) Action, Impact, Desire and Ability
    (c) Attention, Interest, Desire and Action
    (d) Attention, Internet, Direct and Action

19. Measuring communication effectiveness call for:
    (a) Collecting information
    (b) Collecting Money
    (c) Collecting advertisements
    (d) Collecting Feedback
20. Buyer readiness stages include:
    (a) Awareness and Conviction
    (b) Awareness and Conduction
    (c) Awareness and Constitution
    (d) None of the above

Answers

1. (c)	2. (d)	3. (a)	4. (a)	5. (b)	6. (c)	7. (a)	8. (b)	9. (c)	10. (d)
11. (a)	12. (c)	13. (d)	14. (b)	15. (a)	16. (b)	17. (c)	18. (c)	19. (d)	20. (a)

(D) Project Questions:
1. Design a creative advertisement for an educational institute launching a new Masters Programme in Business Management.
2. Discuss the factors that you will consider while deciding on the advertising budget for an established brand of a two-wheeler that has been launched in the market two years ago. Make necessary assumptions.
3. What type of a sales promotion campaign would you recommend for an organisation that is selling laptops? Give reasons for your answer.
4. The major mass media, that is, newspapers, magazines, radio and television are extremely different in their ability for dramatising the message, credibility and attention-getting. Discuss these media along with their advantages and disadvantages.
5. Explain the uses of publicity and public relations in an attempt to salvage the image of an organisation that has taken a beating having had to recall some products from the market.

Case Study

The Marketing Mix of Haldiram's
Products

Haldiram offer a wide range of products to its customers. The product range includes sweets, sharbats, bakery items, dairy products, papad and ice-creams in addition to its namkeens. However, namkeens remained the main focus area for the group contributing close to 60% of its total revenues. By specialising in the manufacturing of namkeens, the company seemed to have created a niche market for itself.

Haldiram's sought to customise its products to suit the tastes and preferences of customers from different parts of India. It launched products, which catered to the tastes of people belonging to specific regions. For example, it launched 'Murukkus,' a South Indian snack, for south Indian customers and 'Bhelpuri,' keeping in mind customers residing in western India. The organisation also offered certain products such as 'Nazarana,' 'Panchratan,' and 'Premium' only during the festival season in gift packs.

Pricing

Haldiram launched namkeens in small packets of 30 grams, priced as low as ₹ 5 (easily affordable to all classes and convenient to be carried for travel as well). They also launched namkeens in five different variants with prices varying as per the weights of the snacks. The prices also varied on the basis of the type of namkeens and the raw materials used to manufacture it. The cost of metalised packing also had an impact on the price, especially in the case of snack foods. The company revised the prices of its products upwards only when there was a steep increase in the raw material costs or additional taxes were imposed.

Place

Haldiram developed a strong distribution network to ensure the widest possible reach for its products not only in India but also overseas. From the manufacturing unit, the company's finished goods were passed on to carrying and forwarding (C&F) agents. C&F agents passed on the products to distributors, who shipped them to retail outlets. Haldiram also had exclusive distributors in the international market.

Although the company had exclusive showrooms owned by Haldiram, they also offered their products through all kinds of retail outlets such as supermarkets, sweet shops, provision stores, bakeries and ice cream parlors. Apart from this the products were also found to be available in public places such as railway stations and bus stations that accounted for a sizeable amount of its sales.

Despite being a traditional organisation, Haldiram's did not restrict its distribution strategy to the traditional and conventional channels of distribution. Haldiram's offered its products through the Internet as well. The company tied up with *indiatimes.com*, a website owned by the Times of India group to sell its products over the Internet. Haldiram's products could be ordered through a host of other websites in India and abroad.

Giftstoindia.com, giftssmashhits.com, tohfatoindia.com and channelindia.com enabled people residing abroad to send Haldiram's gift packs to specified locations in India. Region-specific websites also enabled people to send gifts to specified regions.

Promotion

Haldiram's product promotion had been low key until competition intensified in the snack foods market. The company tied up with an advertising agency for promoting its products. Consequently, through the agency, attractive posters, brochures and mailers were designed to enhance the visibility of the Haldiram brand.

Some of the famous punch lines for haldiram's products were 'Always in good taste.' These were very well appreciated by the consumers. Advertisements depicting the entire range of Haldiram's sweets and namkeens were published in the print media (magazines and newspapers). These advertisements had captions such as 'millions of tongues can't go wrong,' 'What are you waiting for, Diwali?' and 'Keeping your taste buds on their toes.'

To increase the visibility of the Haldiram's brand, the company placed its hoardings in high traffic areas such as train stations and bus stations. Posters were also designed for individual producers. These included captions such as 'yeh corn hain' (this is corn), 'chota samosa - big mazaa' (small samosa - big entertainment), 'yeh Kashmiri mix khoob jamega' (this namkeen item will get well) and 'oozing with taste' (for Rasgoolas).

Since namkeens were impulse purchase items, attractive packaging in different colours influenced purchases. Haldiram used the latest technology to increase the shelf life of its products and ensure that they provided value for money. While the normal shelf life of similar products was under a week, the shelf life of Haldiram's products was about six months. The packaging became a unique selling proposition for the company and gave it a competitive edge.

Posters highlighting the shelf life of its products carried the caption 'six months on the shelf and six seconds in your mouth.' Also true to its traditional origins, during festival season, Haldiram's products were sold in attractive looking special gift packs. The showrooms and retail outlets of Haldiram gave importance to point of purchase (POP) displays. Haldiram's snacks were displayed on special racks, usually outside retail outlets. The showrooms had sign boards displaying mouth-watering delicacies with captions such as 'Chinese Delight,' Simply South,' 'The King of all Chats.'

Issues

Although the company was doing very well, analysts felt that, Haldiram's would have to come up with newer strategies in the market, given the competitive situation in the industry.

The competition in the ready-to-eat snack foods market in India was intensifying. Frito Lay India Ltd. (Frito Lay), one of Haldiram's major competitors, was expanding its market share. Instead of directly competing with the market leader Haldiram, the company launched innovative products in the market and backed them with heavy publicity.

Frito Lay's range of products included a mix of traditional Indian and western flavours which appealed to both the younger and older generations. Its products included Leher Namkeens, Leher Kurkure (snack sticks), Lays (flavoured Chips), Cheetos (snack balls), Uncle Chips and Nutyumz (nut snacks).

Another competitor, SM Foods, introduced a range of innovative products. The company launched India's first non-wafer chips in 1988. SM offered products under two main brands - Peppy and Piknik.

Under Peppy, it had sub brands such as Cheese Balls, Ringos, Hi Protein Crispies, Potato Rackets, Hearts, Veggie Treat, Mixtures and Minerette. Under Piknik, it had Protein Pin, Junior and Corn Puffs. Haldiram also faced tough competition from domestic players such as Britannia Industries Ltd., Bikanerwala Foods and ITC.

Market analysts felt that Haldiram lagged behind competitors in offering variety of snack foods targeted at children, who were always eager to try new flavours in every product category. They felt that the company concentrated too much on traditional Indian items such as Bhujia Sev and Moong Dal.

Haldiram had in fact, taken steps to fill the gaps in its portfolio. Rajendra Agarwal, the owner of the Nagpur unit said, "We want to expand our market by introducing snacks that will appeal to younger people. There will be no growth in the traditional snacks category." The unit planned to launch products such as flavored ready-to-eat popcorn and a product similar to Leher Kurkure.

Haldiram had a limited expenditure when it came to promotions while Frito Lay's expenditure on product promotion was much higher. With successful ad campaigns such as "control nahin hotha" (it is irresistible) for the Leher brand of namkeens, the company made sure that it attracted the attention of viewers.

According to media reports, Haldiram lagged behind competitors in the area of customer service. A report in Deccan Herald that Prabhu Shankar Agarwal, the owner of the Kolkata unit, was arrested on charges of manhandling customers caused further damage to the image of Haldiram. The report also mentioned that few of the company's restaurants did not possess the minimum requirements, such as sufficient seating arrangements and adequate parking lots

Haldiram also had to deal with problems created by spurious products. Some companies claiming to be close associates of the original Haldiram's of Bikaner used the Haldiram's brand name in their products. For example the 'Haldiram Madanlal' company claimed that its proprietor, Anil Kumar Agarwal, belonged to the Haldiram's family of Bikaner.

Source:http://www.icmrindia.org/free%20resources/casestudies

Questions:
1. What are the changes that Haldiram needs to make in its promotion mix to overcome the problems?
2. Despite initial success, the Haldiram's brand was slowly losing market share. Cite reasons for this.

Questions from Previous Pune University Examinations

1. Define Sales Promotion. Explain Various Techniques of Sales Promotion and its Importance. **[M.B.A. Dec. 2010]**
2. Explain in detail the Different Tools of Promotion Mix. **[M.B.A. Dec. 2011]**
3. Write Short Note:
   (a) Personal Selling. **[M.B.A. April 2007, 2011]**

■■■

Chapter 5...

Marketing Planning and Control

Contents ...

Introduction

5.1 Marketing Planning

    5.1.1 Scope of Marketing Planning

    5.1.2 Importance of Marketing Planning

    5.1.3 Components of Marketing Planning

    5.1.4 Essential Requirements of Marketing Planning

    5.1.5 Difficulties in Marketing Planning

5.2 Product Level Planning

    5.2.1 Introduction

    5.2.2 What is a Plan?

    5.2.3 Preparation and Evaluation of Product Level Marketing Plan

    5.2.4 Nature of a Marketing Plan

    5.2.5 Contents of a Marketing Plan

5.3 Marketing Evaluation and Control

    5.3.1 Marketing Implementation and Evaluation Skills

    5.3.2 Controlling the Marketing Activity

    5.3.3 Profitability Control

    5.3.4 Strategic Control

    5.3.5 Marketing Audit

    5.3.6 Marketing Excellence Review

    5.3.7 The Ethical and Social Responsibility Review

- Points to Remember
- Questions for Discussion
- Project Questions
- Case Study

Learning Objectives ...

In the preceding four chapters we have learnt in detail about Product, Price, Place and Promotion. These constitute the marketing mix. In this chapter we will learn the essential aspect of planning and control. The learning objectives of this lesson are:
- To understand the concept of Marketing Planning and Control
- To study the need for a marketing plan
- To understand the Product Level Planning process
- To study the evaluation process for a plan
- To identify the nature and contents of a marketing plan
- To understand the process of marketing control
- To study the various types of control

Introduction

A marketing plan clarifies the key marketing elements of a business and maps out directions, objectives and activities for the business and its employees.

The marketing plan draws on the broader perspectives outlined in a firm's business plan. The business plan states how a company will take a product idea and transform that into a commercially viable proposition.

The marketing plan focuses on issues related to the four Ps: product, price, promotion and place.

Marketing planning is the starting point of any business activity. Planning is deciding at present what is to be done in the future. It involves not only anticipating the consequences of decisions but also predicts the events that are likely to affect the business.

The primary aim of Marketing Planning is to direct the company's marketing efforts and resources towards present marketing objectives like growth, survival, profit maximisation, service to customers etc. However the marketing activity and objectives are the deciding factors on which all other activities of a company are based. Thus the entire activity of a company is actually based on the premise of the marketing plan.

According to **MacColm H. B. Me Donald**, *"Marketing Planning is a logical sequence of activities leading to the setting of marketing objectives and formulation of plans for achieving them."*

In the words of **Wendell R. Smith** *"Marketing Planning is the exercise of analysis and foresight to increase the effectiveness of marketing activities."*

In a nut shell any Marketing Planning is a managerial function that determines the future course of marketing action based on the analysis of past events so that the marketing objectives can be achieved. It is basically concerned with the allocation, development and future use of the marketing resources.

5.1 Marketing Planning

Marketing planning can be used:
1. To assess how well the organisation is doing in its markets.
2. To identify current strengths and weaknesses in these markets.
3. To establish marketing objectives to be achieved in these markets.
4. To establish a marketing mix for each market designed to achieve organisational objectives.

Marketing Planning Process

The marketing planning process involves both the development of objectives and specifications for how they will be accomplished. There are five basic steps in the process.

1. **Determination of Organisational Objectives:** The basic objectives, or goals, of the organisation are the starting point for marketing planning. They serve as the foundation from which marketing objectives and plans are built. These objectives provide direction for all phases of the organisation and serve as standards in evaluating performance. Soundly conceived goals should be S.M.A.R.T – specific, measurable, attainable, realistic and time-specific.

2. **Assessing Organisational Resources:** Planning strategies are influenced by a number of factors both within and outside the organisation. Organisational resources include capabilities in production, marketing, finance, technology, and personnel. By evaluating these resources, organisations can pinpoint their strengths and weaknesses. Strengths help organisations set objectives, develop plans for meeting objectives, and take advantage of marketing opportunities. Resource weaknesses, on the other hand, may inhibit an organisation from taking advantage of marketing opportunities.

3. **Evaluating Risks and Opportunities:** Environmental factors – competitive, political, legal, economic, technological and social – also influence marketing opportunities. The emergence of new technologies or innovations may open new opportunities for under-marketed products. The marketing environment may also pose threats to marketing opportunities.

4. **Marketing Strategy:** The net result of opportunity analysis is the formulation of marketing objectives designed to achieve overall organisational objectives and develop a marketing plan. The marketing planning effort must be directed toward establishing marketing strategies that are resource efficient, flexible, and adaptable. The marketing strategy is the overall company programme for selecting a particular target market and then satisfying consumers in that segment.

5. **Implementing and Monitoring Marketing Plans:** The overall strategic marketing plan serves as the basis for a series of operating plans necessary to move the organisation toward accomplishment of its objectives. At every step of the marketing planning process, marketing managers use feedback to monitor and adapt strategies when actual performance fails to match expectations.

5.1.1 Scope of Marketing Planning

The scope of Marketing Planning in a company depends on the kind of orientation that the company has adopted. In a market-oriented company, Marketing Planning begins with the consumer needs and problems and covers all the components of the marketing mix. It covers marketing research, product planning and development, selling, distribution channels, advertising, sales promotion, pricing and physical distribution.

Within the broad framework of the company's marketing objectives and policies, plans for each component of the marketing mix are formulated and these are known as area plans or sub functional plans. Each area plan has its own objective, policies and programmes.

Once all the area plans are formulated they are integrated together and one master marketing plan is made which guides the marketing objectives of the company. However, while developing this master marketing plan not only area plans considered, but due attention is also given to the programmes of intermediaries operating in the company's indirect channel. This helps the company in developing its vertical marketing system. Thus the scope of marketing planning covers both: those operations that are controlled by a company's marketing department and also those controlled by the company's intermediaries, in so far as these are relevant to the company's products.

5.1.2 Importance of Marketing Planning

The importance of marketing planning lies in the fact that it brings definite benefits to both the marketing planners and the business house. If activity is not preceded by planning then the actions taken will be disorganised and haphazard. Hence in order to have an orderly conduct of operations planning is definitely required. Apart from various other benefits following are the specific benefits which accrue from planning.

1. **Helps to foresee future developments:** Planning is the process of thinking before" doing. When the marketing planners undertake planning they are naturally compelled to think. This results in them analysing the past and predicting the future. This in turn leads them to identify probable events of relevance to the firm with a reasonable degree of accuracy so that they can formulate the relevant course of action to be taken well in advance so as to meet the marketing needs.

2. **Makes possible knowing of opportunities and preparation for handling of threats:** While identifying future developments management planners undertake a

scanning of the environment. This leads to both, locating the opportunities as well as identification of problem areas. This gives a chance to the management to consider the various areas of opportunities and threats well in advance so that best possible solutions can be formulated in time and as a result non rational responses to unexpected events and happenings will be considerably reduced. And considered and well thought out actions will be taken.

3. **Focus on Objectives:** When the marketing activities are planned, the marketing objective is the focus around which all the marketing policies, programmes, strategies, and procedures are built. As the marketing objectives serve as a measure of standard they will highlight all deviations whether good or bad. Thus timely corrective action will be possible and this will lead the company moving in the right direction that is towards the achievement of its objectives.

4. **It makes management by exception possible:** When marketing operations are planned the whole marketing programme is scheduled in terms of time and resources. This makes it possible for the marketing manager to delegate authority to his subordinates. He can thus concentrate on vital and important matters. This delegation and decentralisation brings in management by exception which in turn bring about the much desired efficiency in the organisation.

5. **Optimum utiltsation of resources:** When marketing operations are planned the time and resources available with the company are employed most economically and rationally. As a result there is optimum utilisation of resources and maximisation of the return on investment.

6. **Facilitates Co-ordination:** Marketing Planning facilitates co-ordination both horizontally and vertically. This is because any person located at any level in the marketing organisation can come to know through the marketing plan what the other has been doing at what time period. As a result, the jobs are synchronised in terms of time and content, and the overall marketing operation is integrated for maximum market impact.

7. **Cost Economy:** As marketing planning leads not only to an optimum use of resources but also to integrated working, the cost of the entire marketing programme' is considerably reduced. Thus planning' actually results in economy in cost.

8. **Planning acts as a basis for control:** Planning is the basis for control. A plan lays down standard of marketing performances against which the management measures and evaluates the organisation's performance. All deviations can be noted and corrective actions can be taken. In fact the complete control exercise is rooted in marketing planning.

5.1.3 Components of Marketing Planning

Marketing planning is composed of three basic components. They are: Objectives, Policies and Programmes.

1. Objectives: The first component of a' marketing plan is the marketing objective. The objective is the end towards which all marketing activities are directed. The marketing objectives usually answer the question where are we heading? Or What are we aiming at. In order to facilitate understanding marketing objectives may be divided into three parts, namely basic objectives; goals and targets. The basic objectives define the long range fundamental purpose of the company's marketing operations. They are not bound by time, nor are they quantifiable. Some examples of basic objectives are given below.

- To develop and maintain product leadership;
- To win the loyalty and co-operation of dealers;
- To improve and strengthen the company's long range profit outlook.

The marketing objectives may also be expressed as goals and targets. The marketing goals and targets are specific and not vague or philosophical like the basic objectives. The marketing goals are statements of specific. achievement standards whereas targets are the quantified expressions of these standards to be achieved within a given time frame. The basic marketing objectives, goals and targets are closely inter-related, the basic objectives shape goals which in turn shape targets.

2. Policies: Marketing policies are broad guidelines which guide the marketing personnel in decision making. Policies are general statements or understandings which guide or direct the thinking and decision making process of the subordinates. A policy limits the area of action. The examples of marketing policies include statements like the following:

- We will be competitive in price but not be a price cutter".
- Our after sale service will be most comprehensive".
- Wholesaler-retailer channel of distribution will be the king-pin of our distribution system".

3. Programmes: A marketing programme is a sequence of pre-determined marketing actions made after taking into account the time and resources available. A programme has to be formulated within the limits of the policies of the organisation and it should be designed in such a manner that it achieves the marketing objectives. A marketing programme is made up of procedures, rules and budgets.

5.1.4 Essential Requirements of Marketing Planning

The primary purpose of marketing planning is to increase 'managerial effectiveness'. Planning is nothing but a systematic approach for the management to consider the possible alternatives it faces. In recent years, planning has become' more formalised. There is a well-established procedure for management to follow for marketing planning. However a procedure that provides a technique should have the following characteristics or essentials.

1. **Planning should be simple:** The planning process or procedure should be simple. The planned programme works, only if the average manager is capable. of using it in spite of the day to day work-pressures that he has to face and in the absence of intensive training. In today's business world that is becoming more and more complex and competitive, it is very important that simplicity be maintained in planning. However simplicity should not be at the cost of producing results.

2. **Planning should be practical:** The planning process should be practical. It should be such that every manager at whatever level he may be benefits from it. If the benefits of planning accrue only to the top level managers then the lower level ones will extend only reluctant compliance and this will be followed by unwanted resentment. Thus it is very essential that planning be practical and beneficial to all. To make planning beneficial even to the average manager, the marketing manager should develop a practical process and should provide background information, training and technical assistance.

3. **Planning should be selective and adaptive:** The planning process must be so selective and adaptive that all the managers are covered. An eligibility to participate must not force the participants to use planning more than it is required specially in this area so that different areas of planning of each manager can be co-ordinated and consolidated.

4. **Planning should be flexible:** The planning process must be so flexible that it should be possible to change any portion of planning conveniently, with least cost, if anything happens warranting a change.

5. **Planning should be precise:** Future planning should be precise in terms of goals and objectives. In fact the future cannot be predicted with a high degree of accuracy, and further into the future you try to predict the less accurate you are. However there are three ways of expressing expected results namely general, specific and dynamically quantified. The third is the best way as it is the way in which precise statement is made so that the problem can be easily recognised. It facilitates quick and easy identification, detection and measurement of possible deviations.

6. **Planning should be based on reliable information:** For planning to be sound there is a requirement of reliable information on a continuous basis. The future estimate is neither a forecast nor a prediction but, a temporary hypothesis regarding an important, probable future development that could not be predicted with accuracy. The planner needs to have continuous feedback of information so that he can revise the estimate whenever there is a significant deviation.

7. **Planning should be synthesising and synchronising:** The planning process should be such that it co-ordinates and integrates all types of plans and planning. In each functional area there should be perfect synchronisation and synthesisation of functions. If planning does not co-ordinate and integrate all the subfunction in each area, the firm will have to pay a high price for time, effort, confusion, resistance, resentment and frustration.
8. **Planning should be motivating:** Planning in order to be effective needs the active participation of the managerial personnel. Planning will encourage people to participate provided they are motivated. Any properly designed planning process will motivate the personnel because, it will result in the following:
   - It gives the workers' a real sense of participating in the planning for their own future density.
   - It relieves apprehension by converting the unknown to known.
   - It provides security as to their position in the organisation.
   - It develops pride amongst the personnel to be part of an organisation that knows where it is, where it wants to go and how to get there.
9. **Planning should be accompanied with the least amount of paper work:** An effective planning system is one which gets all the work done with the least amount of paper work. All planning should not be reduced in writing. In fact the writing work can be reduced by following discussions and outlining; giving only the information that is required; avoiding duplicacy of information by providing common information from a common source
10. **Planning has to have a direction:** In order for the planning process to be most efficient, a special director for planning should be appointed whose only job will be not to do planning but only to oversee how it is working and show how it should work. He should be a planning specialist and should dedicate all his time only to ensure that successful and efficient planning takes place, and is properly implemented.

5.1.5 Difficulties in Marketing Planning

The planning process described above is a logical and rational way of determining the future course of marketing action in any company. It analyses the past, considers the present and projects the future so as to facilitate the marketing management of a company. However the process of planning is not without its problems. Some of the major problems faced by a marketing planner are highlighted below.

1. **The problem of accuracy in projecting the future:** One of the major problems in marketing planning is to accurately project the future on which the whole structure of planning is based. As far as projecting the future is concerned problems arise on two accounts. First and foremost there is a lack of reliable data and applicable

tools on whose basis sales and other marketing results are forecast. Secondly the market forces whose behaviour is to be predicted are very dynamic. In India reliable market information is not available and the facilities to process it are inadequate. As a result of this reliable and timely future predictions become difficult. This makes marketing planning problematic. However two alternatives have been suggested to overcome this problem. First the management may develop alternative sets of premises and alternative plans based on them so that major changes in future events may be readily reflected in action. And, second, management should be ready with detours in planning to allow for unforeseeable events. However, both the alternatives need flexibility of plan.

2. **Corporate Inflexibilities:** Another problem faced by a marketing planner is the inflexibilities built in the corporate working. Corporate inflexibilities refer to rigidities' and 'resistance of persons and systems operating in the company with regard to the changes contemplated by the marketing plan. These may be both internal-as well as external. Internal inflexibilities 'refer to the mental frame, attitudes, perceptions and behaviour of marketing and other personnel. The behaviour of the personnel may be so conditioned over a period of time that they may develop inflexibility and resist changes which a plan has envisaged. This is particularly so in old and established business houses. Similarly marketing systems policies, procedures, and rules tend to become so secure that there is an aversion to any change in them. Even investments made can act as impediments in marketing planning for e.g. the management may be very keen to recover the investment made in training of a particular salesman and may resist a marketing plan that writes of this training.

Apart from this internal inflexibilities marketing planning is plagued by external inflexibilities also. The external inflexibilities are rooted in the external environment of a company over which the marketing management has little or no control. These inflexibilities arise from the changes taking place in the culture and behaviour patterns of society, political climate, labour organisations and technological frame within which the organisation operates.

3. **Loss of Initiatives:** A closely knit comprehensive marketing plan stifles initiative because the participants are strictly tied to the set goals, targets, authorities and responsibilities. This discourages working with a free and open mind and therefore diminishes innovations in the marketing operations.

4. **The problem of work pressure:** One of the important problems faced by marketing planners is that marketing personnel are so much preoccupied with execution of marketing functions and solving day to day problems that they are

not left with sufficient time and energy to think and plan marketing operations. Such job pressures are normally caused by enlarged span of control, non-delegation of authority, and reluctance to plan. It is a problem which encourages management by crisis and does not let planning take off the ground.

5. **The cost of planning:** In order to come up with an effective marketing plan the company has to spend in terms of time, money and talent. The specific and logical steps required in marketing planning, all consume a good deal of money, time and talent. With all this the benefits of marketing planning are not available immediately. It has its own payoff period which is usually quite long. This discourages firms from undertaking marketing planning in the most systematic and scientific way. In spite of the above problems the relevance of marketing planning cannot be denied and no company should attempt action without a plan.

5.2 Product Level Planning

5.2.1 Introduction

The Marketing Environment is ever changing and dynamic. To be able to cope in such an environment, organisations need to not only create and retain satisfied customers, but also need to adapt to the continuously changing marketplace. This calls for a marketing plan.

5.2.2 What is a Plan?

A plan is the starting point of all activities. It is the means to achieve an objective. It is a stepwise approach to completion of any task. It is the road map of going from where we are to where we want to go.

A marketing plan basically is a systematic stepwise approach to achieving the marketing objectives. Here are some definitions of a Marketing Plan.

Definitions of a Marketing Plan
 (a) It is a sequential schedule of activities to achieve certain goals/objectives.
 (b) It is a process by which an organisation seeks to achieve its desired objectives with the optimum blend of available resources.
 (c) The part of the business plan outlining the marketing strategy for a product or service.
 (d) The marketing plan includes information such as the product or service offered, pricing, target market, competitors, marketing budget and promotional mix.

Before we proceed, we need to look at the concept of strategy and how it can be helpful in the planning process.

Strategy is defined as the art of defending yourself in the face of a competition. While preparing a plan it is of utmost importance that marketers prepare the plan keeping in view the competitive issues that are likely to arise and the alternatives that can be adopted to solve these problems.

5.2.3 Preparation and Evaluation of a Product Level Marketing Plan

Market Oriented Strategic Planning: It is the managerial process of developing and maintaining a viable fit between the organisation's objectives, skills, and resources and its changing marketing environment. The aim of strategic planning is to shape and reshape the organisation's businesses and products so that they yield target profits and growth.

Market Oriented Strategic Planning calls for organisations to work in three crucial areas. These areas are:

1. Managing the Organisation's business as an investment portfolio: The idea here is that each business has a different profit potential and allocation of resources amongst businesses, should be done according to this potential.

2. Assessing each business by considering the market's growth rate and the organisation's position to fit in that market. Basically the two parameters of the market growth rate and the organisations position in that market are key indicators that indicate if the organisation is doing well or not. Understanding the market position and alteration of plans to strengthen or consolidate the market position can be achieved through this.

3. The third key area is Strategy: The strategy is a game plan that the organisation must develop for achieving its objectives.

Most businesses operate at four levels. These are the,

- Corporate Level
- Divisional Level
- Business Unit Level
- Product Level

The Corporate Headquarters of the Organisation are responsible for designing the Corporate Strategic Plan to guide the entire organisation towards a profitable future. Each division establishes a divisional plan covering the allocation of funds to each business unit within the division. Each business unit further develops a business unit strategic plan to carry the business into a profitable future and finally each product level within the business unit develops a product specific marketing plan for achieving its objectives in the given product market.

A marketing plan operates at two levels. These levels are the,

- strategic level and the
- tactical level

The strategic marketing plan develops broad marketing objectives and strategies based on the analysis of the current marketing situation in terms of the opportunities that are available to the organisation.

The tactical marketing plan looks at the specific marketing tactics that include the promotions, the pricing, the merchandising, the channel management etc.

We can say that the marketing plan is the main tool or instrument for managing the entire marketing effort. In most organisations, the marketing departments would prepare the marketing plans; these plans are then implemented at the appropriate time and at the appropriate levels. Results are then monitored and corrective actions or changes to the plans are made as required.

The complete planning, implementation and control cycle is shown in Fig. 5.1 below:

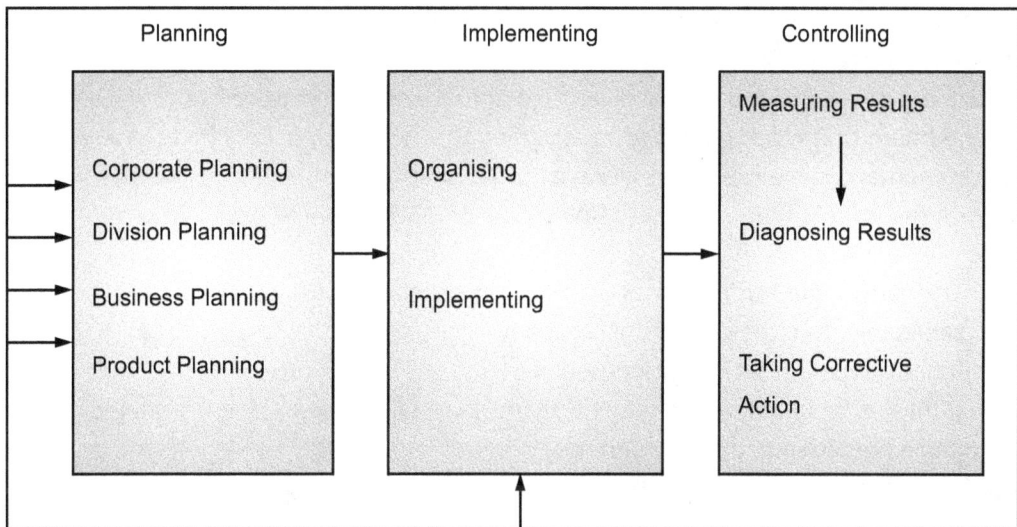

Fig. 5.1: The Strategic Planning, Implementing and Control Process

Let us study this process in detail:

Corporate and Divisional Strategic Planning: As mentioned earlier the Corporate Headquarters are responsible for the corporate plans and also for setting the planning process rolling. There are four basic activities that must be undertaken for this purpose. They are:

Defining the Corporate Mission

Defining the Corporate mission involves articulating the Business that the Organisation is in, defining who the customer is, defining the value that the organisation wants to give to the customer and also mentioning the future of the business. The Organisation's mission is shaped by five elements. These are:
- History of the Organisation
- Current preferences of the Owners and the Management
- The market environment
- Distinctive Competencies

Organisations share their mission statements with all the Top Management personnel, the Stakeholders as well as customers. The Mission statement provides the organisation with a clear purpose and direction to carry out its activities.

A good mission statement will have three basic characteristics. They are:
- They will focus on limited number of goals
- Emphasise the major policies and values
- Define the major competitive scopes within which the organisation will operate like the scope of the industry, the products and the application scope, competence scope, market segment scope, the vertical scope and the geographical scope.

Establishing Strategic Business Units

Most organisations today are diversified into several businesses and it needs to be mentioned here that what applies to one business or what works for one business, may not work for another. Hence it is necessary that organisations treat every business as a separate entity or a separate Strategic Business Unit (SBU). An SBU has three basic characteristics. They are:
- They are single businesses or a collection of related businesses that can be planned separately from the rest of the company.
- It has a separate set of competitors.
- It has a separate management team that takes care of its strategic planning, implementation and profit earning.

Assigning Resources to each Strategic Business Unit

The main purpose behind having separate strategic business units is to develop separate strategies and allocate or assign appropriate funding. In every business unit, one will find a portfolio of products. Of the entire portfolio of products, some products will be those that are not performing too well, while there will be some which are the star performers and yet others that perform at an average level. The organisation needs to allocate resources to each product in the portfolio depending upon its capability to earn profits or depending upon its profit potential.

Methods of Portfolio analysis

There are a few common methods that are used to carry out portfolio analysis. Let us take a look at these methods:

(a) BCG Matrix: BCG matrix is a chart that had been created by Bruce Henderson for the Boston Consulting Group in 1968 to help corporations with analysing their business units or product lines.

The BCG matrix has a relative market share on one axis and the growth rates on other axis. The graph has four quadrants and the products are classified as Stars, Question marks, Dogs and Cash Cows depending on the quadrant they fall into.

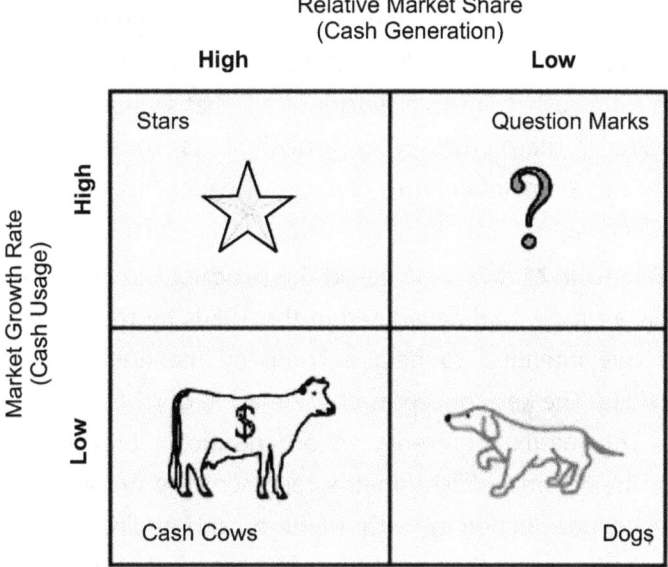

Fig. 5.2: BCG Matrix

- **Cash cows** are products with high market share in a slow-growing industry. Typically they generate cash in excess of the amount of cash needed to maintain the product business. They are regarded as staid and boring, in a 'mature' market, and most organisations would be thrilled to own as many as possible. They are to be 'milked' continuously with as little investment as possible, since such investment would be wasted in an industry with low growth.

- **Dogs**, or more charitably called *pets*, are products with low market share in a mature, slow-growing industry. These products typically 'break even', generating barely enough cash to maintain the product's market share. Such products are generally considered worthless, not generating cash for the company. They depress a profitable company's 'return on assets' ratio used by many investors to judge how well a company is being managed. *Dogs*, it is thought, should be sold off.

- **Question marks** (also known as problem child) are growing rapidly and thus consume large amounts of cash, but because they have low market shares, they **do not generate much cash**. The result is a large net cash consumption. A question mark has the potential to gain market share and become a star, and eventually a cash cow when the market growth slows. If the question mark does not succeed in becoming the market leader, then after perhaps years of cash consumption, it will degenerate into a dog when the market growth declines. Question marks must be analysed carefully in order to determine whether they are worth the investment required to grow the market share.

- **Stars** are products with a high market share in a fast-growing industry. The hope is that *stars* become the next *cash cows*. Sustaining the product's market leadership may require extra cash, but this is worthwhile if that's what it takes for the product to remain a leader in the market. When growth slows, stars become *cash cows* if they have been able to maintain their category leadership, or they move from brief *stardom* to *dogdom*.

(b) Life Cycle Portfolio Matrix: Also called the **product life cycle portfolio matrix** and the **ADL matrix**, it is a simple tool developed in the 1980s by the professional services firm Arthur D. Little. It was intended to help a company manage its collection of product businesses as a portfolio. The key concept is consideration of where each product is within its business life cycle. The matrix represents an organisation's products in a 2-dimensional matrix. In this case, the columns of the matrix represent the growth stage of the business product (embryonic or introduction, growth, maturity, and ageing or decline) and the rows represent the product's competitive position in the market place (dominant, strong, favourable, tenable, or weak or non-viable). This results in a 4 by 5 matrix with 20 cells. The company's various products are placed within the matrix, and the positions are associated with logical business strategies as shown below.

Life Cycle Stage

Competitive Position	Embryonic	Growth	Mature	Ageing
Dominant	All out push for share. Hold position.	Hold position. Hold share.	Hold position. Grow with industry.	Hold position.
Strong	Attempt to improve position. All out push for share.	Attempt to improve position. Push for share.	Hold position Grow with industry.	Hold position or harvest.
Favourable	Selective or all out push for share. Selectively attempt to improve position.	Attempt to improve position. Selective push for share.	Custodial or maintenance. Find niche and attempt to protect it.	Harvest or phased out withdrawal.
Tenable	Selective push for position.	Find niche and protect it.	Find niche and hang on or phased out withdrawal.	Phased out withdrawal, or abandon.
Weak, non-viable	Up or out.	Turnaround or abandon.	Turnaround or phased out withdrawal.	Abandon.

- Broad spectrum of strategic options
- Selective development
- Withdrawal to niche, divestiture or liquidation

Fig. 5.3: Life Cycle Portfolio Planning Matrix

The distribution and trajectory of the businesses across the matrix helps indicate whether the firm's product mix is well-balanced now and in the future. For example, the company will need to maintain a continuing set of mature businesses in order to generate cash to support new embryonic and growth operations.

(c) GE Matrix: The GE/McKinsey Matrix was developed jointly by McKinsey and General Electric in the early 1970s as a derivation of the BCG Matrix. GE, by that time, had approximately 150 different business units and was disappointed with the profits derived from its investments. While exploring new models to implement, GE started to be interested in visual strategic frameworks like the Growth-Share Matrix created by the Boston Consulting Group (BCG) a few years before. However, the BCG Matrix proved to have some limitations. It was not found to be flexible enough to include all the issues that a company would face while operating in a fast changing global environment. The GE/McKinsey Matrix solves most of the issues of the BCG model and proposes a more sophisticated and comprehensive approach to portfolio analysis.

The nine-box matrix provides decision makers with a systematic and effective framework for a decentralised corporation to make better supported investment decisions, and for developing strategies for future product development or new market segment entries. Instead of looking solely at each unit's future prospects, a corporation can adopt a multi-dimensional approach based on two components that will indicate how well the unit will perform in the future. The two components used to evaluate businesses/products, which also serve as the axes of the matrix, are the 'attractiveness' of the relevant industry and the unit's 'competitive strength' within the same industry. Each axis is then divided into Low, Medium and High.

External factors affect Market Attractiveness	Internal factors affect Competitive Strength of a SBU
• Market size • Market growth rate • Market profitability • Pricing trends • Competitive intensity / rivalry • Risk returns in the industry • Entry barriers • Opportunity to differentiate products • Demand variability • Segmentation • Distribution structure • Technology development	• Strength of assets or competencies • Relative brand strength (marketing) • Market share • Market share growth • Customer loyalty • Relative cost position (cost structure compared with competitors) • Relative profits margins (compared to competitors) • Distribution strength and production capacity • Record of technological or other innovation • Quality • Access to financial or other investment resources • Management strength

Fig. 5.4: Factors that influence the axes of the GE/McKinsey Matrix

Although the GE matrix is primarily used in Portfolio Analysis for various businesses, it has also been successfully applied to the product portfolio for various organisations.

Resource allocation recommendations can be made to grow, hold, harvest or divest certain products.

Invest/ Grow: The first zone represents an opportunity to grow through investment and expansion. It is characterised by the presence of both business/product strength and industry attractiveness. The organisation should invest in and grow strong businesses/products in attractive industries, average businesses/products in attractive industries and strong businesses/products in average industries.

Earn Selectively: This zone represents a mixed situation in which a large growth potential does not exist. Here, the company should earn selectively by holding average businesses/products in average industries, strong businesses/products in weak industries and weak businesses/products in attractive industries.

Harvest/Divest: The third zone is a clear situation where the organisation needs to stop. Here the ideal strategy would be to withdraw from the business. In harvesting, the withdrawal is not immediate. The organisation needs to harvest weak businesses/products in unattractive industries, average businesses/products in unattractive industries and weak businesses/products in average industries. Within the harvest zone, the organisation may think of quickly divesting itself of a weak business/product in an unattractive industry.

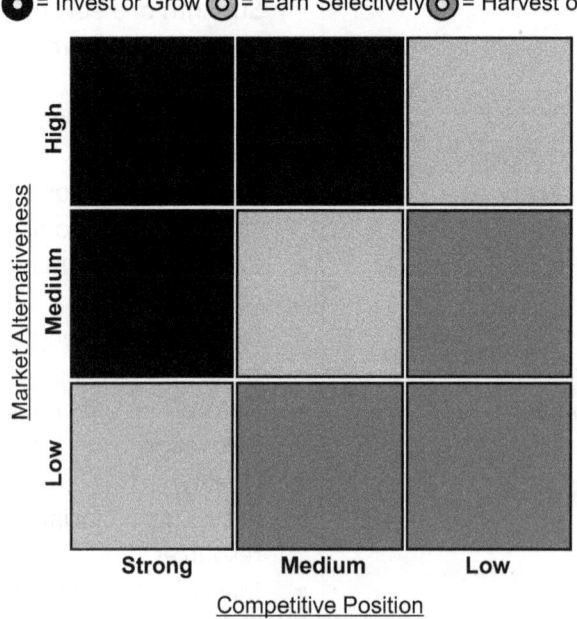

Fig. 5.5: GE Nine Cell Matrix

Appraisal of Portfolio Analysis Models:

(a) Portfolio models are easy to use and give the organisation an idea of the strong and weak products in the product portfolio. However, many a time, there is a chance of laying too much emphasis on the market share while ignoring other relevant factors.

(b) Many products often end up with a position in the middle of the matrix, making it difficult to adopt a particular strategy for the product.

(c) The portfolio analysis models do not take into consideration the other market factors like inflation, which do have a bearing on the cash flow and profitability of the business.

(d) An organisation having varied product lines might find it difficult locating the product in the correct market segment.

(e) Finally, it is also seen that the top management might find it difficult to induce the organisation to accept the idea of strategic portfolio analysis approach.

Business Strategic Planning:

After studying the Corporate Management's Strategic-planning tasks, we can now focus on the strategic planning tasks that managers of individual business units are required to undertake. The Business-unit strategic planning process is an eight step process. It includes the following:

- Business Mission
- External Environment Analysis (Opportunities and Threats)
- Internal Environment Analysis (Strength and Weaknesses)
- Goal Formulation
- Strategy Formulation
- Programme Formulation
- Implementation
- Feedback and Control

Diagrammatically this process can be shown as follows:

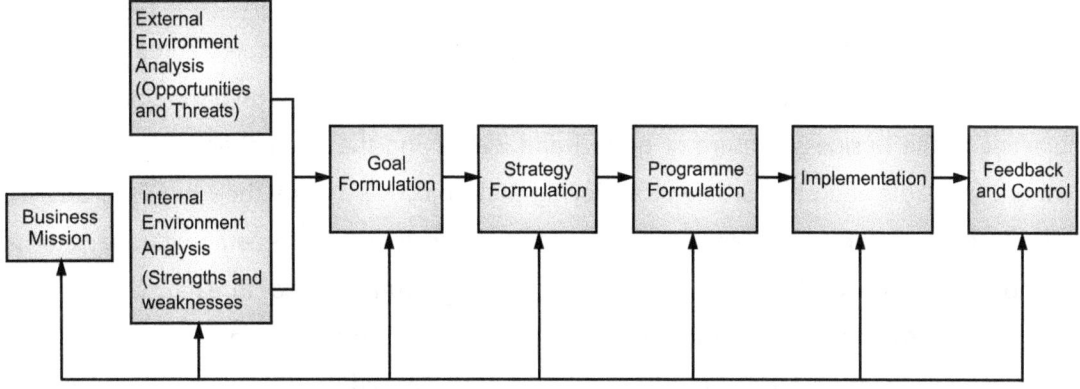

Fig. 5.6: The Business Strategic Planning Process

Business Mission

Each Business Unit needs to define its mission and this mission should be within the broad framework of the organisation's overall mission. In other words, the business unit needs to align its mission with the organisational mission.

SWOT analysis

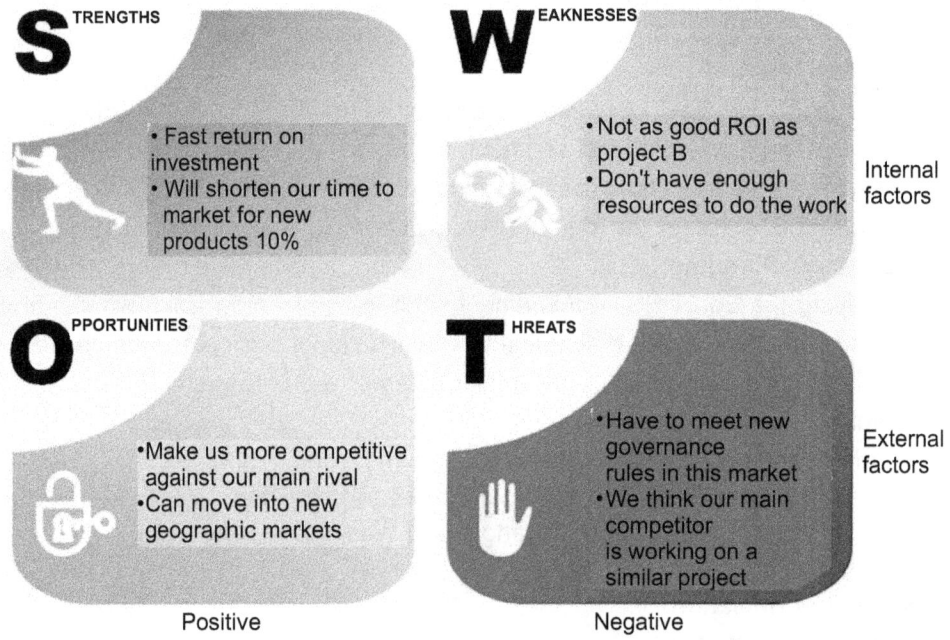

Fig. 5.7: SWOT Analysis

A tool that identifies the **S**trengths, **W**eaknesses, **O**pportunities and **T**hreats of an organisation. Specifically, SWOT is a basic, straightforward model that assesses what an organisation can and cannot do as well as its potential opportunities and threats. A SWOT analysis can be carried out for a product, place, industry or person. It involves specifying the objective of the business venture or project and identifying the internal and external factors that are favorable and unfavorable to achieving that objective. The method of SWOT analysis is to take the information from an environmental analysis and separate it into internal (strengths and weaknesses) and external issues (opportunities and threats). Once this is completed, SWOT analysis determines what may assist the firm in accomplishing its objectives, and what obstacles must be overcome or minimised to achieve desired results.

Setting the objective should be done after the SWOT analysis has been performed. This would allow achievable goals or objectives to be set for the organisation.

- **Strengths:** Characteristics of the business or project that give it an advantage over others.
- **Weaknesses:** Characteristics that place the team at a disadvantage relative to others.
- **Opportunities:** Elements that the project could exploit to its advantage.
- **Threats:** Elements in the environment that could cause trouble for the business or project.

Identification of SWOTs is important because they can help in forming later steps in planning to achieve the objective.

First, the decision makers should consider whether the objective is attainable, given the SWOTs. If the objective is not attainable a different objective must be selected and the process repeated.

Users of SWOT analysis need to ask and answer questions that generate meaningful information for each category (strengths, weaknesses, opportunities, and threats) to make the analysis useful and find their competitive advantage.

SWOT analysis aims to identify the key internal and external factors seen as important to achieving an objective. The factors come from within a company's unique value chain. SWOT analysis groups key pieces of information into two main categories:

Internal factors: The strengths and weaknesses internal to the organisation.

External factors: The opportunities and threats presented by the environment external to the organisation.

Analysis may view the internal factors as strengths or as weaknesses depending upon their effect on the organisation's objectives. What may represent strengths with respect to one objective may be weaknesses (distractions, competition) for another objective. The factors may include all of the 4Ps; as well as personnel, finance, manufacturing capabilities, and so on.

The external factors may include macroeconomic matters, technological change, legislation, and socio-cultural changes, as well as changes in the marketplace or in competitive position. The results are often presented in the form of a matrix.

SWOT analysis is just one method of categorisation and has its own weaknesses. For example, it may tend to persuade its users to compile lists rather than to think about actual important factors in achieving objectives. It also presents the resulting lists uncritically and without clear prioritisation so that, for example, weak opportunities may appear to balance strong threats.

It is prudent not to eliminate any candidate SWOT entry too quickly. The importance of individual SWOTs will be revealed by the value of the strategies they generate. A SWOT item that produces valuable strategies is important. A SWOT item that generates no strategies is not important.

External Environment Analysis: Macro Environmental forces like the demographic forces, economic forces, political and legal forces and Micro Environmental factors such as, Customers, Competitors, Distributors and suppliers all affect the Business. Organisations need to continuously monitor these forces and factors, to be able to identify suitable opportunities and probable threats.

A Marketing Opportunity is an area of potential interest in which the organisation can perform well and has sustainable competencies. After spotting the opportunity the Organisation needs to conduct a Marketing Opportunity Analysis (MOA) to determine the attractiveness and success probability of the opportunity.

Internal Environmental Analysis: To be able to take advantage of the available opportunities, it is necessary that the organisation evaluate its own strengths and weaknesses. The major decision to be taken here is whether the organisation should restrict itself to only those opportunities where it possesses the required strengths or consider better opportunities where it does not have all the requisite strengths and would have to develop these strengths.

Goal Formulation

Once the SWOT analysis has been done, the organisation can now proceed to develop goals for the specified period. Goals are the objectives of the organisation within a specified time frame. They could relate to Market Share Improvement, Sales Growth, Profitability, Innovation or other similar areas. The Business units first set the objectives and then Manage by the Objectives (MBO). For MBO to work there are four characteristics that the objectives must have. They are:

- Objectives must be arranged hierarchically
- Objectives must be in definite terms and wherever possible quantitatively
- They should be realistic
- They should be consistent

Strategy Formulation

Goals/Objectives: Goals and objectives entail what the organisation is trying to achieve and its aim. Strategy on the other hand is the game plan for ensuring that the goals are achieved. Each organisation must prepare a strategy of a marketing strategy, a complementing technology strategy and a sourcing strategy.

Porter's Generic strategies are used by many Organisations as a starting point for their strategy formulation exercise. There are three basic strategies that Porter has given. These are:

Overall Cost Leadership: Here the strategy focuses on achieving the lowest production and distribution costs to be able to grab a large market share through lower costs.

Differentiation: In this strategy the organisation focuses on being different from other competitors by achieving superior performance in an area that is valued by the customer. The organisation works towards achieving those strengths that will lead to the superior performance.

Focus: In this strategy, the organisation does not look for a large market share, but focuses on a narrow market segment and tries to develop either cost leadership or differentiation for that segment.

Program Formulation and Implementation: Once the strategies have been formulated they need to be worked out in detail with the help of detailed supporting programmes. These supporting programmes should include all details about the costs as well as the implementation process.

Good strategies if not implemented properly can lead to a disaster.

Feedback and Control: As the implementation process begins, the organisation needs to track and monitor the results at every stage. Monitoring the performance and taking corrective action at every stage is an essential component of the Business Strategic planning process.

Product Level Planning: We have seen that each product level, within a business unit must develop a marketing plan for achieving its goals. For this the organisation needs to prepare a Marketing plan within the Business Unit.

5.2.4 Nature of a Marketing Plan

The marketing plan is an important output of the entire marketing process. It is a blueprint of what has to be achieved and how it is to be achieved. It is a stepwise systematic approach in achieving the goals and objectives for every product in the business line.

The marketing plan is futuristic and flexible by nature. It also acts as an interface or linkage between various departments of the organisation.

  (i) **Futuristic:** A plan is always prepared for something that is yet to happen. It is made for a future event. Hence by nature the marketing plan is futuristic. It does not have a retrospective nature. It is always about the future.

  (ii) **Interface/Linkage:** Any plan requires that all the components (departments of the organisations, people) of the plan work together in tandem. A plan by nature establishes linkages and acts as an interface.

(iii) Flexible/Dynamic: Since the plan is about the future and the future is always uncertain; by nature the plan must be flexible and dynamic. The marketplace, the consumers are ever changing. In such a situation, it may be required that the original plan be modified or changed. The plan has to have this inbuilt flexibility.

5.2.5 Contents of a Marketing Plan

Having seen the nature of the marketing plan, let us now see what the marketing plan really looks like and what are the contents of the marketing plan. The marketing plan begins with an executive summary and ends with the specification of the controls that are required to make the plan successful. The sections of the marketing plan are as follows:

- Executive Summary and Table of Contents
- Current Marketing Situation
- Macroenvironment Situation
- Opportunity and Issue Analysis
- Objectives
- Marketing Strategy
- Action Programmes
- Projected Profit and Loss statements
- Controls

1. **Executive Summary and Table of Contents**

   Any plan that has been made and needs to be implemented must have the approval of the top management. In cases of the marketing plan, the top management would comprise of the General Manager Marketing or the Vice President Marketing or the Director Marketing (depending upon the organisation). An Executive summary is prepared to give an overview of the entire plan. The members of the top management are usually very busy and would not want to waste their time on reading through the entire plan. The executive summary gives them an overview enabling them to decide if the entire plan is worthy of their time and attention.

   The marketing plan generally begins with a brief summary mentioning the plan's main goals and recommendations.

2. **Current Marketing Situation**

   The current marketing situation informs the person reading the plan, about the details of the market situation, the product situation, the competitive situation, the distribution situation and the macro environmental situation.

   - **Market Situation:** This section presents the reader with an overview of the market. The planner presents data on the target market. The present size of the market and the rate at which the market is currently growing. This data is also presented for the past several years to enable the reader to build an understanding of the growth trends in the market. Also data on consumer behaviour, buying trends and various geographical segments are presented.

- **Product Situation:** The plan will have a description about the product, its features, its unique selling proposition and why there is a need for the product in the market and the market potential. In addition to this the sales, prices, margins and net profits for each major product in the product line for the past several years are shown.
- **Competitive Situation:** The plan will also mention about competing or substitute products in the market. The market share that these products claim and reasons as to why the organisation's own product will work in the market. The major competitors are identified and described in terms of their size, their market share, the product quality and other characteristics that are relevant in the market.
- **Distribution Situation:** The plan will mention regarding the current distribution scenario, available channels of distribution and also about the probable channels that can be adopted. This section will present data on the size of the various distribution channels and how they can be used.

3. **Macro environment Situation**

    The plan will also give a brief summary about the macro-environmental situation, highlighting the trends in the macro-environment. It will highlight the demographic, economic, technological, political and legal and socio-cultural trends that are likely to have an impact on the future of the product.

4. **Opportunity and Issue Analysis**

    Here the planner will carry out a SWOT analysis. That is an analysis of the strengths, weaknesses, opportunities and threats that the product line is likely to encounter. The plan will detail about what opportunities exist in the market, what are the issues facing the organisation in context of the plan and how the plan if implemented, can help the organisation to avail the opportunities and tackle the issues. On the basis of the SWOT analysis the plan goes ahead to discuss the issues that the organisation needs to address.

5. **Objectives**

    Having said this, the plan will now entail the main objectives of the entire project and also state how these objectives concur with the overall objectives of the organisation. Here the two major objectives must be set. They are the Financial Objectives and the Marketing Objectives.

    - **Financial Objectives:** The financial objectives are in terms of the financial figures that need to be achieved like the annual rate of return on investment, the net profits, the cash flow etc. The financial objectives are further converted into marketing objectives.
    - **Marketing Objectives:** Here the plan specifies the marketing objectives again in terms of figures so that there is clarity about what needs to be achieved.

    The marketing objectives cover the total sales volume, total sales revenue, the market share etc.

6. Marketing Strategy

In the next step the plan will lay out the marketing strategy in terms of what will actually be done and how the competition will be tackled. In short the broad game plan to achieve the desired results is laid down. The Marketing Strategy is generally presented in a list form. To cite an example for a high end cell phone it would be as follows:

- **Target Market:** Upper Middle class and Upper class.
- **Positioning:** The most technologically advanced cell phone with never before features.
- **Product Line:** Two lower priced models.
- **Price:** Above competition.
- **Distribution Outlets:** In all multi-gadget electronic stores as well as exclusive brand outlets.
- **Sales Force:** Expand by 5%.
- **Service:** Available 24X7 and quickly.
- **Advertising:** Develop a new campaign and increase budget by 20%.
- **Sales Promotion:** Increase sale promotion budget by 10% and participate in all trade shows.
- **Research and Development:** Increase expenditure by 20% to bring out more innovative features.
- **Marketing Research:** Increase expenditure by 5% to get more information about consumer buying behaviour.

7. Action Programmes

The action programmes in this plan will further narrow down on each aspect of the marketing mix and give an insight into what will be done with regards to each of the marketing mix elements. Each element of the strategy is worked out with respect to what will be done, how it will be done, who will do it, when it will be done etc.

8. Projected Profit and Loss Statements

The plan will also include projected profit and loss statements. These statements would enable the Top management to evaluate the plan from a financial perspective.

9. Controls

Controls would specify the validity and check points to ensure smooth running of the plan.

In short the marketing plan is a blueprint that will tell the organisation, what to do, why to do, when to do, how to do and what will be the outcome.

5.3 Marketing Evaluation and Control

No marketing process, even the most carefully developed, is guaranteed to result in maximum benefit for a company. In addition, because every market is changing constantly, a strategy that is effective today may not be effective in the future. It is important to evaluate a marketing programme periodically to be sure that it is achieving its objectives.

Having prepared all the pans it is now time to implement these plans. This process is known as marketing implementation.

Marketing Implementation is the process that turns marketing plans into action assignments and ensures that such assignments are executed in a manner that accomplishes the plan's stated objectives.

5.3.1 Marketing Implementation and Evaluation Skills

The organisation needs to possess specific skills to effectively implement any marketing programme. These skills are:

- **Allocating:** Allocating skills are extremely important from the point of view of allocating budgets and planning the various available resources like money, personnel and time.
- **Monitoring:** Monitoring skills are required to evaluate the results of the marketing plan and to check whether they are in line with the plan.
- **Organising:** Organising skills are required to build an organisation that can carry out all the tasks effectively.
- **Interacting:** Last but not the least is interacting skills. These are required to get things done by influencing people. These skills are required not only to motivate the organisation's own people but also to influence other stakeholders like the intermediaries, the suppliers, the research firms, the advertising agencies etc.

Once the implementation of the marketing plan has taken place, the next step would be controlling the market.

5.3.2 Controlling the Marketing Activity

In spite of the best efforts, there are always chances that things may not happen as per the plan in the implementation stage. As a result, plans would need to be continuously monitored and altered to ensure that things do not go wrong.

This is known as **marketing control**.

The Control process for all types of controls involves four steps:

1. In the first step, the Management or the person who has been allocated the responsibility sets the objectives, the goals or the targets for a pre-decided period.
2. In the second step, the Management monitors its performance in the market place.

3. Based on step no. 2, the Management determines the causes for major or serious performance deviations.
4. In the last step, the Management takes corrective actions to close the gaps between goals and performances.

Annual Plan Control

The aim of this control is to ensure that the organisation achieves its targeted sales, profits and other goals for the said annual period. The basis of annual-plan control is managerial objectives—that is to say, specific goals, such as sales and profitability that are established on a monthly or quarterly basis. Organisations use five tools to monitor plan performance.

These are:
(a) Sales Analysis.
(b) Market Share Analysis.
(c) Marketing Expense to Sales Analysis.
(d) Financial Analysis.
(e) Market Based Scorecard Analysis.

(a) Sales Analysis

This involves measuring the actual sales in comparison to the set targets or goals. The Two specific tools used in the sales analysis are:
(i) Sales Variance analysis and
(ii) Microsales analysis.

(i) **Sales variance analysis** measures the relative contribution of different factors to a gap in sales performance.

Example: Suppose as per the annual plan an organisation is supposed to sell 12,000 note books for the entire year at the rate of ₹ 70/- per book, for a total revenue of ₹ 8,40,000/-. At the end of the two months it is seen that only 500 books are sold at a rate of ₹ 50/- per book to generate a total revenue of ₹ 25000/-.

Here the organisation needs to know how much of the sales variance is due to the price; and how much is due to the quantity.

So we know:

12,000 notebooks @ ₹ 70 → ₹ 8,40,000

But end of 2 months:

Only 500 sold at ₹ 50 → ₹ 25,000

Hence,

Variance due to decline in price is (₹ 70 – ₹ 50) (500) = ₹ 10,000

Variance due to decline in volume is (₹ 70) (2000 – 500) = ₹ 1,05,000

(ii) **Microsales Analysis:** The sales of specific products, territories, sales persons etc who have failed to perform up to the expected set target level.

(b) Market Share Analysis

Organisations need to know how they are performing in relation to their competitors. This can be done in three ways:

- **Overall Market Share:** It is the organisation's sales expressed as a percentage of the total market sales.
- **Served Market Share:** It is the organisation's sales expressed as a percentage of the total sales to its served market. The served market comprises of all buyers who are willing and able to buy its products. The served market share is always larger than the overall market share.
- **Relative Market Share:** It can be expressed as a market share in relation to the biggest competitor. If the relative market share is over 100%, it means that the organisation is a market leader.

Another useful way to analyse the market share, is in terms of four components

$$\text{Overall Market Share} = \text{Customer Penetration} \times \text{Customer Loyalty} \times \text{Customer Selectivity} \times \text{Price Selectivity}$$

Customer penetration is the percentage of all customers who buy from the organisation.

Customer Loyalty is the purchases from the organisation by its customers, expressed as a percentage of their total purchases from other suppliers of the same products.

Customer Selectivity is the size of the average customer purchase from the organisation, expressed as the size of the average customer purchase from an average organisation.

Price Selectivity is the average price charged by the organisation, expressed as a percentage of the average price charged by all the organisations.

A reduction in the overall market share means that the organisation is not performing well on any of the above four parameters.

(c) Market-expense-to-sales ratio

It is necessary to monitor that an organisation is not overspending to achieve its sales targets. For this the marketing expense to sales ratio must be monitored. There are several components of this ratio like expense-to-sales ratio, sales force-to-sales ratio, advertising-to-sales ratio, sales administration-to-sales ratio and marketing research-to-sales ratio.

(d) Financial Analysis

The expense-to-sales ratio should be analysed in the overall financial framework to determine how and where the organisation is making its money; which simply means, look into the areas which are profitable.

Financial analysis can be used by the Management to identify those factors that affect the organisation's rate of return on its net worth. The main factors that affect the organisation's rate of return on the net worth and their calculations are as follows:

- Profit Margin = Net profits/Net Sales
- Asset Turnover = Net Sales/ Total Assets
- Return on assets = Net Profit/Total Assets
- Financial Leverage = Total Assets/ Net Worth
- Rate of return on net worth = Net Profits/ Net Worth

Basically the rate of return on the net worth is a product of the organisation's return on its assets and the financial leverage.

To increase the rate of return on the net worth, the organisation must increase either of these two factors:

(i) Return on assets or
(ii) The financial leverage.

For this the organisation will be required to analyse the composition of its assets and see if the asset management can be improved.

Return on assets can be improved by improving the profit margin. For improving the profit margin, the organisation must increase profits by increasing the sales or by cutting the costs in some way.

Similarly return on assets can also be improved by improving the asset turnover ratio. This can be done by increasing the sales or reducing the assets (e.g. inventory, receivables etc) that are held at a given level of sales.

(e) Market Based Score Card Analysis

The measures that we have studied so far are mostly financial in nature. However, financial factors are not the only indicators of the Organisation's health. The organisation can also look at other different measures like the Market based Score Card.

The Market Based Score Card is made up of two kinds of scorecards:

- Customer Performance Score Card
- Stakeholder Performance Score Card

The Customer Performance Score Card will look at various measures such as:

- New Customers
- Dissatisfied Customers
- Lost Customers
- Target Market Awareness
- Relative Product Quality
- Relative Service Quality
- Target Market Preference

The Organisation should set a benchmark or target figures, for each of these parameters, and monitor them, to ensure that they are as desired.

The stakeholder score card will look at monitoring the stakeholders of the organisation like:

- Employees
- Suppliers
- Banks
- Distributors
- Retailers
- Stockholders
- Shareholders

Their opinion should be monitored from time to time and dissatisfaction should be registered and taken care of.

5.3.3 Profitability Control

Profitability control and efficiency control allow a company to closely monitor its sales, profits, and expenditures. Profitability control demonstrates the relative profit-earning capacity of a company's different products and consumer groups. Companies are frequently surprised to find that a small percentage of their products and customers contribute to a large percentage of their profits. This knowledge helps a company allocate its resources and effort..

Marketing Profitability Analysis is a four step process. This includes

(a) **Identifying the Functional Expenses:** The functional expenses includes expenses that are incurred to sell the product, expenses that are incurred to advertise the product, expenses that are incurred to pack and deliver the product etc. The other expenses like salaries, rent, supplies etc are then allocated to the functional expenses. For e.g. If the salary of the sales person is ₹ 25,000/- and that of the advertising Manager is ₹ 35,000/-, then ₹ 25,000/- is allocated to selling and ₹ 35,000/- is allocated to advertising.

(b) **Assigning Functional Expenses to the Marketing Entities:** The next step is to measure how much functional expenses was associated with each type of channel. This is done by calculating the sales made by each channel. The selling expense for each channel and selling expense per call through that channel is also determined.
Similarly the advertising expense can be calculated on the basis of number of advertisements allocated to each channel.
Packing and Delivery expense is allocated based on the number of orders placed by each type of channel.

(c) **Prepare a Profit and Loss Statement for each Marketing Entity:** Based on step number (b) above, a separate profit and loss statement can be prepared for each type of channel. This analysis will tell the organisation about those channels through which it is losing money and those channels that are the profitable ones.

(d) Determining the Best Corrective Action: Based on the results seen in the profit and loss statements, the organisation can choose to stop selling through the loss making channels or take some corrective action in those areas and concentrate on the profitable ones.

Similarly the same exercise can be carried out for products or territories or other marketing entities.

Efficiency Control: Efficiency control involves micro-level analysis of the various elements of the marketing mix, including sales force, advertising, sales promotion, and distribution. For example, to understand its sales-force efficiency, a company may keep track of how many sales calls a representative makes each day, how long each call lasts, and how much each call costs and generates in revenue. This type of analysis highlights areas in which companies can manage their marketing efforts in a more productive and cost-effective manner.

This includes an analysis of:
- Sales force Efficiency.
- Advertising Efficiency.
- Sales promotion Efficiency.
- Distribution Efficiency.

In short we can say that efficiency control monitors the efficiency of all the areas where there is spending on marketing activities like salespersons, advertising and sales promotion.

Sales Force Efficiency: It is necessary for Managers to monitor the performance of their sales persons. Some of the Key Performance Indicators (KPI's) for sales force personnel are:
- Average number of sales calls per day.
- Average sales-call time per contact.
- Average revenue per sales call.
- Average cost per sales call.
- Entertainment cost per sales call.
- Percentage of orders per 100 sales calls.
- Number of new customers added for a specified period.
- Number of customers lost for a specified period.
- Sales force cost as a percentage of the total sales.

These measures will give the organisation an insight into those areas that are lacking in performance and necessary improvements can be made accordingly. For e.g. If it is found that while the average number of sales calls per day for most sales persons are between 5 to 8. However some salespersons are able to do only 2 calls per day. Then these sales persons can be sent for training to improve their efficiency.

Advertising Efficiency: Although the task of determining the output or measuring the results of advertising investments is a difficult one, organisations can try to keep track of the following:

- Advertising cost per thousand target buyers reached by the media vehicle.
- Percentage of audience who noted, saw or associated and read most of each print advertisement.
- Consumer opinions on the advertisement's content and effectiveness.
- Before and after measures of attitude towards the product.
- Number of inquiries generated by the advertisement.
- Cost per inquiry.

If it is found that there are issues in any of the above mentioned areas, the Management can take corrective action to improve the advertising efficiency. This can also be done by positioning the product better, defining objectives, pretesting the messages, using computer technology to guide media selection, try to get better media buys and also conduct post testing.

Sales Promotion Efficiency: Each sales promotion campaign entails some cost to the organisation. To improve the efficiency of sales promotion activities, the Management needs to monitor the costs for each campaign and the impact of the promotion on the sales. For this the following key parameters need to be monitored:

- Percentage of sales sold on deal.
- Display costs per sales rupee.
- Percentage of coupons redeemed.
- Number of inquiries resulting from demonstration.

An analysis of these parameters will also provide insights into the most cost-effective sales promotion method.

Distribution Efficiency: To be able to bring about efficient distribution, the organisation needs to monitor all the components of the distribution system like inventories, warehouse location and transportation modes. It should monitor and measure:

- Logistics cost as a percentage of sales
- Percentage of orders filled correctly
- Percentage of in time deliveries
- Number of billing errors.

The main task here is to reduce inventories while speeding the order-to-delivery cycle.

5.3.4 Strategic Control

Apart from control of various areas like sales force, sales promotion and advertising, organisations need to monitor and control the overall marketing effectiveness with terms to achievement of the goals.

Strategic control processes allow managers to evaluate a company's marketing programme from a critical long-term perspective. This involves a detailed and objective analysis of a company's organisation and its ability to maximise its strengths and market opportunities. Companies can use two types of strategic control tools. The first, which a company uses to evaluate itself, is called a **marketing-effectiveness rating review**. In order to rate its own marketing effectiveness, a company examines its customer philosophy, the adequacy of its marketing information, and the efficiency of its marketing operations. It will also closely evaluate the strength of its marketing strategy and the integration of its marketing tactics.

Marketing Effectiveness Review: Marketing effectiveness review includes judging or assessing the performance of the Marketing Department based on the five major parameters:
- Customer Philosophy,
- Integrated Marketing Organisation,
- Adequate Marketing Information,
- Strategic Orientation,
- Operational Efficiency.

The table 5.2 below lists four major types of marketing control.

Table 5.2: Types of Marketing Controls

Sr. No.	Type of Control	Who is responsible for controlling	What is to be achieved through the control	Approaches for control/Check points
1.	**Annual Plan Control**	Top and Middle Management	To examine whether the planned results are being achieved.	- Sales analysis - Market share analysis - Sales to expense ratio - Financial analysis - Market based scorecard analysis
2.	**Profitability Control**	Marketing Controller/ Head of Marketing	To examine where the organisation is losing money	Finding profitability by - Product - Territory - Customer - Segment - Channel

contd. ...

3.	**Efficiency Control**	Line and staff management /Head of Marketing	To evaluate and improve the spending efficiency and impact of marketing expenditures	Efficiency of • Sales force • Advertising • Sales promotion • Distribution
4.	**Strategic Control**	Top Management/ Marketing Auditor	To examine whether the organisation is on the right path with respect to the opportunities that are available.	• Marketing Audit • Marketing excellence review • Marketing-effectiveness rating instrument • Ethical and Social responsibility review

5.3.5 Marketing Audit

The second evaluation tool is known as a marketing audit. This is a comprehensive, systematic, independent, and periodic analysis that a company uses to examine its strengths in relation to its current and potential market(s). Such an analysis is comprehensive because it covers all aspects of the marketing climate (unlike a functional audit, which analyses one marketing activity), looking at both macro-environment factors (demographic, economic, ecological, technological, political, and cultural) and micro- or task-environment factors (markets, customers, competitors, distributors, dealers, suppliers, facilitators, and public).

The audit includes analyses of the company's marketing strategy, marketing organisation, marketing systems, and marketing productivity. It must be systematic in order to provide concrete conclusions based on these analyses. To ensure objectivity, a marketing audit is best done by a person, department, or organisation that is independent of the company or marketing programme. Marketing audits should be done not only when the value of a company's current marketing plan is in question; they must be done periodically in order to isolate and solve problems before they arise.

A marketing audit is a comprehensive, systematic, independent and periodic examination of an organisation or its business units, marketing environment, objectives, strategies and activities with a view to unearth the problem areas and opportunities and recommend a plan of action to improve the organisation's overall performance.

As mentioned in the definition above, Marketing Audit has four basic characteristics. Let us discuss these characteristic in detail:

- **Comprehensive:** The marketing audit encompasses an audit of all the departments within marketing and all major activities that are carried out by these departments. Hence it is a comprehensive audit. It is not restricted to a few areas or a few problems areas or issues. As such it is a comprehensive auditing and hence helps in locating the real source of the problem or the root cause of the problem.
- **Systematic:** The audit involves a step wise and orderly examination or checking of the environmental factors affecting the marketing organisation, the goals and objectives of the marketing organisation, the various strategies and action plans that have been designed and implemented by the organisation, the marketing systems that have been developed by the organisation and all the related marketing activities. This kind of an audit calls for a very systematic approach. Moreover only if the approach is systematic, can the auditors point out the real problems and issues and suggest improvements in the problem areas.
- **Independent:** Generally it has been observed that the real purpose of conducting the audit is served when the auditing agency is an outsider or an outside consultancy. An organisation can have its marketing audit done through many sources. The following are commonly used:
    - **Self Audit:** The manager uses a checklist to rate his own operations.
    - **Audit from across:** A counterpart from another department usually at the same level conducts the audit.
    - **Audit from above:** A senior or someone from Top Management conducts the audit.
    - **Audit by the organisation's auditing office:** Organisations that have a separate auditing office can have their office conduct the audit.
    - **Organisation's task force audit:** The task force of the Organisation conducts the audit.

    Although various sources can be used for auditing, they lack the objectivity that such an audit requires. Hence it is preferred to get the audit done from an outside agency or an outside auditing consultancy.
    - **Periodic:** Ideally audits should be carried out periodically as they are able to warn the organisation about deviations well in advance before things blow out of proportion. Ironically most audits are conducted only when the sales have fallen, and there is an issue or a problem.

Let us now see what a marketing audit actually does. The Marketing Audit looks at six major components or elements of the organisation's marketing situation.

Table 5.3 given below gives the details of these six elements that are audited

Table 5.3: Six Major Components in the Marketing Audit

Sr. No.	Element/Component being audited	What is checked
(I)	**Marketing Environment Audit**	
	Macroenvironment	
(a)	**Demographic**	• Major developments and trends that pose opportunities/threats. • Actions taken by the organisation in response to these developments.
(b)	**Economic**	• Major changes in price, savings, income, credit and how the organisation has responded to the changes.
(c)	**Environmental**	• Requirement of the organisation in terms of natural resources. • Concerns regarding pollution and energy conservation. • Steps that are taken by the Organisation.
(d)	**Technological**	• Major changes in product and technology. • Available substitutes.
(e)	**Political**	• Changes in law and regulations that may affect the marketing strategy. • Recent happenings in areas of product safety, equal employment opportunity and other things that affect the strategy.
(f)	**Cultural**	• The general attitude of the target audience towards the product and the business. Changes in customer lifestyles and values.
	Task Environment	
(a)	**Markets**	• Trends in market size, geographical distribution, profits, market segments.
(b)	**Customers**	• Customer needs and buying behaviour. • Customer perception about the company and its products.
(c)	**Competitors**	• Major competitors. • Competitors Strength, Weaknesses, Opportunities and Threats (SWOT) Analysis.

contd. ...

(d)	**Distribution and Dealers**	• Main trade channels. • Their growth potential and efficiency levels.
(e)	**Suppliers**	• Availability of key resources. • Latest trends amongst suppliers.
(f)	**Facilitators and Marketing Firms**	• Cost and availability for transportation services, warehousing services, etc.
(g)	**Publics**	• Which segment of the public represents opportunities/threats?
(II)	**Marketing Strategy Audit**	
(a)	**Business Mission**	• Is the mission statement clear in terms of marketing?
(b)	**Marketing Objectives and goals**	• Is there clarity of marketing objectives, and goals to facilitate marketing planning?
(c)	**Strategy**	• Is there a clear marketing strategy in place for ensuring that the goals are met? • Has the strategy been formed depending upon the product Life Cycle? • Is the segmentation, targeting and positioning done clearly? • Is resource allocation done properly to ensure that objectives are met?
(III)	**Marketing Organisation Audit**	
(a)	**Formal Structure**	• Is the organisation structure proper from the point of view of authority and responsibility for carrying out all marketing activities?
(b)	**Functional Efficiency**	• The efficiency of the marketing systems to ensure smooth functioning of all departments like sales and marketing department. • The linkage with the production department and its ability to meet desired production levels and profit levels.
(c)	**Interface Efficiency**	• Are there any problems between various departments and in their working relationships that are hampering the growth of the organisation?

contd. ...

(IV)	**Marketing Systems Audit**	
(a)	**Marketing Information System**	• The accuracy and reliability of the Marketing Information system and the usage of data provided by MIS for decision making.
(b)	**Marketing Planning System**	• Conception and usage of Marketing planning system. • Availability of decision support systems for managers. • Output of the planning system in terms of acceptable sales targets.
(c)	**Marketing Control System**	• Adequacy of control procedures to ensure achievement of objectives. • Periodic profitability analysis of products, market territories etc.
(d)	**New-Product Development System**	• Generation of new product ideas. • Adequacy of testing prior to launch of new products.
(V)	**Marketing Productivity Audit**	
(a)	**Profitability Analysis**	• Profitability of products, markets, territories and channels. • Identify segments that need to be expanded, contracted or withdrawn.
(b)	**Cost Effectiveness Analysis**	• Cost benefit Analysis and feasibility of employing cost-reduction measures.
(VI)	**Marketing Function Audits**	
(a)	**Products**	• Analysing Product line decisions like necessity of line stretching or line pruning.
(b)	**Price**	• Pricing objectives, strategies and procedures. • Customer perception about the price. • Meeting of objectives of the channels of distribution with the given prices.
(c)	**Distribution**	• Distribution objectives and strategies. • Adequate market coverage. • Effective distribution of channels.
(d)	**Advertising, Sales Promotion, Publicity and Direct marketing**	• Advertising Objectives. • Advertising and other Marketing communications spend. • Choice of media.
(e)	**Sales Force**	• Objectives of the sales force. • Proper allocation of territories. • Proper methods for target setting. • Proper methods for performance evaluation.

5.3.6 Marketing Excellence Review

Another method to rate the performance is to benchmark the performance of the organisation against the best in the Industry or the market leaders. Here the benchmarking can be done on various parameters like product quality, price, features etc. Based on the results the organisation can identify the areas that it is lacking in.

5.3.7 The Ethical and Social Responsibility Review

Organisations need to evaluate themselves on their being ethical and socially responsible. It is necessary to be an ethical business organisation if the business excellence is being sought.

Points to Remember

- **Introduction**

    The Marketing environment is ever changing and dynamic. To be able to cope in such an environment, organisations need to not only create and retain satisfied customers but also adapt to the continuously changing marketplace. This calls for marketing planning.

- **What is a Plan?**

    A plan is the starting point of all activities. It is the means to achieve an objective. It is a stepwise approach to the completion of any task. It is the road map of going from where we are to where we want to go.

- **Definitions of a Marketing Plan**
    - It is a sequential schedule of activities to achieve certain goals/objectives.
    - It is a process by which an organisation seeks to achieve its desired objectives with the optimum blend of available resources.

- **Corporate and Divisional Strategic Planning**

    As mentioned earlier the Corporate Headquarters are responsible for the corporate plan and also for setting the planning process rolling. There are four basic activities that must be undertaken for this purpose. They are:
    - Defining the Corporate Mission
    - Establishing Strategic Business Units
    - Assigning Resources to each Strategic Business Unit
    - Business Strategic Planning

- **Nature of a Marketing Plan**

  The marketing plan is an important output of the entire marketing process. It is a blueprint of what has to be achieved and how it is to be achieved.
  - Futuristic
  - Interface/Linkage
  - Flexible/Dynamic

- **Contents of a Marketing Plan**

  Following are the sections of the marketing plan
  - Executive Summary and Table of Contents
  - Current Marketing Situation
  - Macroenvironment Situation
  - Opportunity and Issue Analysis
  - Objectives
  - Marketing Strategy
  - Action Programmes
  - Projected Profit and Loss statements
  - Controls

- **Marketing Implementation**

  Marketing Implementation is the process that turns marketing plans into action assignments and ensures that such assignments are executed in a manner that accomplishes the plan's stated objectives.

- **Marketing Implementation and Evaluation Skills**

  The organisation or the marketers need to possess specific skills to effectively implement any marketing programme. These skills are:
  - Allocating
  - Monitoring
  - Organising
  - Interacting

  After implementation of the marketing plan, the next step is control.

- **Marketing Audit**

  A marketing audit is a comprehensive, systematic, independent and periodic examination of an organisation or its business units, marketing environment, objectives, strategies and activities with a view to unearth the problem areas and opportunities and recommend a plan of action to improve the organisation's overall performance.

Questions for Discussion

(A) Long Answer Questions:

1. Define a marketing plan. Discuss the nature and scope of a marketing plan.
2. With the help of suitable examples, discuss strategic planning at the Corporate Level.
3. With the help of a diagram, describe the Planning, Implementation and Control Cycle.
4. What do you understand by Portfolio Analysis? Describe any two methods of Portfolio Analysis.
5. Enumerate and explain the various steps in Business Strategic Planning Process.
6. Explain the contents of a Marketing Plan.
7. Describe the concept of marketing control. What are the various methods of marketing control?
8. Discuss the rationale for marketing control. Describe the various aspects of financial analysis in marketing control.
9. Explain in detail Marketing Profitability Analysis.
10. Describe the various parameters that are monitored in Efficiency Control.

(B) Short Notes - Write Short Notes on:

1. Nature of a Marketing Plan
2. Contents of a Marketing Plan
3. Corporate Mission
4. Strategic Business Units
5. Portfolio Analysis
6. BCG Matrix
7. Life Cycle Portfolio Analysis
8. GE nine cell Matrix
9. SWOT analysis
10. Marketing Implementation and Evaluation Control
11. Annual Plan Control
12. Market based Score Card Analysis
13. Marketing Environment Audit
14. Marketing Systems Audit
15. Marketing Effectiveness Control

(C) Multiple Choice Questions:

1. By nature the marketing plan is:
   - (a) Inbuilt
   - (b) Futuristic
   - (c) Basic
   - (d) Scholastic

2. The Marketing plan operates at two levels. They are:
   - (a) Big Level and small level
   - (b) Macro and Micro level
   - (c) Strategic and analytical level
   - (d) Strategic and tactical level

3. Most Businesses operate at:
   - (a) One level
   - (b) Two levels
   - (c) Three levels
   - (d) Four levels

4. The four levels at which most Businesses operate are:
   - (a) Corporate, International, National and State
   - (b) Corporate, Analytical, Operational and tactical
   - (c) Corporate, Divisional, Business Unit and Product
   - (d) Corporate, Divisional, National and Business unit

5. Contents of the Marketing Plan include:
   - (a) Corporate Decisions
   - (b) Action Programmes
   - (c) Decisions regarding profitability
   - (d) Analytical process

6. Skills required for effective implementation of the marketing plans include:
   - (a) Good Allocating skills
   - (b) Good profiteering skills
   - (c) Good preparatory skills
   - (d) None of the above

7. Marketing Control includes:
   - (a) Annual
   - (b) Profitability
   - (c) Efficiency
   - (d) All of the above

8. Annual Plan Control includes:
   - (a) Efficiency Analysis
   - (b) Profitability Analysis
   - (c) Marketing expense to sales analysis
   - (d) Sales to promotion analysis

9. Market based score card analysis is a part of:
   - (a) Annual Control
   - (b) Profitability Control
   - (c) Efficiency Control
   - (d) None of the above

10. Average number of sales calls per day is a measure of:
    (a) Profitability control
    (b) Safety Control
    (c) Sales Force efficiency control
    (d) None of the above

11. In the marketing plan the Current Marketing situation comprises of details about:
    (a) Profits Situation
    (b) Action plans
    (c) Macro Environmental Situation
    (d) None of the above

12. Four Quadrants of the BCG matrix include:
    (a) Stars, Question Marks, Dogs and Cash Cows
    (b) Moon, Question Marks, Dogs and Cash Cows
    (c) Stars, Tick Marks, Dogs and Cash Cows
    (d) Stars, Question Marks, Monkeys and Cash Cows

13. The number of cells in a GE matrix are:
    (a) Eight
    (b) Nine
    (c) Ten
    (d) Eleven

14. SWOT analysis stand for an analysis of:
    (a) Structure, Wisdom, Options and Trends
    (b) Stability, Weakness, Offers and Threats
    (c) Strengths, Weakness, Operations and Troubles
    (d) Strengths, Weakness, Opportunities and Threats

15. Marketing Audit is a part of:
    (a) Systematic Control
    (b) Effective Control
    (c) Strategic Control
    (d) Profit Control

16. A Corporate Mission Statement will focus on:
    (a) Many Goals
    (b) Limited number of Goals
    (c) No Goals
    (d) None of the above

17. Marketing Productivity Audit comprises of:
    (a) New product Audit
    (b) Goals Audit
    (c) Cost Effectiveness audit
    (d) International Audit

18. Distribution Efficiency measures:
    (a) Logistics cost as a percentage of Products
    (b) Logistics cost as a percentage of sales
    (c) Logistics cost as a percentage of Cost
    (d) Logistics cost as a percentage of number of goals
19. Advertising Efficiency measures:
    (a) Advertising time per thousand buyers reached by media vehicle
    (b) Advertising function per thousand buyers reached by media vehicle
    (c) Advertising frequency per thousand buyers reached by media vehicle
    (d) Advertising cost per thousand buyers reached by media vehicle
20. Customer Performance Score Card measures:
    (a) Lost Customers
    (b) Found Customers
    (c) Unfound Customers
    (d) None of the above

Answers

1. (b)	2. (d)	3. (d)	4. (c)	5. (b)	6. (a)	7. (d)	8. (c)	9. (a)	10. (c)
11. (c)	12. (a)	13. (b)	14. (d)	15. (c)	16. (b)	17. (c)	18. (b)	19. (d)	20. (a)

(D) Project Questions:

1. As a Manager of an organisation that wants to launch a new range of Photocopiers in the market, you are required to prepare a marketing plan for selling the photocopiers. Prepare the plan.
2. A diversified organisation has 5 strategic Business Units.
   Following are the details:

SBU No.	Sales (in Crores ₹)	Number of Competitors	Sales of Top three Organisations in that sector (in Crores of ₹)	Market growth Rate
1.	100	10	120, 120, 100	10%
2.	150	25	150, 150, 120	13%
3.	180	11	180, 120, 110	7%
4.	320	5	320, 120, 110	4%
5.	105	9	150, 120, 110	4%

Using the BCG Matrix portfolio analysis model find each SBU's relative market share and also determine the overall health of the company.

Case Study

M/s Strands is a medium sized organisation located in the Industrial belt of Vashi in Navi Mumbai. The organisation manufactures a variety of hair care products. The Management of Strands is worried because in the last two years their sales and profits have declined considerably. The Management feels that the Sales Force is responsible for this decline as they have not been putting in their very best and not giving 100% to the organisation.

To rectify the situation, the Management plans to introduce a new incentive based compensation plan and also provide training through a hired trainer, in the modern techniques for selling and negotiation skills. However, before launching this plan the Management decides to hire a Marketing Consultant and get an audit done.

The Auditing firms conduct in-depth interviews with Managers, Customers, Dealers, and Sales Personnel and also checks the various records and data available. The findings are represented below:

- The Organisation's product line comprises of 15 products, mostly shampoos. The three leading brands are Gloria, Pearls and Vella. These account for 80% of the Organisation's total sales. The Organisation has been thinking of moving into the moisturiser and fairness creams markets for a long time now.
- The target customer group of Strands includes people from the lower middle class and lower class. When customers were introduced, they found the quality of Strands products to be average.
- The main channels of distribution for Strands are the small kirana shops. It has good penetration with small kirana shops that are found in every locality in every city. However, Strands has not been very successful in persuading a lot of modern format retailers to carry its product line.
- The marketing and promotional budget of Strands is fixed at 15% of the Total Sales. However, in the hair care sector, most competitors spend close to 25% of the total sales on marketing and promotional expenditure. Advertising is the major thrust area on the promotional front.
- The Organisation has a policy of internal promotions and both the VP-Sales and VP-Marketing have risen from the ranks. The VP- Sales is responsible for setting targets and assigning territories whereas VP-Marketing is responsible for all marketing and promotional activities.

After a thorough study, the Auditor has given a report stating that the problems of the Organisation will not be solved by the proposed plan of training the sales force and the incentive scheme.

Question:

1. If you were the Auditor, what would your recommendations be for the Management of M/s Strands?

Note: Marketing Planning and Control being a new chapter has no Questions from Previous Years Pune University Examinations.